# Dedication

This book is dedicated to the Master Entrepreneur Salesperson, and professional sales people in general around the world, who understand that the answer to owning and managing a successful business is largely dependent upon his or her ability to sell.

# Author's Disclaimer

This written work is designed to provide competent and reliable information regarding the subject matter as is contained in each chapter covered. However, this book is sold with the clear understanding that the author is not engaged in rendering legal, financial or any other professional advice. Laws and practices will vary from country to country, province to province and state to state around the world and if legal or other expert assistance is required, the services of a professional should be considered. The author therefore specifically disclaims any liability that is incurred from the use or application of the contents of this written work.

Trevor K. Whittaker

# ENTREPRENEURSHIP
# $ALES 101

AUSTIN MACAULEY
PUBLISHERS LTD.

ISBN 9781785549434 (Paperback)
ISBN 9781785549441 (Hardback)


www.austinmacauley.com

First Published (2015)
Austin Macauley Publishers Ltd.
25 Canada Square
Canary Wharf
London
E14 5LQ




Printed and bound in Great Britain

# Contents

# Acknowledgments

From the time that I could remember I was being taught one lesson after the other and endured many challenges throughout my life. While trying to find my way, like you, some of the lessons I learned were sweet, some were "bitter sweet" and some were just plain bitter. While we go through the good or sweet times we feel that we are on top of the world-as I did. However, when things go wrong the human and wrong reaction is to find someone else to blame. I questioned God on many occasions but somehow always knew that I was the master of my own demise in almost all of my failures in life.

Having been brought up in an environment which most would consider being poor and destitute I most certainly may have been numbered amongst the criminal elite should I have allowed my early influences to overcome me. In fact, even at an early age I recognized that there was something or someone greater than me, and if I was to remain "on the straight and narrow", I would need to have His influence and protection as long as I lived. Having been walking the Christian life for so many years now, I can honestly inform you today that my life has been guided, protected and directed by my Heavenly Father for as long as I can remember. Therefore, for this book, and the lessons which I have learned in the business environment and the rest of my life, I give praise, honor and glory to whom it truly belongs – God the Father, God the Son and God the Holy Spirit.

My dear, dear wife, Sunly-Ann, I pay a special tribute to in that she has been my earthly inspiration for this second book. I have never; in all the time that I spent on putting pen to paper so to speak in order to complete this work heard a single complaint from her. Instead, what I received from my loving wife is a tremendous amount of encouragement and a woman who "stood in the gap" at the office every Wednesday and Thursday so that I could write this and my first book in the peace and quiet of our lovely home which we designed and built together. Thank you, baby, and as I have always said: "You are the best!" My friend, my lover and my greatest supporter!

I want to say a big thank you to all of my children Donovan, Ricky, Kristen, Natasha and Shamarie who have spent time encouraging me to produce this, and other works but more for the lessons which each of you continue to teach me every single day of my life. Please never forget that if you walk with the Lord, focus on the task at hand, and NEVER give up you will achieve your dreams. Savannah and Taylor-Reece your "Grampy" loves you so much and your free spirits astound me. Matthew, my amazing new born grandson – you make me so proud. To our departed little Ashton, I continue to miss you handsome! Thank you for the tremendous lessons of courage which you taught me through your debilitating illness which finally took you from us but placed you into the loving arms of our Heavenly Father. I love you and we will not forget!

To my brothers and sisters wherever you may find yourselves, thank you for the "fights" which taught me to say sorry and thank you for the lessons which made me strong. I would not change you for the world and no matter what we all went through as children God saw it all and loved us despite our circumstances.

Lastly, (but most certainly not least) to my dearly departed mother Alma, Mom I know that you are proud. You taught me so many lessons for which I shall be eternally grateful. You were the greatest sales manager a young boy could have. When we had no food you would make "special treats" and then train me to go out to the neighbors and sell these so that we could eat. You motivated me to do more and to sell more so that we could eat more and pay the rent. You taught me that if you don't work then you don't eat and I can honestly tell you that those days of selling, your eternal optimism and motivation have not left me to this very day. You taught me to love when things are at their worst, and you taught me what it feels like to rely upon other people for help. However, most of all you showed me how to laugh and to understand that a sense of humor in all of life's events is like a "spoon full of sugar making the medicine go down". I miss you and will always love you!

# Introduction

While the entrepreneur has many challenges, as can be seen in the book, authored by me namely, ENTREPRENEURSHIP (*minus*) 101 (Publisher: Austin Macauley-ISBN 978 1 78455 148 3 Paperback; ISBN: 978 1 78455 150 6 Hardback www.austinmacauley.com) there is no greater threat to your success than that of your inability to sell. The old adage once again comes to the fore and that is simply this – *NOTHING HAPPENS WITHOUT A SALE!*

With this in mind, and remembering all those entrepreneurs who have gone out of business because they have simply never understood this concept, this book, ENTREPRENEURSHIP $ALES 101 is considered by me a way to get you, the entrepreneur to use effective selling methods to grow your business so that you do not become a negative cash-flow statistic and a casualty of losing your business and everything else that you own. You and I both understand that there are many sales books which have been written over time, and largely, these have been directed at sales organizations and the corporate environment. I have also seen many good books directed at the individual sales person with the purpose of enhancing his/her sales skills. I think that as time goes on you should look for these and read these if you feel that they will help you in any way at all. My feeling is that any action from your side which will enhance your ability to both understand sales and to sell will be good for you and in particular if you are an entrepreneur who has never been exposed to professional selling skills up until this moment. You may have just said: "So there he goes, just like the rest of them, always dealing with PROFESSIONAL sales. Why can't I find someone who understands that I have no sales experience at all and all I am looking for right now is to get the BASICS so that I am able to move by business forward one day at a time?"

You are right, of course, and that is why I am telling you that ENTREPRENEURSHIP $ALES 101 is the book which you have been looking for. Each and every word and chapter has been carefully selected only with you in mind. If the book helps the individual and any other organization then I will be pleased; however, this entire book was put together by me personally and specifically with the entrepreneur in mind. This means that I will have to understand that you may have never been exposed to any sales training at all in your life. I would also have had to consider the fact that you may have already been in business for a while now and that you are struggling and have finally come to the conclusion that you have recognized the real reason for the current decline in your turnover and cash-flow and that is the lack of sales in your business. I must have also thought of the fact that you have now concluded that as an entrepreneur you have decided that "the buck stops with you" and not being able to sell and to rely on others in your organization is not a good situation to be in at all and you now want to do something about this. While I will obviously congratulate you for getting to this point where you are wanting to do something about your weakness in sales the point that I want to make about this book is as follows:


ENTREPRENEURSHIP $ALES 101 is your book!


I know that you do not have the time to become complicated. I understand that "time is money" to you and going on a three to six month training course at the local college is not on at this time. Your time and the cost of any formal course at this point in time are not even in your budget. If you in fact had the money you may need to spend these funds on keeping your cash-flow positive as opposed to any other activity. Therefore, I want you to know that this book is not designed to be complicated. Each chapter has been chosen in order to ensure that you will be able to implement the techniques immediately and with limited resources if this is your need. The idea then is to uncomplicate the selling process for you the entrepreneur and to only focus on the areas that are needed (desperately in some cases I know) to show immediate results. However, should you be a salesperson, with no interest in owning your own business but are employed by a company to produce sales then I will of course highly recommend that you read, absorb and practice the skills contained in this book. I can assure you that you will not be sorry that you did! Thus, as you read the pages of this book you will understand the "back to basics" philosophy and the need to keep things simple.

The markets within which you and I operate may be considered complex for some but yet basic in its make-up. Your target market and mine may have both broad, and yet, peculiar needs. Your client base, and prospective customer base is big in size and vast if we are dealing from an international sales basis and as you are aware these people and their companies are in a constant state of flux. This means that we will be dealing with needs that are "on the move" and that change regularly and if we are not aware and professional from a sales point of view then we will be left behind and lose sales to those more adept at identifying needs and closing the sale. We will thus conclude that your selling cycle and mine may be both complicated and yet basic at the same time. While you may feel that the previous statement is a contradiction in terms you will soon see as we progress through the book together that I am not wrong and neither is my assessment of your target market.

With the above in mind it then becomes imperative to prepare yourself as an entrepreneur/salesperson in a well-balanced, flexible and a professional manner ready, willing and able to meet the diverse challenges which lie ahead of you. The following simple mission statement has been adopted to reflect the goal of this book and the outcome of what you may learn. This mission statement may apply to you personally and may be adapted as you grow as a salesperson and as you develop a professional sales department in your business.

*To be the most professional entrepreneur salesperson and to develop the best and most professional sales team ever to come out of my business; willing and ready to be judged on my/our progress and results alone; and to stand by our clients/customers in providing services and products which supersede the concept and realm of the true meaning of the word EXCELLENCE.*

The one idea which I would however like to leave you with right at the start of our journey into sales is that effective and professional sales training and exposure is a never ending process. In today's sales training arena (whether courses, books and seminars) you and I find many different philosophies and techniques as this relates to determining the content and the technical level of sales training methodologies and programs. In fact, there are so many different ideas on sales training within any given marketplace around the world that it would be easy to become confused as to what is really applicable to your situation and mine. The great thing, in our case and hence me writing this book for you, is that ENTREPRENEURSHIP $ALES 101 has been designed very specifically with the entrepreneur in mind. The goal is to get you to maintain a positive cash-flow and a growing business and the only way to do this is to grow $ales, as we have already concluded that *nothing happens without a sale!*

Therefore, once again, taking the very specific needs of our businesses into account, I have decided to present you, the entrepreneur or salesperson, with a sales program which will allow you to get BACK TO BASICS. While many current sales programs are positive in their own right it is my feeling that in the case of entrepreneurs worldwide that these fall short of the very specific and basic needs of the entrepreneur in order to develop the sales skills of the entrepreneur in as short a period of time as is possible. The BACK TO BASICS program as is presented here has a simple philosophy and is based upon three fundamental principles namely:

1. Simplicity.
2. Effectiveness.
3. Focus.

**Simplicity**

You will find that the chapters contained within these pages are filled with a deliberate attempt to keep all programs and systems simple in nature. The reason for maintaining a simple construction on this pillar is to avoid misunderstanding and miscommunication. It is common knowledge that misunderstanding and miscommunication will ultimately lead to frustration and a lack of productivity. While part of the goal of this book will be to ensure that the entrepreneur becomes more effective in his/her own sales effort it must also be understood that the entrepreneur cannot do everything in the business so it will behoove you to also develop your own effective and productive sales force-another goal of the contents as is contained herein. The overall goal then is to develop you and your sales force so that you will become highly motivated and productive. A high sense of motivation and productivity will translate into a higher closing ratio in sales and this in turn should ensure a positive cash-flow not only for your business but in turn to the sales team which you will one day develop. A highly motivated sales team produces more and the more they produce the less of a cash-flow challenge you will have – THIS IS AFTER ALL THE GOAL IS IT NOT?

## Effectiveness

Please remember, and while this philosophy may apply to many other areas, for the entrepreneur and in the course of our current discussion, I have found that the best sales plans in the world become the worst plans simply because they are not practical in the roll-out process. When you read and understand the program and techniques contained in this book it is imperative that you understand that I have structured the same in such a way that you will easily able to apply the contents in a practical way so that these can work for you without too much trouble at all. If you are not able to implement what you learn then the plan will be of no use and most certainly cannot be considered "effective" now can it? The plans in this book and the associated targets are only effective if they are both practical and achievable and this in essence defines the word effective in my opinion. In any event I do believe that the best part of what I have designed for you here is that each aspect of the sales program that is applicable to a positive result outcome is entirely measurable at all times. The program becomes user friendly only in that all progress or lack thereof is measurable in determining the effectiveness of the sales effort and annual sales quotas/targets together with the production of the individual sales person, the entrepreneur and the rest of the team.

## Focus

The sales program contained between these pages is also specifically and willfully designed to produce FOCUS. The focus spoken of has a direct reference to all staff responsible for sales within your business including you. In other words, no one within or without your business should even be in doubt about where you are headed and your determination to get there. Your direction of your sales effort should be clear to anyone looking in. We all need direction and direction is no more critical, due its direct impact on the bottom line, than in the company sales program. Planning for business must be in writing and this provides a goal and direction which leads to the focus spoken about here and this simply MUST apply to the company sales effort. This book and the programs contained herein are designed to get you this point with ease and to assist you to maintain a clear focus at all times.

Once direction has been established and achieved surely the simple thing to do then is – MAINTAIN FOCUS!

ENTREPRENEURSHIP $ALES 101 will most certainly help you to maintain focus in order for you to achieve your desired turnover through the achievement of your sales goals and quotas. Achieving sales quotas/targets will take a clear understanding of the entire sales process and together with this success comes more confidence and confidence will give your business security in many areas including your personal life. Generating sales means a positive cash-flow and this in turn means that you can continue to pay the bills and use the money to self-finance additional purchases for continued growth. You growing your business is what I am interested in but I can tell you confidently that if you do not feel a need to learn to sell and you have no one else performing this vital activity in your business then I am afraid to tell you that your business will soon have a "heart attack" and die. You want your investment secure and sales will do this for you and I want to show you how to achieve your goal of owning a professional, secure and growing business.

As an entrepreneur you will always be challenged by those around you and by those that care for you to show results and progress within your business. Showing progress and results will not be enough even for you if you only take mediocre steps in this regard. I can assure you that the contents of this book and your willingness to implement the recommendations and programs will enhance your great ability as an entrepreneur. Therefore, I shall have no hesitation in asking you to proceed to the main chapters of ENTREPRENEURSHIP $ALES 101 with a view to learning and applying. I shall also take this opportunity then to remind you that "knowledge is power" but that "knowledge is not knowledge until you put it into practice".

# "OFF THE CUFF"
# A MOMENT OF MADNESS IN ENTREPRENEURSHIP ADVICE

This morning I was watching national television and I am compelled to share this with you my fellow entrepreneur.

The story goes as follows! I was watching two "entrepreneurial gurus". The one guru was in from the United Kingdom and the other from somewhere up in North Africa-both had authored books and were obviously using the opportunity to promote their books and the fact that they were in the country to "speak to entrepreneurs and to encourage them". True to form the TV personality on at the time had some searching questions for the gentlemen who were dressed in quality suits that you and I only dream of. Neither of the gentlemen wore a tie and sat very relaxed on the couch as they were interviewed. I listened intently as I was curious as to the questions to be asked first of all and then I was even more curious as to the answers which would inevitably be forthcoming.

It was not the interim questions and answers that concerned me a great deal as these related mainly to their books and much was said in order to encourage people to go out and purchase the books as apparently they contained a "great deal of wisdom" regarding the contents. In fact, please forgive me for this but you will know from **ENTREPRENEURSHIP (*minus*) 101** (Publisher: Austin Macauley-ISBN 978 1 78455

148 3 Paperback; ISBN: 978 1 78455 150 6 Hardback www.austinmacauley.com) that I tend to say things as I see them, when they were asked very pertinent questions as to chapters and contents of their books they seemed to flounder around for the answers – this surprised me as when one writes a book surely one will have an idea of its contents? Be that as it may the following two questions were good but the answers given by the gurus astounded me to the point where I became concerned for entrepreneurs out there who may believe these answers and take them as fact.

1. "What do you consider the main reason for young business failing in the first year?"

2. "What advice would you give someone who wants to become an entrepreneur and wants to achieve this quickly?"

**The answers given by the "gurus" were as follows (I will quote their exact words):**

Question 1: "They become exhausted".

Question 2: "They need to follow someone around in that business".

The following is my opinion as it relates to the answers given to the interviewer's questions as stated on national television.

"They become exhausted?" Really! For me then I have to ask how it is even possible to become exhausted before the first year of business is done. Many established entrepreneurs have been going at it for twenty years or more and will tell you that they are not close to being "exhausted" yet. They will also tell you that they are qualified to be an entrepreneur, studied to be a business person or gained the necessary practical skills to be an entrepreneur. They actually know what they are doing! They are not "exhausted" as they know and love what they are doing – they found their passion! In my humble opinion these people don't lose their businesses because they are "exhausted" they lose their business because they were never qualified to be in business in the first instance – read

**ENTREPRENEURSHIP (*minus*) 101** (Publisher: Austin Macauley-ISBN 978 1 78455 148 3 Paperback; ISBN: 978 1 78455 150 6 Hardback www.austinmacauley.com) and you will see exactly what I am referring to. I tell the reader that these "unqualified business people" will be out of business soon after they begin and I share with the reader why.

"They need to follow someone around in that business" Wow! Wow! Wow! Is this not just the best advice from a man who obviously has no clue as to what he is talking about and he dares to write a book on what he does not know!? Why don't you and I analyze this statement for a little while? Who must he "follow" (maybe he means "shadow" who knows?)? I have an idea on this! My feeling is that he may be following a new entrepreneur and that this is why many new businesses fail. There are too many prospective entrepreneurs following (shadowing) new (baby) entrepreneurs and this may be the very reason why these people are becoming "exhausted" before the first twelve months is completed. Do you realize that you and I may have found the very reason then for the consistent failure of new business within the first year worldwide? The answer then is simple, let's prevent the "blind leading the blind" and we will have many more successful businesses around the world. Hooray!!!

On a more serious note of course, and while we may agree that shadowing is a good way to learn it is not and cannot be the only way to ensure that the correct training is given and received BEFORE the prospective entrepreneur is "qualified" for the role ahead. Not everyone qualifies to be an entrepreneur and while government and financial institutions are consumed with developing business for their own reasons I can tell you that it would be far better to ensure that the person intending to go into business actually is qualified for the same. It would be better to promote the development of business leaders and entrepreneurs from a young age than to sit back and do nothing in this regard and then feel proud of the fact that one is developing statistics regarding new business failure.

Again, please read my book **ENTREPRENEURSHIP (minus) 101** in order to see if you actually qualify as an entrepreneur. You will also see then why this book is now before you. ENTRPRENEURSHIP $ALES 101 was promised in the previous book as I am convinced that the majority of businesses may fail for various reasons; however, the biggest and most serious reason for new business failure in my opinion is the lack of sales and a lack of focus on sales, and thirdly, the fact that the entrepreneur himself/herself does not know how to sell. We will now go through each step in the sales process in order of events to ensure that you have all the necessary tools and knowledge to remove the greatest threat to your business success – A LACK OF SALES!

# Part 1

# Basic Psychology of $ales

# Chapter 1

# $ales: Nine steps to successful selling

## Introduction

We have spoken about developing a simple sales program and strategy which would help you and me to become more successful (or simply successful in some cases) in business and sales. We have also by now made it clear that there are many good books on the shelves and on the internet which can assist the individual to become more "well-rounded" in the selling environment. Some of these resource materials, we have also concluded, are technical and complicated in nature and we don't have the time to first decipher another person's mind before we are able to sell or establish a sales department within our businesses. This is the very reason that you and I have decided to go BACK TO BASICS in our approach when it comes to sales and achieving in this area of our business life.

With this in mind I do want to share with you some of the people whom I have employed over the years and who have come to me from all walks of life, and when I say this, I include the corporate environment where they seemingly have no shortage of funds to ensure that their sales people receive only the very best sales training available in the market place today. I mean, I am talking about hundreds of thousands of Dollars (budgeted for annually by the way) in order to ensure that their sales staff are exposed to only the best and MOST EXPENSIVE ("expensive" by the way is many times associated with the BEST in the corporate environment) gurus in the world as far as this relates to sales training. My goal is to show you that all you need to pay is the price of this book to get going and be successful in sales – IMPLIMENTATION IS THE KEY! Psychiatrists and Psychologists have written many wonderful theories, processes and included the most complex of matrices (a new name for charts) in order to explain the selling process without ever having sold a single item as a "normal" sales person would. Many, not all, of the so called sales gurus out there have never sold a day in their lives, and yet have written books on the subject, and have become very, very wealthy on the back of their writing and speaking talents, but they have never actually held down a sales position ever. The other thing of note to mention here is that many of these wealthy speakers and authors have never experienced entrepreneurship in any form and thus have no experience as to what you and I have to deal with on a daily basis. The other issue with the "remedies" as presented by these people is that their solutions to your selling challenge cost a fortune to implement. We will not be going down this route.

Susan (not her real name) applied for a sales position with me one day and I proceeded with doing the usual checks and balances as this related to her claims on her CV. I was impressed! My business operates in a very competitive environment within the service industry and I am focused on sales all the time and am always on the look-out for professional sales people who are able to match their mouths when it comes to producing sales. Susan's CV revealed that she had a current position with one of our biggest competitors and a corporate giant within our industry. In fact I would venture to say that they are so big that they have forgotten who their client base is as the amount of complaints which we get about this corporate is good for our business. The long and the short of my idea here is to let you know that my feeling was that Susan would be a distinct advantage for my business and so I progressed through the checks with eagerness. Believe it or not all checked out and I was happy from the paperwork side of things and felt comfortable in getting her into my boardroom for a one on one interview.

The day came and Susan was sitting around the boardroom table and the discussion began in earnest. I found out more about Susan and her experiences both in life and the selling environment and she found out more about me, my expectations and our business which, she claimed to be familiar with through the market place. I was particularly curious as to Susan's certificates which she had taken great pains to include in her CV package and also brought it up during the interview process. You name the sales guru and through her company Susan had been exposed to them through seminars and sales conferences – I was impressed!

I asked Susan to sell me one of the samples of our product which I had deliberately placed onto the boardroom table. I want to inform you before you judge me that I did choose a product which she was selling at present with her current company. Here is the news my friend! She could not sell me the product at all! I was absolutely amazed at her inability to distinguish between simple things such as benefits and features of the said product. She floundered to the point of embarrassment and I was forced to stop the entire process. I looked over at her and said "unfortunately I cannot offer you a position with us, but please tell me how you have attended all of the sales training which you have and yet, as you will agree, you cannot sell?" I also asked her to explain to me how she was able to maintain her position in a company (her current employer) which all competitors looking in from the outside deemed to be the most successful in the industry without being able to sell professionally?

You will be amazed at her answer just as much as I was. I was told that the current company has a reputation big enough to generate sales leads at a high rate simply because they are seen in every washroom in the country. She manages her day by working on sales leads alone. I did say that even sales leads need to be closed professionally to which she replied: "I have so many sales leads and I hand out so many proposals (quotations to some) that it does not matter if they say 'no' to my proposal as I am assured that at least one or two of the many which I hand out will be accepted by the prospect." She was smiling as she recounted her sales philosophy and principles to me. My thought was that no wonder she was not able to actually perform a single part of the selling cycle including the most critical known as CLOSING. I asked her what she would do if the company ever stopped generating the current level of sales leads and she replied "this is what is happening at that present moment" and that is why she is looking for another job. Pretty honest don't you think – for an interview? She had no clue – despite all the thousands of Dollars spent on her – as to what the selling cycle was, as all she had received, despite all of her certificates, was motivational speaking without a plan to becoming a better salesperson, more professional and more focused on closing the great sales leads which were being provided by what I determine as a great competitor.

My friend, this book may have its motivational moments but I can assure you that as an entrepreneur you will need more than motivation; you will need to understand the selling process and have a clear cut system for moving your sales effort forward. While I do understand that sales philosophies will differ from one company and/or salesperson to the next I can only present in this book what I have seen work for me (and those around me) for the last thirty-five years or so. I have come to the conclusion then that the entire selling process/cycle consists of the following nine steps:

# CLOSING

| Step 1 | SUMMARIZE THE *NEEDS* |
| Step 2 | SUMMARIZE THE *BENEFITS* |
| Step 3 | *ASK* FOR THE ORDER |

## OBJECTIONS

| Step 4 | PAUSE |
| Step 5 | ACKNOWLEDGE |
| Step 6 | ISOLATE |
| Step 7 | QUESTION |
| Step 8 | ANSWER |
| Step 9 | CLOSE |

## Conclusion

The first part of this book will deal with the psychology of sales and is centered on helping you to understand that the sales process is simple and that you could easily complete the entire sales cycle by using the nine steps presented above. I simply cannot get more BACK TO BASICS than this! I will reveal the secret of understanding the difference between a need, a feature and a benefit and will show you how these get confused by even the "best" of sales gurus today. Back to basics to you and me then will also mean that you will be taken "back" to the good old days when we used to refer to a selling process called "need satisfaction selling". Many salespeople easily become confused with the simple difference between the feature and the benefit of a service and/or product but the good news is that after you have read and understood (and applied) this book you will no longer have an issue with the same confusion which you will see in the very same sales people whose companies have spent hundreds of thousands of Dollars (if not millions over time) on training their sales staff to understand this phenomenon.

When you have completed all the steps/work prior to this point you WILL need to ask for the order and this you will see is commonly referred to as the CLOSE. Do you have any idea as to how many "salespeople" are approaching prospects every day and do not understand the closing procedure and thus walk away with no sales thereby costing their respective employers millions in lost revenue over a period of time? YOU will not have this problem after you consider applying the contents of this book to your business sales effort. Sales objections, or the thought or word, is enough to send chills down the spine of the unprofessional sales person. However, you, as the Master Entrepreneur salesperson cannot have such a fear as the "fear" referred to here has more to do with ignorance brought about by a lack of knowledge than anything else. You will never fear objections ever again as I will reveal a tried and tested method of how you can make objections work *for* you instead of *against* you.

We will now begin the "dissecting" part of explaining each step as stated above. "Hold onto your hat" so to speak as you are ready to now observe some of the greatest secrets of the selling environment as we go back to sales basics.

# Chapter 2

# Selling Benefits
## *Back to need satisfaction selling*

**Introduction**

A very good friend of mine called me a short while ago and shared with me a challenge which he felt was hindering his sales force and costing him a fortune in lost revenue.

Instead of dealing with the matter over the phone we set up a time to meet, away from his office, in order to discuss his challenge as this related to his non-performing sales force. We arranged to meet at a favorite coffee shop close by and he almost immediately (other than the usual handshake of course) started to vent regarding the frustrations which he was experiencing with his sales staff. Apparently, the biggest issue for him being their inability to close the sale and turn company generated sales leads (or any sales lead for that matter) into business. Obviously, as he explained, this lack of production in sales was severely impacting on his "bottom line" with the negative impact being felt on his cash-flow situation. According to him he was paying good money out to salespeople who really had no ability to bring in sales. Sales quotas/targets were set but not being achieved. He had hired a sales manager who, according to Keith (my friend), was more of a sales "damager" and had no ability to identify the cause of the current crisis. I asked Keith if he had done his "due diligence", as I like to call it, on all sales staff and the sales manager BEFORE employing them. He assured me that he had been very careful to scrutinize all CV's including that of the sales manager and that he had taken previous advice from me to call a minimum of three contactable references for each new member of the sales team.

The sales manager, according to Keith, was "top of his class" and his references were impeccable, to the point that when each reference was asked, they would be more than happy to re-employ the sales manager given the opportunity. The situation, I could see, was a cause of great concern and frustration for my friend and I wanted to help. Keith's sales team had grown from his time as the sole salesperson, being a good entrepreneur understanding that *nothing happens without a sale*, to twelve team members including the "sales damager", sorry, I meant the sales manager. We arranged that I would meet with his team as to me this would be the only way to do an assessment as to where things were going wrong. I arrived in the company training room on the day and was impressed with what I saw – a great bunch of people, well-meaning and willing to work with me in finding a permanent solution to the current crisis when it comes to closing the sales deal. From the outward appearance I could not fault what I could see as they were all dressed according to company policy and in a professional manner. I asked each one to introduce themselves to me as though I were a prospect; this was our first meeting and I could not fault them on their professionalism here either and thought that the sales manager (who by now I understood to be Clive) had done a great job in training this into his team – "well done", I said! So what was the problem?

When I receive an SOS such as the one which I received from Keith (or any other concerned client) regarding the inability of a sales team to produce, I almost instinctively go to two issues which are, in most cases, a constant when productivity is lost.

1. An unprofessional inability (unwillingness/reluctance) to ASK FOR THE ORDER.
2. An unprofessional inability to understand the difference between a FEATURE and a BENEFIT.

As Clive was the sales leader and mentor for the company I asked him to explain his training on both of the two critical phases in the sales process. The answer which I got will explain why so many salespeople struggle with sales and ultimately fail. The same feedback given by Clive will also explain why so many companies are wasting valuable resources when it comes to paying unprofessional, untrained and lazy salespeople who are always on the look-out for a "short-cut" for everything in their lives. Let me tell you, my friend, in sales there are basic skills to be learned and practiced but THERE ARE NO SHORT-CUTS! You either do it right by always ensuring that the basics are done professionally or you lose and a loss in sales will be very costly to you as an entrepreneur and it could very well cost you your business. Big corporates feel the "pinch" on a daily basis and instead of going back to sales basics they hire motivators and gurus who are intent on complicating the sales process which is not necessary in my opinion.

Closing the sale is a simple procedure requiring three things as we have stated in this book and which we will continue to put before you throughout this book. However, should you not follow the simple procedures then you will fail-NO SHORTCUTS!

Let's go back to the training room with Clive and his team. I chose three salespeople to role play the exact way which they have been taught to close, and guess what, I saw three different closing techniques none of which were professional or effective at all. I asked Clive how it was possible to get three variations of an ineffective closing procedure and his answer astounded me: "I have never done role play with the team to check the closing procedure as you have". While the three chosen closers were performing their role play closing techniques I was recording the entire process with the intention of playing these back to the entire team. The idea was to critique the close in a written structured format which I had passed out to one and all. I was not surprised when not one of the three showed any proficiency at all in effectively closing their own sales manager (acting as a prospective client). They could also not display a clear professional sequence which would lead up to an effective close.

While I could go on and on as to all the negatives which came out of that session on the day I was not there to focus on the negatives so I had seen enough to help me and my friend Keith to know where his challenges were coming from. In a nutshell they had no concept of the basic sales principal known as *need satisfaction selling*. In fact, when I asked the question: "Has anyone here heard of an age old sales principle known as need satisfaction selling?"; the answer which I received back will tell you why professional sales is under sever threat and why companies are wasting good money on lazy and ineffective salespeople. The answer went something like this if I remember correctly: "no, we have never heard of need satisfaction selling so it must be 'old school' and we don't do old school any more"! Wow! Wow! Wow! I immediately realized who I was dealing with and one word came to my mind namely "arrogance". However, when I explained to them that the "new school" thought was not working for them they asked me to explain myself. This was the invitation that I had been waiting for and so I made them consider making a commitment to using the principle if it made sense to them, and to my surprise, whether out of desperation and/or failure, I received a positive answer from one and all. You see, what I discovered within a very short space of time was that while other areas of their sales process needed attention, I can tell you as I told them on the day, need satisfaction selling means that you will have to discover the needs and once you have discovered the needs the salesperson would then have to apply the associated benefit but that one could only do this if we understand the difference between a feature and a benefit. The current lack of knowledge regarding the difference between a feature and a benefit was the crux of the challenges faced in the sales department currently under the leadership of Clive. Without this knowledge there was no hope of ever discovering the prospect's wants/needs. If we do not have the ability to draw out what the prospect's wants, needs and desires are then there will never be a successful close because the process of need satisfaction selling is just that, discovering the needs and then "covering" these with the benefit of your company's product or service – a basic and simple principle that will ultimately make the difference between success and failure as an entrepreneur or salesperson.

My goal is to get you to understand what I am trying to get across to you and that you will see the sense in what I am saying, and this, for the good of your business and future success. Thus, I have dedicated this and the next chapter of this book to help you to understand the process of need satisfaction selling and that understanding the fundamental differences between a feature and a benefit is the secret to making all of this come together for you in a practical and simple way. The professional then will have to grasp the difference between a feature and a benefit, and so, let's discover the secret that may help you become more professional when dealing with the prospect.

## Foundation Statement

The key to your success lies within a process called *need satisfaction selling*. Being able to identify the needs of a prospective client and finding a way to satisfy those needs is what will determine whether you succeed in the sales process or fail. Contrary to popular opinion (in the mind of the unprofessional only) one cannot satisfy a need by selling the *features* of doing business with your company. We then also understand that you and I cannot sell our services or products based upon the features of the same alone as sooner or later we must translate the features into tangible benefits as this will satisfy the prospects needs ultimately. As a reminder then, once the prospect has revealed a definite need it is your job and mine, as salespeople to satisfy the need as soon as is possible during the closing presentation-do this professionally and you WILL succeed.

While we will go into more detail during the next chapter, the goal here will be to lay a basic foundation before we move on. We will discuss in simple terms what is meant by a feature and a benefit.

**Feature (Basic Rules)**

1. The selection of which features to present must be directly related to the needs which were expressed by the buyer.
2. Once you have selected the features of your product and/or service you must then convert these into appropriate benefits.

A feature then will describe the service or product as it will deal with what it IS more than what it DOES. A feature then is a characteristic of what something is and in essence describes what you will be giving to the client. For instance, the following examples depict features offered by a service related business:

- An on-site control file.
- Anti-theft brackets for air fresheners.
- Color and uniformity of washroom products.
- We only install low-profile bait stations.
- Our Insect Lights Traps have pheromone glue boards.
- We use gel-bait when eliminating Cockroaches.

The goal now after understanding that a feature is clearly what something IS must be to "translate" these into something that DOES.

## Benefit (Basic Rules)

Features must be converted first of all into their relative importance to the prospect or the buyer. In order to do this you and I must follow the following basic rules:

A benefit will and must describe WHY the service and/or product are important to the prospect.

A benefit always describes what something (a feature) DOES.

It will SOLVE the specific buyer's expressed want and need.

A benefit will CLEARLY describe the satisfaction which the prospect will receive.

It will most certainly satisfy the buyer's DOMINANT motivation for wanting to change service providers or to purchase a product.

## The Hidden Secret behind the Feature and the Benefit

All I am going to ask you right now is to read with a view to retaining and understanding the subject matter at hand as I can assure you that before you reach the end of the next chapter you and I will be in sync. While I am about to bring in a third component as this relates to features and benefits you must understand that this third component will play no part in changing the definitions already presented, rather, the next component will show you the "how and the why" of the feature and the benefit.

## Net Gain (Basic Rules)

"Net Gain Benefits" are those benefits that the buyer desires, wants and needs and perceives (and has communicated this to you verbally or in writing) are critically important in getting his/her problem solved. Net gain benefits are usually unique to your business, and to you, as they describe the actions that solve the prospect's needs and wants, and are also clearly what sets you apart from your competitor. Let's define this just a little more shall we? A net gain benefit is described as follows:

A net gain, as is perceived by the prospect, represents the difference (or gap) between what the buyer NEEDS and what the buyer GAINS.

The "net difference" then may be the clear and distinguishable difference between your service and/or product and that of your competitor.

A net gain may also be likened to a unique feature which has been translated into a benefit.

A net gain can also be considered a service and/or product which the prospect cannot either do for themselves or obtain elsewhere.

In other words, a net gain benefit is a unique, incremental benefit which the prospect needs and cannot get elsewhere.

The Business Directory.com defines net gain as follows: *The overall improvement observed in some measure after all positive and negative influences have been fully accounted for.*

The word improvement here helps us to understand what the basic premise of the term net gain must be taken to mean as surely this denotes a way to make the status quo better? The prospect has a challenge and has expressed the same as a need. The simple fact of the matter then is that we need to turn the challenge or need into a benefit and in doing so we have made his or her situation better, and this in itself must denote to a net gain over the status quo. The enhancement then between the status quo and the benefit is determined to be the net gain.

## Conclusion

The foundation has now been laid in order for us to continue on in our journey to more fully understand the critical aspects of wants, needs, features, benefits, and then, most importantly to nurture your ability to understand and to implement and talk net gain benefits to your client. After all, what is the point, to our prospects then in making a change to their business and leaving the current supplier if you cannot point out the real reasons for doing so? The real reasons referred to here will make direct reference to the benefits and the net gains between what you are able to offer him/her and what they are receiving from their current supplier. Make sure that gains match the benefit which you are offering, and this coming from the feature of your product and/or services. In order to get to all this though, you will need to discover the needs right up front and NEVER FORGET THESE during the sales and closing phases. The next chapter will continue with most of what we have just discussed; however, you will also see that the contents will help you to cement your thoughts in this regards and to implement in practical terms the "gold nuggets" which you have discovered here.

# Chapter 3

# How to ASK FOR THE ORDER
*Basic $ales closing for success*

**Introduction**

Recently I had a very pleasant supplier salesperson in my office (I admire salespeople a great deal; however, I have exceptions as you will see later in the book) as we were looking to add some critical equipment for one of our growing branches. I had received a few proposals/quotations from a few competitor companies with a view to obtaining not only the best price, but more importantly, the ability to service the equipment in time, on time and without any issues regarding a stock of spare parts should the need arise. I was happy with all three of the proposals but decided to call the salespeople in as the pricing was pretty close and so were the other needs which I had. My feeling was that it would come down to making a decision to go with the most professional salesperson who is able to convince us that they are better suited to provide the necessary after sales service meaning the one who listened upfront when I clearly outlined our needs with regards to all the aspects of this particular sale. You may not know me (or maybe you do from reading my previous book) but I will more often than not have some of my key personnel sit in on such decisions as "many heads are better than one" they say.

The salespeople set up the necessary appointment professionally and started to make their final pitches obviously, we thought, with a view to closing the deal.

## Salesperson One

We shall name this person Mary. Mary met with at least four of our company representatives (including me) in our boardroom and began her session in the correct manner in my opinion and that was to "break the ice" so that we could all get onto a comfortable level. She was friendly, outgoing and spent quite a bit of time going through her proposal which I had personally been interested in from the very beginning. However, during the meeting I raised an objection regarding the pricing, she became nervous and stated that she would have to discuss my concerns with her sales manager and get back to me. She could not and did not try to close the deal but promised to come back once she had an answer. Needless to say I was disappointed as I did not have any time to waste as the decision needed to be made soonest as the site needed the equipment.

## Salesperson Two

Robert sat down and immediately did the guy thing and got onto the weekend's sporting activities which included the events at the world cup soccer and the latest golf being played around the world. This went on for more than ten minutes and it seemed to me that we would never get to the point of discussing the matter at hand – my intended purchase of the equipment needed for our branch. However, I was then forced to direct matters and finally got Robert to focus on the proposal and the reason for the meeting. I did not hold his exuberance against him and decided that if what he tells us is good and if he asks for the order then we would probably go with his equipment as the brand had a good reputation for being reliable. The first issue which we all faced was that Robert "forgot" the proposal package at his office so I had our office assistant make him a copy of mine. Once we gave Robert his copy of the proposal he seemed confused as to the size of the machine which he proposed and felt that it would not meet our needs. I asked him to give us feedback as to what he felt our needs were just so that we were all on the same page. What we all heard from the salesperson this day had very little to do with our needs at all, and in fact, we all concluded that he was mixing us up with some other client whom he was busy with on the sales side. His apparent confusion left him on "the back foot", embarrassed and visibly shaken. He, too, had to leave in order to sort out the challenges which he had created for himself – another disappointment and we could not get a decision made.

**Salesperson Three**

When this third salesperson walked into the boardroom early the next morning she exuded confidence and professionalism from her manner of dress to her ability to communicate and in her obvious organization. Chantel was a bubbly person but understood the need to get on with things. She had done her homework and had expected the objection on the pricing. Chantel reminded us all of a statement which she had made during previous meetings:" My pricing may not be the lowest but what I will tell you is that our service matches the price". She then proceeded to show us all why she was considered the best in her industry. By the time that Chantel was done with her presentation we had decided to move ahead with the agreement so that we could get the job done and get the much needed equipment to our branches across the country.

A week later, at the weekly management meeting, I decided to use the opportunity to discuss and analyze Chantel's meeting in detail. Obviously there were more managers present than at the actual meeting with the supplier salesperson but I thought it a good idea to involve everyone nonetheless. Sam was the Operations Manager present during Chantel's meeting and was the first to respond to my question: "Why did we buy from her?"

Sam went on to explain that her level of professionalism made him comfortable and her product knowledge set him at ease. The proposed equipment, according to Sam, was "a perfect fit". John, a man that has been with our company since inception really was also impressed with level of professionalism; however, for John it had more to do with her ability to remind us constantly throughout the meeting that she had listened to our needs and proved that the equipment was a great fit. The point made by John was that he felt the price was quite a bit higher than her competitors, but the fact that Chantel spent a great deal of time outlining the great service support seemed to reduce the actual price without really reducing the price, "if you know what I mean", he said. I said, "I know exactly what you mean and exclaimed that I had got the same impression and as service support was important to us this proved that she had listened to our major need from the very beginning of our relationship". When I asked Judy to give her feedback I was astounded at her perceptiveness and ability to clearly state events in fact just as they happened. Judy said: "What I saw was a young woman who looked the part and could play the part right down to the close!" She continued: "It has been a long time since I have been exposed to someone of this caliber in that she was organized and took time to repeat our needs so that she assured us that she had got these down; she also took time to once again clearly distinguish the difference between the features of the machine and the benefits which matched our needs down to the last screw. I absolutely loved the way that she closed the sale once all was said and done. There was nothing left for us to say but let's go ahead as she had concluded matters so professionally!" John came back and said, "Sorry I want to add something!" I asked him to share and he was immensely impressed with the fact that she handled our objections like a true professional and did not feel threatened when we raised these, and in fact, she made it clear that we were quite within our right to raise questions [objections] as she is more than willing to give us the additional information as this may be critical to us when making an informed decision". Wow! John exclaimed.

All wondered how Chantel had become such a great person to deal with and how she had obtained her level of professionalism in her presentation and the entire selling process. I had no objection in sharing a little secret with them and that was that Chantel and I had known one another for many years and that I had been her sales manager at a company which we both worked at many years ago. I also shared that I knew that we would eventually purchase the equipment from Chantel but that I did not say anything for fear of jeopardizing the process in play. Needless to say Chantel is now in our employ after us losing contact for so many years.

I was then asked to give my assessment and stated three clear actions from Chantel's entire presentation: She had clearly:

1. Summarized our needs.
2. Summarized the associated benefits related to her equipment and our needs.
3. Closed the sale by asking for the order.

We will now "dig" for diamonds in doing whatever we can to understand the process as stated above and as was so professionally followed by Chantel. This is the first step in understanding the basics of how simple it is to close the sale. You may think it strange that we would start our journey at the so called end of the selling cycle but you will soon see that the close is actually the beginning of it all.

# HOW TO CLOSE

# STEP ONE SUMMARIZE THE NEEDS
## *Definition of needs*

A need, within our context must be taken to mean a *requirement*. It may also be deemed to mean within the sales environment a *want*, a *demand* by the client who is desperately in need of very specific wants. The customer is desperately trying to tell you and me that he/she currently lacks something and he/she is asking us if we have the ability and capability of fulfilling these as the current supplier is not or may not be. While the client may not tell you and me this they are in fact desperate to the point where the need may be so great that they in a sense *yearn for, long for and may even crave for* a solution to their current crisis and they are relying or depending on you and me to fill the gap. In fact, it may be that the need is what we would determine to be a *have to have.* The need becomes, within the sales environment, essential, a necessity and a prerequisite to a successful conclusion during the closing process. They have a current challenge and need and YOU have to resolve the same. Collins dictionary describes this state of mind as: "the condition of lacking something".

It is my personal philosophy, which I have tried and tested over and over again over the years, that should a salesperson be able to uncover the needs at the very beginning of the sales process, and remember these, (writing these down while the client is telling them to you will be a good idea-trust me!) and remind your client of these throughout the selling process then you will have discovered the secret to successful closing. One of the best ways to uncover the client's needs is to discover the reason that you are sitting in front of your prospect. The idea here is simply to state: "John, thank you for meeting with me today! I am curious, I see that you currently have a service provider which competes against us for the same service so may I ask why you invited me to meet with you today?"

If this is considered the "usual" sales call, and once you have asked this question then simply sit back and allow the prospect to share his/her so called "concerns" with you. The reason I use the term "concern" here is that inevitably the prospect will now begin a process which we all have come to know as VENT or VENTILATE. I thought that Collins Dictionary was spot on with the definition of the term vent: *A small opening in something through which fresh air can enter and fumes can be released.* I must admit within the context of our discussion I feel, while hilarious if you really think about it, that Collins is absolutely spot-on if you truly understand what some prospects are capable of feeding back to you during this phase of the selling cycle. Collins continues to add humor to my goal here of getting you to understand the importance of allowing the prospect to vent as in the venting process you are going to find the gold nuggets, if you will, called NEEDS. The Dictionary also defines the word and action vent in the following terms: *The shaft of a volcano through which lava and gases erupt.* My friend, I simply must share this one with you as when we put all of the "definition pieces" together you will understand the humor of it all, and while I'm at it, this will not be the last time you hear me mention this, using humor in the sales process is like a breath of fresh air and you should never be afraid to use humor when appropriate (using humor when you are selling caskets/coffins will probably not be one of those "appropriate moments" which I mentioned earlier). Getting back to my promise of yet another definition think on this one please: *The anal opening of a bird or other small animal.*

Taking the above definitions into account I want to share with you some sales moments whereby you will clearly see how these take on a very personal nature and meaning.

I had the opportunity to present my company's services to a major corporation which had been with one of our biggest national competitors for years. We had tried to gain business from this corporate for a long time but to no avail as they had built loyalty between one another which was virtually impossible to sever. However, I was called in to do a presentation of our services and set up in the boardroom as I was told. My impression was that I was only meeting with the decision maker (you must ALWAYS only deal with decision makers at first or you will simply be wasting your time); however, upon my arrival I soon realized that I would be presenting to a boardroom full of the company's senior executive management team. This was not a problem to me as I know my stuff so to speak and have dealt with boardroom situations before no matter how challenging they became and they most certainly can be very challenging, but I will show you how to deal with this later on in the book.

The management settled into their seats, I was introduced and I politely got up and asked permission to ask my very first question after I spent a minute or so outlining my goals for the presentation. My wanting to start out by asking a question was approved and I then proceeded with: "Ladies and gentlemen, I am aware that you have been dealing with our esteemed competitor for many years and while I most certainly appreciate you agreeing to meet with me today, I am curious as to why I am here?" I want to be honest with you we could all hear a pin drop as they say as the room fell into utter silence. The CEO spoke first and stated: "A straightforward but good question Trevor! I shall let my team share with you why you are here if you don't mind?" He looked at his team and said one word: "GO!" I am able to report to you that for the next twenty minutes at least I took notes as they spent time in the process called VENT.

The mood was one of frustration and in some instances I heard anger and all I did was say: "Really! Tell me more!" By this time I had asked for permission to take notes and had to write very quickly in order to place down all of the areas of discontent. In this case being (1) poor or non-existent service at some of their branches (2) invoicing frustrations(3) additional price increases which were not authorized(4) the unauthorized use of sub-contractors. There were more areas of discontent and I encouraged the venting process until I felt that I had them all down and that I understood the prospect's frustration. I can tell you that when the CEO said the word "go" it was like lighting a keg of dynamite as the shear anger and frustration was most apparent and at times I thought that I was the target of their frustration. It was like a volcano had built up pressure and it exploded all at once – RIGHT IN FRONT OF ME! I felt the "release of gases" spoken of by Collins and the volcanic gases erupting around and of course, while the bird did not release its "load" on me I most certainly felt that it had as the management team "gave it to me" in no uncertain terms. After all, it was I who had dared to ask such a first question and many would say that I asked for trouble and I would agree; however, how else does one discover the very needs which could add millions on a yearly basis to one's business? This is how important this first question is as not only do you take some form of abuse (I can assure you) but you also allow the prospect to vent so that you are able to then deal with a more calm personality and while they vent you write. After taking all of the above mentioned "abuse" can you imagine that I asked if I could ask a second question? The CEO looked at his team and said: "Guys, Trevor is a sucker for punishment isn't he? Trevor go ahead ask your question", as he looked at his staff members with a smile on his face.

My next question went something like this: "According to my list, you have mentioned at least twenty-five areas of discontent. May I just say that I shall be reviewing all of these with our staff; however, I am once again curious as to which of these areas that were mentioned could be considered the most important in order for us, as a start, to come out with the top five concerns for my company to target and ensure your satisfaction – your COMPLETE satisfaction will be all that I am after." I can assure you that they had no problem with arriving at the following five areas of discontent as their most important:

1. The current service levels were not matching company expectations.
2. Confusion as to who was managing the account.
3. Multiple unauthorized price increases throughout the year.
4. The unauthorized use of sub-contractors.
5. Multiple invoices for workplace services thereby complicating payments leading to late payment penalties being levied.

I HAD WHAT I WANTED! I had the very areas of discontent which has caused them frustration over a number of years which has led to me making the presentation on the day, and now, all I needed was the level of professionalism which would allow me to close the sale whilst throughout the selling cycle reminding them of their areas of discontent (their needs) and attaching my solution (our company and service BENEFITS) to the same. I will have to satisfy their needs (areas of discontent) with the benefits of doing business with my company and this is what is known as NEED SATISFACTION SELLING amongst professional salespeople and Master Entrepreneurs. I continued on with presentation that day and constantly reminded them of their areas of discontent and how I was going to solve them.

My solutions to the above were accepted by the prospect who later became my new profitable client, and after many years now we still maintain a loyal relationship between us all. The only reason that this is so is that we identified solutions to the prospect's areas of discontent (as stated above) and have since managed these to the client's satisfaction to date.

1. The current service levels were not matching company expectations. (Add SLA as a solution)

**Benefit to match Need**: We proposed matching an SLA (Service Level Agreement) with the client's needs and expectations to maintain high service levels and both parties would appoint company representatives to meet bi-weekly in order to ensure compliance by both companies.

2. Confusion as to who was managing the account.

**Benefit to match Need**: We agreed to appoint a Senior Accounts Service Representative who would establish a professional communications protocol and deal with any and all complaints and compliments from the client. We also agreed to have the account file discussed at weekly senior management meetings in order to ensure compliance with the accepted written protocol.

3. Multiple unauthorized price increases throughout the year.

**Benefit to match Need**: We agreed to place an additional clause in our contract/s or agreement/s which would limit any price increase to one per year and that annual written notification of such an increase would reach the client no less than thirty (30) days prior to the implementation.

4. The unauthorized use of sub-contractors.

**Benefit to match Need**: It was pointed out that our company did not make use of outside contractors to do the work as all work was performed by company staff and the same is stated in the current written legally binding agreements.

5. Multiple billing/invoices for workplace services thereby complicating payments leading to late payment penalties being levied.

**Benefit to match Need**: It was pointed out that we were one of only a handful of companies nationwide who are able to perform most workplace services as was required by the prospect, and due to this, all services were performed under one "umbrella", with one responsible person and all services placed onto one bill/invoice prior to presentation for payment.

## STEP TWO ⟶ SUMMARIZE THE BENEFITS

We have seen how important it is to extract the areas of discontent from the prospect – ask the right question, sit back and take notes as the prospect will not hold back particularly if they are frustrated. However, the prospect does not have to be frustrated for you and I to uncover the needs as EVERY prospect has needs, and guess what, sometimes they are able to state these clearly but there are those times that the prospect has to "search" for what he or she is ultimately looking for and what they need and expect in a service provider and/or product. The major reason why you and I are so interested in obtaining the needs is to apply the benefits of our services and/or our products. It stands to reason, and even you must agree, that if there is no reason (benefit) to make a purchase then why do so? The one thing that I will have to make clear at this juncture is that there is a huge difference between a FEATURE and a BENEFIT. While we have studied this difference in the previous chapter I want to inform you that while the definition is quite simple for both words there are many unprofessional salespeople out there who still do not understand this critical difference:

1. Benefit: what something DOES.

2. Feature: what something IS.

For instance, when buying a house the agent points out that the house has an amazing fireplace and is set in a marble design. You may ask then is the fireplace, which is set in a beautiful marble design, a feature or a benefit? You must also ask yourself in seeking the answer to your valid question is the fireplace in this state able to do something for the owner or is it just something that is in the house at present? What will then need to happen in order to make the fireplace do something and in doing so what will it need to do in order to be of some benefit to anyone including the prospect that is currently looking to purchase the home? In the first instance was the fireplace ever mentioned during the identifying needs phase of the selling cycle as an actual need? Who said that the agent was instructed to find a home with a fireplace? However, should the existence of a fireplace within the home be at the instruction of the prospect (identified during the needs analysis stage) then the salesperson will have the added task of "making the fireplace come to life" so to speak.

The fireplace: something that IS.

The fire place is thus a feature in its current form if you and I have understood the definition of the term "feature". However, in order to make sure that you understand the term "feature" let's define the term further.

Features are prominent and noticeable to us all. It is thus something that we can see and these stare us in the face. For instance one's face has certain aspects such as a nose, mouth, lips, forehead, cheeks, eyes, teeth, and if you want to include these as a part of your face then the ears. Other aspects of the face will include zits (if you have any), freckles, skin color, skin tone and facial hair (if you are a male). All these previously mentioned items are what we consider someone's facial features to be, and in fact, we all refer to these parts as "features" when describing someone – police departments around the globe do the same thing. With this in mind and to give you some practice the face and its components are to be considered features of a human face. It is what these features do (as they all have a purpose) that add benefit to having them.

Parts of the face: something that IS.

Another way to describe the term "feature" is to state that it represents the characteristics, facets, details, aspects, peculiarity, quality and trait of something which IS. A *characteristic* then is a distinguishing feature of an object (for the sake of our exercise as things that are not tangible such as a training program for instance will also have features and benefits) having certain attributes, certain aspects, properties and hallmarks. Enough! I think that you now understand that a feature is simply something that IS! A feature then does nothing of its own accord until you and I consider the part as a sum of its whole and turn it into something that DOES which we call a benefit. I cannot tell you the cost to companies when sales people cannot distinguish between a feature and a benefit. As an entrepreneur, should you wish to become a Master Entrepreneur then you will force yourself to understand the difference as in this understanding you will directly affect your sales closing ratios in the positive and in so doing you will positively affect your ability to create turnover, cash-flow and profit.

A benefit: something that DOES

The face has a nose but the nose is not only for the looks as the benefit of having a nose is that you and I are able to smell all kinds of things using this organ and that it also assists in performing a life function called breathing. These aspects then are considered what the nose (a feature) DOES (a benefit). Surely this cannot be that difficult to understand, and yet, dare I suggest that you ask a salesperson or an entrepreneur to describe the differences to you!? I am sure that you will be as surprised as I am on a constant basis as to the enormous lack of ability in this regard.

The fireplace then as a feature has certain benefits, the biggest one being that when filled with wood and set on fire the fireplace (feature) will give of heat (benefit). The added benefit of a fireplace that actually works is that the heat fills the home and ensures that the family is kept warm during cold days and nights. In some parts of the world a fireplace giving off heat is essential to survival so the benefit goes on as long as the fireplace DOES. With this in mind I performed a Google word search and while the definition did not say much at all I do agree with the following from Google, and feel that the short sentence describing what a benefit is will be sufficient to add value to our discussion: *an advantage or profit from something* [that does]. Collins states that the definition in their opinion is: *something that improves or promotes* [our client's wants and needs]. The term benefit then must also be taken to mean a *gain*, an *asset* to something or someone, a *convenience* to anyone particularly our prospects businesses or those of our clients, it is also *beneficial* to those who need such a benefit and to *profit* those people and businesses to whom the appropriate benefit may apply.

We shall touch on features and benefits again a little later on, however, it must be understood that when summarizing the benefits you should clearly state the features and then demonstrate the benefits of the same. As the prospect will not buy features from you as he/she will not have need of these; however, the prospect will most certainly appreciate you understanding his wants (areas of discontentment) and satisfying those with solutions (benefits) that actually work.

During a presentation performed by one company, and after a need analysis was done, the salesperson concluded that they could satisfy the prospect's needs based upon their wants. They did so as follows:

*Paul, the benefit of having our hygiene service* [feature] *team come in monthly to perform specialized hygiene services will mean that you will never have to deal with the malodor in your washrooms again* [benefit]. *We will upgrade your washroom rental products* [feature] *to where it not only meets international standards but we will also ensure that you comply with all relevant local and international legislation in this regard* [benefit]. *Our services* [feature] *are designed to deal with your problem areas and increase staff morale* [benefit].

### STEP THREE ───────────→ ASK FOR THE ORDER

Step three is surely the logical conclusion to all of your work to date? Why would one not ask for the decision or order at this point in the selling process or cycle? You would have performed all of the following functions prior to this question being raised meaning that you have done all that was asked of you by the prospect, and more, so surely you deserve to know whether you have approval to start the services or deliver the order? There is only one way to find out – ASK!

1. You have uncovered the needs by doing needs analysis.
2. A professional presentation of services and/or product was performed.
3. The client requested a site survey with a view to preparing formal proposals/quotations.
4. The proposals/quotations were then presented to the prospect.
5. As a professional entrepreneur salesperson you presented the NEEDS.
6. You also presented the BENEFITS.

Step seven is to ASK FOR THE ORDER so why would you stop at point 6 above? Can you imagine that I have to deal with salespeople and entrepreneurs every day that are afraid to ask for the decision or the order? How ridiculous to perform all the necessary tasks and then to fall short in asking for the decision – the most critical action of all? Yet, this happens every day and this lack of professionalism is costing us all productivity and profit. The other consideration here is that due to this unprofessionalism and fear the salesperson or unprofessional entrepreneur will never be able to take the prospect to the next step in the selling cycle namely: OBJECTIONS. It has been noted by many of us professionals that it can take (depending on the situation and salesperson) up to six closes or more before a transaction is finalized. SIX CLOSES OR MORE! The question then is that if the unprofessional do not want to perform the first close which is a very simple question then how on earth are they earning income for themselves and for their respective employers? It is not a wonder that salespeople are only lasting three to six months in certain positions and can you even begin to imagine the cost if the sales department has such a high turnover within any organization and so much worse if this happens within a new business where finances and the allocation of cash-flow is critical for the survival of the business. Hiring the wrong salesperson may be the worst mistake which you can make as the drain on the business income could be catastrophic.

Let's consider the word ask shall we?

To ask, according to Collins Dictionary, I am not surprised, is a fairly simple procedure: *to say or write (something) in a form that requires an answer.* Wow! So to get an answer to a question all we have to do is ASK!? You and I will then have to ASK why salespeople do not spend more time in ASKING the closing question particularly in light of the fact that we are told that it takes six or more questions (closes), in most cases, before a successful close is achieved. While there are many people who will have as many views on the meaning of the word "ask" I want us to stay within the context of the use of the word within the sales process. I would like to present to you that the word "ask" within our context may also be taken to mean an "invitation" – an invitation to do business with the salesperson and his/her organization. How hard can this be? By asking for the order the salesperson is declaring that all that has been required and requested of him/her has been completed "so where to from here Mr. Prospect?" The salesperson will technically be soliciting an answer, by asking for one, as to the way forward. The question MUST be asked in order to determine the way forward because the way forward may mean dealing with an objection or with an answer in the affirmative which will ensure a successful conclusion to the selling process and progress in getting the new order processed.

Closing questions come in all different formats and may be determined upon the services and/or products being offered; however, the following questions may be considered and adapted for use during the closing cycle:

1. *We are able to plan your installation for next Tuesday-would that suite you, Susan?*
2. *David, are you satisfied with the proposal?*
3. *Jacky, when would you prefer that we start the services – the 1st of the month or the 15th?*
4. *Shane, if I could deliver the consignment before your international visitors arrive next Friday would you be prepared to conclude the paperwork with me right now?*

## Conclusion

The selling cycle, and in particular the closing process need not be complicated at all, however, some have sought to overcomplicate this with the very purpose of financial gain. Instead, and in my humble opinion, of helping salespeople they have confused them with way too many technical and unnecessary complications. Over the years, moving away from basics in sales has been costly and has raised false expectations to the new generation of salesperson and entrepreneur. Today sales staff has no clue of the selling process in that they have been made to believe that the new way to do sales is on the computer. We have lost the notion of a personal one-on-one meeting with the prospect at the cost of convenience and a non-confrontational approach to both the prospect and the client. We have been falsely led to believe that salespeople are just as effective (even more so in some cases) sitting behind a desk operating the computer in order to generate sales.

We also now hear that the "hard sale is a thing of the past" and that we should not make the client uncomfortable during the selling process. Apparently asking for the order is a big "no-no"! It is not a wonder therefore that salespeople are getting away with murder nowadays and that poor performance is tolerated. Tolerating a lost or directionless salesperson will cost us all dearly as the natural crux of many unprofessional salespeople is that they are "lazy" (short-cut crazy). They are lazy to prospect, they are lazy to abide by the systems in place to assist them (always a new short cut), they are lazy when it comes to administration and they are most certainly lazy when it comes to achieving sales quotas/targets and feel offended when the sales manager or the entrepreneur places pressure on them to perform according to quotas and/or targets. The moment pressure is applied they quit and move on to the next company that will tolerate their slothfulness. This is a shame as we are creating a "monster" and soon, if business is to survive, we are going to have to go back to basics when it comes to sales training and expectations as far as productivity is concerned.

We have started this book some would say backwards. However, I believe that we have done the right thing by starting at where sales are made and productivity is assured- THE CLOSE. Asking the closing question is a logical step and a basic progression once all the "homework" has been completed. Summarizing the needs is vital and must be aligned to the appropriate benefit-"need satisfaction selling". Steps one and two in the closing cycle naturally lead even the most reserved salesperson to the logical question of asking for the decision. What is even more logical is when the closing question is asked and the answer comes back as "no" then the very next question to ask is "WHY!"

When the closing question is asked and the answer is "no" it means that a second question such as "why" must be asked – LOGICAL! If the salesperson cannot go ahead with the proposal then we consider this to be the next phase of the selling cycle called HANDLING OBJECTIONS.

# Chapter 4

# When the Prospect says "NO!"
## *Six steps to handling $ales objections*

**Introduction**

John was a new salesperson and unfortunately found himself selling houses for a newly found agency who did not understand the concept of sales training. John was not trained professionally and neither did he attend sales courses which could help him to succeed. We all know of companies who take on salespeople, hand them a computer and a briefcase, and then they are told to "go sell". While John was not sales trained he was given a quota and he was now into his third month of below quota production figures – his job was now under threat. By the time that I started to mentor the young man he was mentally and physically drained but desperate for guidance and for answers – every sales trainer's dream. The first thing that struck me about John was his pleasant demeanor; going by outward appearances only, it would seem that he was a person that I could build trust with had I been a prospect. He only had a short time to build a rapport with me and I was impressed by his self-taught style of presenting himself to someone he does not know at all. He was outspoken and most certainly not shy to ask for help as was his initial plea to me once the ice had been broken.

What was John's greatest fear? He was afraid to ask for the order. I shared with John that he was in good company as most salespeople today have the same problem. I asked him why he was afraid to ask for the order and he gave me the standard answer – "I am afraid that I will not know what to do if they say 'no!'

A very good friend of mine astounded me one day when he revealed that he had been madly in love with a girl whom he had met in high school. I was told by Michael that he had fallen in love the moment he met Maggie in grade eleven. I asked if he had ever asked her out on a date and he said that he wanted to in grade eleven but "the moment didn't present itself" as she was always around friends. I asked him if he heard of a communications device called the telephone and after contemplating how to respond to my obvious sarcasm he stated that he could not muster the courage to give Maggie a call and pop the question. While I do understand that there those who are more reserved than others I could not get myself to understand a man who had spent the large part of his young life loving someone so intensely (according to him anyway as if I loved someone that much I would be the kind of guy to make the approach and probably would not even think twice about it), and yet so afraid to ask a simple question. In all honesty, for John, you or me, what would it take to ask someone you like out on a date? Apparently Maggie had in fact given John the necessary positive "buying signals" on a few occasions and decided to give up and move on when John did not make the connection.

Why would a person not want to ask the love of his/her life a simple question about going out on a date? Well, the same question may be posed to salespeople who do not ask for the order as is the case with our property sales agent namely John and many others like him all over the world. The answer to this question is far easier for the likes of John and Michael to answer than it would be to actually ask the dreaded question itself. Here is the answer as to WHY good, well-meaning people don't want to ask the closing question-whether in love or in business.

THE ABSOLUTE FEAR OF REJECTION! In other words they are so afraid of the "no" answer that they rather not ask the question to begin with!

John needed help and his first step was to ask me a closing question: "Trevor, would you help me?" I saw him close his eyes just before he got the last word out and his shoulders bent over in anticipation of the dreaded word, and then, against all odds according to John, I said "yes". He was astounded and I was happy that I could help. The first question which I asked John was "why" he had a problem with asking a closing question, and again, I was not surprised by his answer as I have heard the same thing many times in my career and from many well-known people which may surprise you should I ever reveal their names. I was told by John, and many people making sales a career will tell you the same thing: "I am not as afraid of asking the question as I am of the response which I may receive". My response: "so you assume that the response may be negative despite the fact that you have done all, and more, for the prospect in order to get yourself to the point of the close?" The answer was a convincing "yes!" I then asked John to explain to me how many answer variables he may experience when asking the closing question to which he correctly stated two. I asked him to tell me what he thought those were and he correctly informed me that one would either get a "yes" or a "no" as an answer. "I can work with you, John", I exclaimed!

John was correct, and while the "yes" or "no" answer might come in various forms it will still boil down to a "yes" or a "no". The biggest problem that most salespeople have then is not really asking the question but in the event of a "no" answer they have no clue as to how to respond from that moment on. I have good news for you in that this is exactly what this chapter is about! I am going to reveal to you a tried and tested method used by me and countless other "back to basics" sales professionals in dealing with and overcoming the dreaded "no" answer to your closing questions. The first thing that you need to understand is that in order to use the system I am about to reveal to you there is a prerequisite and that is that you ACTUALLY HAVE TO ASK THE CLOSING QUESTION! The other thing that you must be aware of is that you may have to ask it six times or more with a single client BEFORE you receive a "yes" answer. The way forward then for us is to understand that after receiving a "no" answer there is ALWAYS a next logical question which we use many times a day, and as you may know, the same word which comes out of the mouths of two or three year old toddlers to the point of driving us all crazy: "WHY?"

With our new found understanding of the above let's review the second part of the selling process as was first noted in chapter one of this book.

## Nine steps to successful selling

OBJECTIONS
Step 1-PAUSE
Step 2-ACKNOWLEDGE
Step 3-ISOLATE
Step 4-QUESTION
Step 5-ANSWER
Step 6-CLOSE

## Pause Defined

Pause is to the sales environment what a yield sign is to the traffic on the road. It does not mean stop but it also does not mean go. A yield sign at an intersection means that you can go if you have made sure that you will not obstruct or hinder oncoming traffic and so in essence in order to achieve this one needs to come to a stop but a very brief one at that. To pause means a similar principle will need to apply in that it means that you stop whatever you are doing just for a brief moment in time – not permanently but just for a moment.

We will also be correct in defining the word pause to be a *slight hesitation*, to *wait*, to *delay*, even to *waiver*. To pause, in our context, may be likened to a "breather", or in contemporary vernacular, "to hang back".

## Step 1-Pause (Explained)

Understand something about objections – THE PROSPECT HAS A RIGHT TO SAY NO! The prospect also has the right to raise questions! The prospect has the right to question your product, your service, your company, and yes, the prospect even has the right to question your credentials and you as a person if he/she feels that this may impact on their decision. As a reminder then: THE CLIENT HAS A RIGHT TO OBJECT! You will hear this concept again and again from me as we progress.

The reason that I need you to understand the rights of the prospect is so that you DON'T TAKE IT PERSONALLY!

Therefore, when the prospect says "no" or raises a question, this will not represent a personal attack on you or the company which you represent, and neither, will the prospect be negatively dissecting your product and/or service? I have been around the proverbial "sales block" many times in my life and I can assure you that when a prospect raises an objection of any kind the underlying psychology is that he/she simply feels that they do not have sufficient information in order to make a final decision. Many of the prospects that you will deal with are as smart if not smarter than you and I so expect to be TESTED! Now that you understand the basic concept of objections you will understand why I say that you will need to PAUSE *before* responding to the prospect. The silence will help you in two areas:

1. Give the prospect time to re-evaluate the objection (is it actually valid?).
2. Give you time to evaluate the objection with a view to formulating an appropriate response.

When you answer too quickly you may come across as being defensive (this happens to unprofessional salespeople who deny that the client has a right to object) and the client will immediately sense this consternation in you. What the prospect needs right now is a cool head from you and not a childish reaction and response. Should you not handle the pause step professionally your client will lose in that he/she will not be associated with your great company and services and/or products. You, and your business, on the other hand have expended a great deal of your energy and time only to walk away not having closed the sale professionally and then you alone will count the costs of your unprofessional actions.

I have on many occasions during the sales process with prospects simply IGNORED an objection if this surfaces during the presentation or any other phase up to the close. I am here going to testify to that again, on many occasions, either the client answers his/her own objection or the same does not resurface again. However, if the objection is a serious or genuine issue I can promise you that it will not go away and you will be forced to deal with the objection at some point in time – to me, preferably at the close as this is the time to both deal with objections with a view to giving the appropriate answer and to close yet again. I have also been bold enough to RESPECTFULLY request the client to give me the time to answer his concern at the end of my presentation. Why? Well he may have forgotten the objection by then or he may have answered it himself/herself during the sales process and/or my presentation of my services and products may provide the answer needed by the prospect.

**Professional tip**: By answering an objection too quickly, you may also be creating an objection that is not real but just a "smoke screen" designed deliberately to get you off track or to throw you off balance.

However, I also want you to know that if the objection is in fact real then it will not go away and the prospect will most certainly be raising the objection again at some stage. Be ready to respond professionally no matter when an objection arises.

## Acknowledge Defined

First of all, as we try to understand the concept of acknowledging someone, you and I must understand that this is a conscious ACT. In order to acknowledge the prospects objection it would thus intimate that you have actually LISTENED and RECEIVED the prospect's objection or question. The acknowledge stage does not only imply that you have listened but that you also view the statement by the prospect as serious enough to acknowledge receipt thereof. Therefore, it is not possible to acknowledge what the prospect has said if you were not listening in the first place and unfortunately it is in the lack of professional communication by the salesperson that the message from the prospect is lost. For instance, a real estate agent was specifically told during the needs analysis phase that the prospect requires four bedrooms and a study, they do not want a house with a swimming pool and the house must be located in a quiet neighborhood. At the time of the close the prospect sends out a clear message of "no". The salesperson at least asked the next logical question: "Why!"

The prospect (if it were me) would be blunt enough and to the point, and would be well within his/her rights to exclaim: "You did not listen to my needs at all! I had very specific requirements which I discussed with you at the outset of our meeting, and forgive me for saying so; I get the clear impression that you have ignored me on all of these. I requested four bedrooms and you have taken us to houses having three. I also made a request for a study as I am an author and work from home on many occasions and you have not shown me one house containing a study. Why are you showing me houses with pools when I specifically requested that a pool be omitted during your search? Finally, many of the houses which you have taken me to are situated in either busy roads or noisy neighborhoods and I was very specific about a quiet area as I need to focus when writing and noise can become very distracting to me!"

The idea is to pay attention at the needs analysis phase, AND TO WRITE THESE DOWN, as only then are you able to meet the needs. Should you not understand the prospects needs then you will have to clear this up at the beginning of the sales cycle. You cannot acknowledge what you don't hear and if you don't listen then you will lose. Many objections come about because salespeople don't listen and apply the knowledge, and because of this, unnecessary obstacles are raised during the most critical time of the selling cycle namely the close. In other words, and I mean this with all sincerity, salespeople become, due to their own unprofessionalism, their own worst enemies and destroy their chances of a smooth close at the end.

Collins Dictionary on defining acknowledge: *To recognize or admit the truth of a statement; to show recognition of a person ...; to make known that a letter or a message has been received.*

Acknowledgment: *The act of acknowledging something or someone.*

The act of acknowledging is an all-encompassing action in that it gives us the ability to acknowledge both negative and positive parts to the sales conversation. If you have said something wrong then this is considered a negative action on your part and acknowledging this as fact will go a long way in building rapport and trust with the prospect. On the other hand the prospect is positive and the salesperson is positive and the objection is positive and a professional salesperson will not hesitate to gain a positive conclusion during the closing process. When the prospect raises an objection and the salesperson acknowledges this as genuine and true, then he/she is simply stating this in one of the following ways: Admit, recognize, accept, grant and concede. Surely this is not that difficult to understand? The worst thing to do though, and this is the crux of the failure of the unprofessional, is to arrogantly DENY the prospect his/her rights during the closing process, which is in essence, is opposite to the spirit of acknowledging the prospects objection. To me personally, one word defines acknowledge best within the context of the closing cycle in sales and that is the word RECOGNIZE. By acknowledging then it must be taken to mean that you and I are professional enough to recognize the prospect's right first of all to raise the objection in the first place and then to acknowledge receipt of the message in this regard.

## Step 2-Acknowledge (Explained)

Within the context of the closing phase of the selling cycle we are acknowledging (recognizing) two critical actions, namely:

1. Concede the prospect's right to the objection in the first place and acknowledging their point of view as real.
2. The prospect has a right to ask questions during the sales cycle and also to express their views with regards to you, your product and/or service and your company which is represented by you.

**Professional tip:** Never give the prospect the impression that you are questioning their rights – in many cases they know exactly what these are!

When acknowledging the prospect's right to raise an objection or a question you must use empathy (the art of placing yourself into the position of the prospect) and understand the kind of words which you would want to hear after you have raised an objection had you been the prospect at that moment. You may develop your very own responses; however, I want to present you with the following responses which I have used effectively over the years. You may choose to use them or develop you're very own and unique acknowledgement responses:

- *John, I understand how you feel.*
- *Susan, I am glad that you brought that question up.*
- *George, There's a lot to be said for your point of view.*
- *Mary, let's think this one through together shall we?*
- *Charles, I appreciate you sharing that with me.*
- *Charlene, your feelings are quite natural at this point.*
- *Jeffrey, I am certain that ultimately you want to make the right decision.*

## Isolate Defined

You will see me refer to a *circle* during this explanation and that is what the prospect will do to you should you not isolate any and all objections as being the only issues to deal with prior to asking the final closing questions. The *circle effect*, so to speak, when asking the closing question has to do with the inability of the unprofessional salesperson entrepreneur during the closing process. The salesperson fails to solicit a successful conclusion due to a lack of understanding of the act of isolation. In answering an objection too quickly without isolating the same as the ONLY reason why the prospect will not move ahead at that time will initiate the *circle effect*.

The word *exclude* comes to mind in my attempt to help you to understand this critical stage of the closing process and how to handle objections. In this context the word exclude will help is to understand that we RULE OUT any possibility that more objections exist in the mind of the prospect prior to asking for the order as a final question. In other words we want to discover and uncover ALL of the potential stumbling blocks (objections) with one purpose and one purpose only and that is to get these out of our way before we ask for the order. The following illustration will help you to understand both the concept and the tremendous frustration that is felt by an unprofessional trying to close without knowledge of how to ISOLATE objections.

**ISOLATION CIRCLE EFFECT (Representing consistent failure to close the sale)**

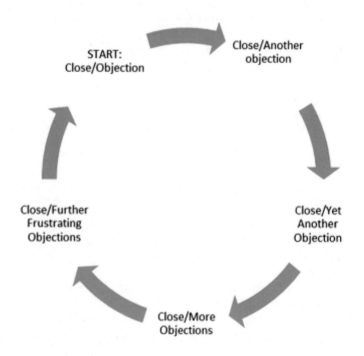

START:
Close/Objection

Close/Another
objection

Close/Yet
Another
Objection

Close/More
Objections

Close/Further
Frustrating
Objections

**Step 3-Isolate (Explained)**

In your and my current understanding of the action to *isolate* we must then do whatever is necessary to ensure that the first objection given by the prospect is the only problem/issue the prospect may have BEFORE attempting to answer it.

**Professional tip:** There is no sense whatsoever in answering one objection until you know how many there are before your final close.

The professional entrepreneur salesperson will not allow him/her to be "taken for a ride" and I don't mean "joy ride" as the Isolation Circle Effect ("ICE") will leave you out in the cold. You will not only frustrate yourself but most certainly the prospect will feel this frustration and soon join you in how you feel-the end result will be nothing less than "lose-lose" situation. The question is HOW do we overcome at this critical juncture and what are the practical questions to ask when one arrive at this point in the sales cycle? To me, and while you may develop many more of your own over a period of time, I have selected two questions which have helped me to isolate objections during the final closing moments and they are:

1. *Paul, other than that, is there any additional problems you see?*
2. *Justine, is there anything else that will prevent you from moving ahead if we solve that problem today?*

Alternative…?

3. *Adam, should I be able to resolve this issue for you would you be prepared to move ahead with the proposal today or do you foresee any other challenges that I should cover for you?*

## Question Defined

To question within this context does not mean that the salesperson need go into "interrogation mode". When you ask the prospect a question during this phase then both your physical demeanor and attitude had better be interpreted by the prospect as "I would really like to know how you feel about that?" You do not talk down to the prospect but yet you come across as a concerned professional. You are not the police department, the CIA, FBI and you are most certainly not a part of MI6 or the Russian KGB. You have a sales prospect in front of you who may be confused or unsure of some aspect of your presentation, proposal, company, services and/or products or even unsure about you so consider this when questioning the prospect. The questioning referred to here has nothing to do with a negative attitude which may come to the fore and prevalent within the salesperson and neither does this action refer to you cross-examining the prospect. Furthermore, you must also understand that this is not the time, due to a negative demeanor and/or attitude, to interrogate (in the negative sense), interview or grill your prospect, and if you feel it necessary to do so then you had better understand that your prospect must never feel that you are.

The idea here is to EXTRACT critical information out of your prospect in such a way that he/she is happy to give you the answers. I feel that the word QUIZ may also apply at this stage as this is more of what you will be doing in that your quizzing the prospect may reveal the very reason he/she feels the way that they do about whatever is bothering them.

My old friend the Collins Dictionary refers: *A form of words addressed* [not aggressively for our context] *to a person in order to obtain an answer; an act of asking; an investigation into some problem.*

Questioning: *Proceeding from or characterized by doubt or uncertainty;* [I love this one] *intellectually inquisitive.*

## Step 4-Question (Explained)

The question is then what are we in fact questioning during this stage of the closing cycle? The prospect has raised an objection, which we have all agreed they have a right to do, and we politely want to know why they feel the way that they do-SIMPLE! In context now then you will understand that the previous step was to isolate the objection as the only objection standing in the way of you concluding business with the prospect, and for the sake of the exercise she has said, "No I have nothing else that I know of standing in our way!" This is great news but you and I will still have to deal with the ONE objection then right? Right!

**For example:** "Thank you for clarifying that there are no further challenges from your side Mary. I understand that you have a concern that we may not be able to meet your national delivery requirements; however, may I ask why you feel this way?"

There are three key aspects of step 4 for you to consider and adopt:

1. Question the prospect as to why he/she feels the way that they do.
2. Understand that prospects may raise a question/objection for some hidden reason.
3. Always try to understand the reason for the question/objection.

When you question the prospect as to why he/she feels the way they do about what you have to offer they may tell you one thing but mean another. For instance, in the previously mentioned example the client feels that you may not be able to meet the national distribution requirements so understand that there has got to be a reason she feels that way. Was it something you said during the presentation process, did she develop a negative impression by visiting the company website or has she had previous bad experiences which made her look bad and her goal is now to protect her reputation? During this process it is important to discover the reason for the objection or you will not be able to move ahead with the close. The idea is to discover the initial objection and answer the objection to the satisfaction of the PROSPECT not you. If you cannot answer the objection the prospect will not feel comfortable to move ahead. Therefore, BEFORE answering the objection make sure that you completely understand the objection. If the salesperson is unclear of the objection or the meaning thereof then it is better to have the prospect repeat the objection to you-rather safe than sorry I would say.

In certain circumstances, it is desirable to probe to the surface the real reason/s for the prospects feelings or thoughts as it is always more effective to question the prospect's position than it is to defend your own. The secret is then to restate (in question format) an objection in less objectionable words even if understanding has not been an issue. This action will help to clarify the actual objection. By restating the objection in less objectionable terms in the form of a question will many times force the prospect to consider the objection as after the question is asked you are going to KEEP QUIET. The added pressure upon the prospect will help you to gently squeeze the answer out of them. The prospect will always have an agenda for why and how they buy and many times buy for their own reasons and not ours or what we think motivates them to a successful close. The other thing that you and I will need to understand about the psychological make-up of the buyer is that he/she considers their reasons for buying to be valid to them at all times. A buyer is not interested in your and my reasons for why they should do business with us but rather their personal goals, aspirations and value systems dictate their buying behavior.


**Professional tip:** It is important to allow the buyer to answer his/her own objection/s as much as is possible.

The above can be accomplished by simply asking the prospect why they feel the way that they do about the objection raised by them or by being silent after the objection was raised in the first place. Silence applies subtle pressure and this pressure makes the prospect think about many things but most of all how to respond to you. In many instances I have had prospects answer their own objections BEFORE I could, and this, all because I was not in a hurry to answer and kept my silence until they responded.

Once you have uncovered why the prospect has raised the objection then in many instances it would be preferable to deal with the underlying reason for the objection, clarify with the prospect that you have satisfactorily answered the concerns and thereby the objection BEFORE asking for the order (the very next logical step).

## Answer Defined

The word "answer", referred to above, has more to do with acknowledgement and response in our context. By answering you have recognized that the prospect's objection is both genuine and serious, and in this light, it deserves a response in order to satisfy the prospect's question and concern in this regard. What you will thus be offering is a solution, remedy and explanation of the legitimate objection raised. You will resolve, solve and explain the objection on behalf of the prospect and your goal is to "get the business of closing" back on track as objections are nothing more than a detour on the road to sales success.

Be very careful how you answer! You need to remain calm at all times as you are a professional remember? You are the one presenting the "way out" of the perceived hurdle by the prospect. As the professional you will be responsible for answering the objection and not defending your position. While at times you may need to refute, rebut and defend yourself the prospect must never feel this in any way at all if you are to conclude successfully. Thus, when you and I finally get to answer an objection raised by the prospect then we had better understand that we need to be accurate in our response, non-defensive in our actions and correct in our answer-anything else will break down the fragile but developing trust between the parties. The prospect may want you to meet certain requirements so the question is can you and the answer you give tell him/her why you are so convinced that you can. Lies and deceit will be detected and will destroy the relationship before it even has time to mature. Your answer then is a solution to a problem so you had better make sure that the answer which you are about to give not only works in practice but satisfies the prospect in totality.

**Step 5-Answer (Explained)**

So far we have spent some time in moving through the critical steps needed in order to professionally handle objections: (1) Pause (2) Acknowledge (3) Isolate (4) Question. While the process of answering the prospect after an objection has been raised is considered a critical step in the entire process I can assure you that if you perform this task in a less than professional manner you may as well leave the prospect's office as you will fail in your attempt to close. Of this fact I am most assured! PLEASE focus now and understand the concept and necessary actions and attitudes at this time. You must understand that the very next step is the all-important final stage, the close, which will either see you get the business or you may walk away, after all of your work and effort, with absolutely nothing.

As you have gone through the various steps as previously dealt with you will now begin to understand that you may not need to perform this step. Why? Because if you read and understood what I have shared with you so far you will understand that the prospect may have already answered his/her own objection-GREAT! However, if this has not happened then you will need to understand the following with regard to answering the prospect's objection as by now you will know that the objection is not a smoke screen and that it will not go away until you answer it or deal with it. Over the years I have developed a few techniques which I have used to answer the prospect's objection. I do want to warn you though that some of these techniques may take practice to perfect and for these to come out in a "smooth" non-offensive manner. However, by now you may have built enough rapport or trust with your prospect in order to achieve your goal and no matter the technique applied. You will also develop your own techniques so don't think that mine are written in stone. I have generally used four techniques namely:

1. The Boomerang.
2. The professional explanation.
3. The counter-balance strategy.
4. The denial method.

While you will need to focus and absorb during this step I will provide you with examples of how to implement these techniques in the actual selling situation.

### The Boomerang

The client comes up with a negative objection for instance: "Trevor, I can't go ahead with your proposal because I need the installation completed by the 1st of the month and you have already indicated that you need seven days' notice from date of signature on the agreement in order to install." When you learn the art of throwing a Boomerang the idea is that it comes back to the hand or arm which you used to let it go during the throwing process.

Collins Dictionary: *An action or statement that recoils on its originator.*

**For example:** As stated above, the prospect may object to the fact that he/she cannot have installation by the 1st of the month (obviously an emergency situation for the prospect because for the sake of our example it is already the 28$^{th}$ day of the previous month) and due to the short notice given by the prospect the company's service department will need at least seven days from date on contract in order to prepare for the installation-they are also busy with other installations and will need the time to accommodate this new project should the prospect decide to move ahead.

The entrepreneur salesperson should reply in all honesty and state that the reason for the seven days' notice is that the installation team/s is usually fully booked seven days in advance and this is unfortunately out of your control as a salesperson. "I do understand that the installation will need to be completed before your home office/head office visit on the 5$^{th}$ of next month and this is of concern to you."

Trying to make this work for both parties is critical so you may want to use the Boomerang technique as follows:

*However Susan, I do want to make this work for us both and therefore May I propose the following? What I can arrange with my managers and service department is that we reduce the four days allotted for the service down to only two days. This will give me time to process the paperwork between us and to get our guys on site by at least the 2$^{nd}$ of August with the completion date set for 4$^{th}$ August which is a day before your corporate visit. May I ask you Susan, should I be able to make all these arrangements would you be prepared to move ahead with the paperwork right now?*

**The Professional Explanation**

There are going to be those times that objections are valid, even in your own eyes, the goal then would be not to waste any more time and get down to presenting a professional answer once you are completely satisfied that you have adequately and professionally analyzed the objection. In order to answer an obvious and valid objection I recommend that you consider doing one or more of three things:

- Analyze from non-company situations (maybe a competitor for instance)
- Answer by using examples from your own company situations.
- Answer by using third-party stories.

**For example:** *Susan, we don't like to rush such an important and large installation as just last week I was called back to a prospect who refused to give me the necessary time to do the installation professionally. I was told by the prospect that the entire installation was botched and many units were installed incorrectly. The long and the short of the challenge for the client was that he had no option but to cancel the new agreement with our competitors and has now finally appointed us as his new service provider. We have completed the installation professionally and the client is now very happy. Should I be able to provide you with the same professional service and installation and saving you time would you be prepared to move ahead with me today?*

**For example:** *Susan, I am able to inform you that while our service and installation department requires seven days' notice of any installation due their workload I have been able to persuade our sales manager, in the past, to take urgent installations up with the service manager with good results. If I am able to make a call to John right now and arrange this for you would you be prepared to authorize the agreement right away?*

**For example:** *A friend of mine shared one of his nightmare stories with me Susan. I want to just share this with you. Apparently, one of his clients needed an urgent installation, and while he was told by his service department that the installation was not possible in the time allotted by his client he went ahead anyway and had his prospect authorize the* *paperwork. My friend, who has now learnt a valuable lesson, achieved his monthly sales quota; however, he did so at the expense of his client. The prospect was under pressure as she had terminated the services of the previous supplier due to poor service levels. The salesperson, my friend, was also under severe pressure to perform and to achieve his quota for the month. This was obviously a recipe for a disaster. Instead of considering the needs and expectations of the prospect he did not and the entire situation from there was a failure. The installation was not done on time and the units were installed in all of the wrong areas on site. These were then taken off and they began the service and installation all over again. I don't want this for you and my concern is your complete satisfaction. Should I be able to promise you a smooth installation based upon you and me working together without undue pressure would you be prepared to come on board with me right now?*

## The Counter-Balance Strategy

One again, we are dealing with objections here which cannot be denied and their validity is beyond question-this will need to be answered professionally. One of the additional strategies which I have used is to compensate for the valid objection by using what I have come to call an over-balancing benefit.

The prospect claims that the cost of your company's housekeeping program is too high.

**For example:** *Paul, when we first met* (needs analysis stage) *you shared that you were frustrated with your current supplier for housekeeping and when I asked you why you shared the following with me. According to you the current supplier frustrated you a great deal and this was because of their lack of quality due to the clear absence of professional supervision. You also stated that it seemed to you that the housekeepers were simply doing their own thing and had no* sense of accountability toward anyone at all. I don't want this for you Paul as your complete satisfaction is of prime importance to me. Our company has amassed many years of experience in our industry and I can assure you that we have seen the kind of frustration currently being experienced by you on many occasions. Company's like yours hire us because we are solution driven meaning that we listen to what your concerns are and then take time to remove these as a source of frustration to you. In your case, and should you decide to move ahead with me today you will find us different in that we are one of few service providers nationally which ensures a minimum of three monthly senior branch office visits made up of the service manager, the area manager and a senior regional service manager. We have also made provision for a permanent and full-time on-site supervisor whose function it will be to manage the site scope of work, the staff and to communicate with you on a weekly basis regarding the housekeeping program. The cost of all these additional quality assurance staff has been included into the proposal and so you will not receive any additional amounts on your monthly bill. You will now also be assured that your housekeeping program on site will be managed professionally meaning that you will be free to focus more of your attention of your core business. Should you be happy with this change and new level of professionalism would you be prepared to authorize the agreement with me right now?

## The Denial Method

This technique is to be used when you simply are left with no choice by the prospect-you will have to deal with the objection head-on. I want to also take this opportunity to warn you as the denial method must be used with respect and with dignity at all times. Should you not use this technique with the utmost professionalism you will, without a doubt sever any possible future relationship which may develop despite your answer to the prospect's objection.

The prospect may brazenly state: "I hear that your company actively bargains on pricing!" You may want to reply as I do and as is stated in the following example.

**For example:** *Maggie, unfortunately someone has misinformed you. Due to the level of service and quality produced by our company this is not possible. I am able to show you details of several other proposals, like yours, which I have presented recently and you will find the pricing structure exactly the same. I hope that this will not stand in our way of moving forward today?*

The denial method must only be used then when the objection is obviously untrue and the use thereof by the entrepreneur salesperson must be considered very carefully. Your answer or response must remain of a professional level at all times as your goal is to always preserve the business relationship for now and into the future. Whatever you do, do not "burn your bridges" with prospects as they may not become your client today but there is always another day. While you "can't win them all" you must leave the door open if your answer and close cannot lead to a business venture between you and the prospect.

**Professional tip:** If you don't believe your answer then the prospect won't either and this means that you have NOT convinced them to move forward. You MUST believe what you are saying so that this aspect can come through in your answer.

### Close Defined

You and I know, and most people will agree, in the sales environment, when the word CLOSE is used it generally means *the end* of the sales cycle. When we close the door we also *shut the door* and feel *secure.* When we close the sale we also close the proverbial door on the sale and the income from the sale makes us feel more secure. To ask for the order is as natural as it is to close the door and in both cases the result is security. The word close means then that we have *concluded* the sales cycle as much as we have closed the door because we have completed a day's work and are now home for the evening. We have *ended something* which we have started and we have *finished* and *concluded* an action which in this case is the sales cycle or the handling of objections. There is also now the *termination* of the discussion with the prospect which hopefully by now has become a client and a *cessation* of the sales pitch has now come to an end and a successful *conclusion.* We have completed and "wound up" the job at hand.

As I have said before, you and I have summarized the needs and the benefits and have gone into the mode of closing the business off. The most LOGICAL thing to do is to ask for the order at this point and the most ILLOGICAL thing to do at this stage is not to close off for the business. Get this in your head and you will never regret it for as long as you live NEVER be afraid to ask for the order as this is how you make a living and provide for your family. Should you fail to understand the importance of not coming to a logical conclusion by asking for the order EVERY time that you are in the selling environment you WILL fail and this is my promise to you. If you say that you are successful without closing then I want to say that you could be so much more successful if you take my advice on closing. I will go as far as to say that professional salespeople that close are true salespeople and the rest are simply order takers and useless in my book in the actual sales call.

The action then is rather than assuming your answer satisfied the prospect's objection-ASK FOR THE ORDER AGAIN!

**Professional tip:** You have not satisfied the prospects objection until you get a positive decision-one simply cannot get more clear-cut than this!

## Step 6-CLOSE (Explained)

1. Summarize the needs AGAIN.
2. Summarize the benefits AGAIN.
3. Ask for the order AGAIN.

Prospects will give numerous objections and many you will hear over and over again within any given industry. The most common objection of all has to do with pricing but I can assure you that if you add as many benefits to the prospects needs and wants as you can the price will look better and better. Remember this in your sales life. The more the net gain value between what the prospects wants and what you have to offer the better the price looks. EVERYONE deals with a pricing objection, and this, in sales all over the world so expect it and be ready to reduce your perceived high price by adding NET GAIN VALUE and by doing so the price will seem more and more competitive.

Just before we conclude this chapter I want to help you to understand that there are certain objections which you will have to deal with. The reason that I present these to you is so that you can use these to practice answering them BEFORE you are in front of a prospect who presents these to you. My hope is that you will see these less as objections and more "a cry for help" by the prospect for more information.

## Some Prospect Objections

**1.** Competitor pricing is better.

You may want to answer these using the following guide:

- Full service as opposed to no service.
- Quality as opposed to savings.
- Net benefits over your competitor
- Point out some exclusive feature, benefit or service looking for the net gain.

- "John, have I not shown you value during our discussion?"

- "Mary, what part of the service would you like me to eliminate so that we are able to come in on budget?"

**2.** Prospect has a friend in a similar business or industry.

You may want respond as follows:

- "Peter, if this is the case then please help me to understand why you have allowed me to meet with you this morning?"

- "Maggie, might I ask you what is more important to you, quality service or friendship?"

- Sean, will prioritizing your personal relationship with your friend help you to achieve your objectives for the company?"

**3.** Prospect believes that your competitor has better marketing and thus believes they are a better company than yours.

Consider the following possible responses:

-Question the competitor's services/products on offer which compete against your offering.

- Prioritize the important services/products and focus on these.

- "Mark, what service were you hoping to receive that I may have overlooked?"

**4.** The prospect says that he/she would like to "think it over".

May I suggest that you consider implementing as below?

- "Sharon, if we resolved the issue that needs some thought would you be ready to make the decision today?"

- If necessary, give the prospect some time alone to consider the issue-sit in the reception if

You have to.


## Conclusion

Before we end this chapter I would like to put in place all the pieces the puzzle in order for you to see clearly how each step of handling objections comes together. While you and I have spent time dissecting each phase of the process I can assure you that if you were to study and apply these I will be able to encourage you, with a great deal of confidence, that you will see a substantial difference in both your closing ratios and your personal confidence. You will go from simply selling to a Master Salesperson and you will go from being simply an entrepreneur to becoming a Master Entrepreneur. I have now given you secrets that have taken some of us Master Entrepreneur Salesperson's decades to discover and have simply "handed" them to you. It is not as much as to whether they will work or not as this fact has been proven many times over; however, what is more important is what will you do with what you have now been given? You have nothing to lose if you ask me! Should you choose to continue on in your current path then that is what you will do but should you embrace my "back to basics" style of handling objections then you should prepare yourself for reaching a new level of sales and professionalism.

With the above said and done then I will now move into an example selling situation which should help you to understand clearly how each piece fits together when handling objections and finally closing professionally.

You have just asked the closing question AFTER you have summarized the needs and the benefits:

*Susan, based upon the presented needs and benefits as was just pointed out I want to inform you that we are able to present an offer to the owner for number 24 Summer Lane tomorrow. Are you happy to move ahead with the paperwork now (closing question)?*

*No Trevor, I am not!* (I would now PAUSE)

*Susan, I hope that you don't mind me asking this question but I am curious as to why you have made this decision?*(close) *Trevor, I have given the house some thought overnight, and while I truly feel that it is a good fit for my family* (buying signal)*, I don't like the fact that it has metal garage doors. Susan,* (I would now ACKNOWLEDGE) *I am glad that you raised this point as I can see that this disappoints you about the house. May I ask,* (I would now ISOLATE and QUESTION) *other than the metal garage door are there any other problems you see or would you be prepared to move ahead* (trial close)*? Trevor, yes, I have also had time to consider the fact that the house does not have a deck around the barbeque area. Please don't get me wrong Trevor I love the house* (buying signal)*! Susan, may I just understand your concerns at this point? You are not happy with the metal garage door and the lack of a deck around the barbeque area and can understand that this may be making you question your willingness to move forward. The good news is that I have hope* (says I with a smile as I trial close)*; however, other than the two concerns which you have raised is there anything else that will prevent you from moving ahead if we solve these issues for you (close)? Trevor, I do have one more thing! I know that I asked you not to show me houses that have a swimming pool; however, I just love the entertainment area* (buying signal) *and the trees in the background* (buying signal) *and I felt that this would be perfect for my grandchildren when they come around* (buying signal)*. Trevor, I hate to do this to you but now I feel that the lack of a pool could become a deal breaker on this house but I absolutely love the house* (buying signal)*. I have no further issues with the house and just hoped that these three areas were covered then I would be happy to authorize the offer right away* (buying signal)*.*

*Susan,* (I would now ANSWER – she has also clearly given me her reasons for feeling the way that she does) *you know that my goal is to make you happy, and that you will come out of this purchase completely satisfied, so may I ask you then that should we be able to rectify the current concerns around the garage door being metal as opposed to solid wood, a deck around the barbeque area and a swimming pool closer to the trees would you be happy to move ahead with me right now (close-SHUT-UP)? Trevor, yes, but how will you be able to make this happen? I don't understand. Susan, I can see that this is the home for you and your family and while I may need a little help from you I think that I could make this happen so that you are happy* (trial close). *Susan, based upon your requirements I will place a suspensive condition clause in the current offer which would take on the following wording: The purchase of this house is subject to the purchaser obtaining three written proposals for (1) changing the garage door from steel to solid wood (2) adding a deck around the barbeque area (3) the construction of a swimming pool. The offer is also subject to the approval by a financial institution of such proposals which shall be included as a part of the first mortgage on the property* (close).

*Trevor, this is great! I never thought that a solution was possible. I do love the house so* (buying signal)*!*

*Susan,* (I would now prepare to CLOSE yet again) *based upon my proposal, are you happy to accept the cost of the changes to the property, as was requested by you, to be added to the mortgage? Yes, I am* (buying signal)*! Are you happy with the suspensive condition clause in the offer protecting you in the event that the bank does not grant the finances for the additions and changes? Yes I am Trevor* (buying signal/close). *Susan based upon your agreement then I would need you to authorize the following documents* (close).

The idea here is not for you to concern yourself with the legal aspects as to my example as certain aspects (legally) speaking may not apply in all countries. However, focus on the example as a whole and see how all the parts come together when handling objections. I can tell you that once you have mastered the technique of handling objections professionally then your entire business and sales life will change.

# Chapter 5

# Understanding Group Decision Makers
## *Who are they?*

**Introduction**

While as an entrepreneur salesperson you will have an opportunity to present your products and/or services to smaller businesses it must also be said that you may find yourself spending more of your time focusing on larger businesses. Even businesses being managed by a husband and wife team could be incorporated under the category of group decision makers as the wife may make the decision at the time and the husband may have been an influence from the beginning of the sales process. However, for the sake of understanding the various parts of group decision making we will accept that generally speaking when we refer to group decision makers we understand this to mean that multiple people are involved in the decision making process somehow.

You may not understand this at this point but the process of making a decision as to whether to go with your proposal or not started once you set up the first meeting with a view to doing a formal presentation of your services and/or products.

You, as a professional salesperson, made a call to the company President and set up an appointment for a meeting. The company President understands, by way of your phone call, that you are to do a presentation of your services, products and the company which you represent. It is thus a common practice within business today, where multiple departments are affected, that the company President will notify all the relevant players to be present at the meeting and your presentation. The question is: "Who are these people attending the meeting and what role will they play in arriving at a favorable decision after your presentation?" This would be a very good question indeed!

The professional salesperson will quickly realize that many decisions to purchase are in fact decided upon by more than one person at a time and this type of buying is performed by group decision makers. With this in mind the entrepreneur salesperson makes it his/her business to understand how to deal with or manage such a buying entity. Groups can contain many different people representing numerous departments within a business and each person will have a very specific role to fulfil within the buying environment. As professional salespeople you and I must understand these roles and also understand how to meet the needs of each person within the group-this is critical if we are to succeed within this environment.

While we have now established that we must have a better understanding of group decision making we must also not erroneously conclude that this is a complex thing to come to terms with. For instance, while I am sure that many of my friends and colleagues out there may disagree with me it is my belief that there are only really four categories making up group decision makers, namely:

1. The Initiator.
2. The Gatekeeper.
3. The Influencer.
4. The Purchaser.

The goal here will be to get you to understand the role of each "player" and that the role may be duplicated around the boardroom table. What I am saying is that it is quite possible to have two Initiators, three Gatekeepers, four Influencers and two decision makers sitting around the same table. My experience though has taught me, which I now give to you, that no matter how many of the "President's men/women" sit around the table you and I are generally able to place them into one of the four categories mentioned above. I also want to warn you that while it may be that only one person will make the final decision the others around the table may say "NO!"

## The Initiator

The Initiator is simply put, in my opinion, a leader while also capable of being quite manipulative when forced to be. This person usually starts out with a challenge which has either been noticed or which has been brought to his/her attention via a third party within the company. The very essence of such a person is to resolve challenges with a clear intention of resolving these PERMANENTLY. The Initiator is most certainly not one who initiates anything which he/she does not believe in and that shows clear signs of not providing a clear and lasting solution. In fact, the Initiator can either be your best friend during a presentation or your worst enemy if during your presentation you do not match your capabilities with the original promise of a lasting solution to his/her challenge. This is also not the kind of person that you want to make a fool of. For instance, if you had made promises and you do not deliver on these and because of this he/she is embarrassed in front of peers then you have simply created and arch enemy.

Some characteristics of the Initiator are that they are generally enterprising individuals-meaning that they are resourceful, daring and bold, if you will. They will find a way to take care of the problem and not be afraid to make a decision to back the prospective supplier until the solution is implemented.

They will not mind bold or radicle changes to the status quo as long as they see a positive outcome. Introducing the wrong suppliers to an organization could be embarrassing and this is not the person that you want to make look bad as they have great memories and will not forgive lies and deceit very easily if at all. Generally (you will get the exceptions to the rule of course as elsewhere in life), the Initiator is a friendly person and will show enthusiastic tendencies mixed together with high energy levels. There are also three further crucial characteristics which help us to identify such a person within the boardroom environment and they are:

1. Imaginative.
2. Creative.
3. Inventive.

Finally, the Initiator is known to one and all as the person who first recognized and identified the initial challenge and that the same needed to be resolved permanently. The Initiator also recognized that you and I may have the potential to take care of his/her challenge and that is why we are now ready to present this to the group in the boardroom. Hence, we can conclude then that should you not make the mistake of embarrassing the Initiator then you and I will have a friend in such a one.

## The Gatekeeper

Simply put then the Gatekeeper keeps or secures entrance to the prospect's business and while some may deem this person a "sales enemy" I tend to disagree. We will deal with the role of the Gatekeeper in more depth during the chapter on handling the telephone I can assure you that making a friend of the Gatekeeper is most certainly not as difficult as is being made out to be. However, our goal now is to understand the person's role within the group.

The Gatekeeper's role is to ask all the right questions which will help him to eliminate you from the company's vendor list. To such a person only the best will do and he/she will interrogate you if they have to in order to ascertain why you claim what you do about your company and product and will want all the necessary reassurances that you are able to deliver. Should there be any doubt in the Gatekeeper's mind as to your personal and corporate integrity then you will find your presentation cut short and will see you packing your bags before you even get to second base. You may liken this individual to the Gatekeeper as was displayed in the movie "Thor". This man was not charged with protecting the realm as such but access to it, which you and I may argue is tantamount to protecting the realm. The task of the Gatekeeper then is focused and is simple in nature but frustrating to those that want to gain access: KEEP THE UNWANTED OUT! Such is the charge of the Gatekeeper whether in the protection of a realm (Thor) or in protecting the corporate image and integrity of the company's purchases.

The Gatekeeper then, within the context of your presentation and your desire to do business with the prospective company, will stand out as the most knowledgeable person on the company's vendors. He may even control and limit the company's vendor list but most certainly will have full knowledge about each vendor. In fact, this person may in fact have been the "father" of the company's vendor list and may have approved each vendor currently doing business with the company-a pretty important person in anyone's book I would say. The Gatekeeper, in this scenario may be a Procurement Manager/Director or VP in charge of purchasing for the company, and as such, will control vendor information which flows within the organization and to other group members.

In a nutshell then the Gatekeeper will ensure that you are on your toes and that you answer all relevant questions throughout the interview process. His/her goal is to ensure that unless you can add the much needed value you and your company will not make it on to his/her vendor list. What he/she is looking to do is to ensure that he/she has a functional vendor list and one which is reliable and productive – he/she does not believe that more is better so getting on to his/her list is what you are on about and he/she is on about keeping you off the list UNLESS you can prove that you are absolutely worthy of this "honor".

## The Influencer

Collins Dictionary on the word "influence": *an effect of one person or thing on another; the power of a person or thing to have such an effect; to have an effect upon (actions or events); to persuade or induce.*

The above clearly reflects that the Influencer wields a great deal of power within the group sales environment. While not the ultimate Decision Maker the Influencer may be likened to a mother's influence over her adult son. She cannot make the final decision for him any longer but she most certainly can and will influence her son to make a decision which she believes will ultimately benefit her son and her family.

Thus in the context of the above and within the boardroom environment the Influencer must be considered to be an important person and part of the boardroom team. Within the context of the prospect's company I can assure you that this person will hold a senior or even an executive position within the organization. This person will show clear signs of authority and you will also notice the unwillingness of others around the table to challenge this person in the forum. He or she will display an attitude of dominance, leadership and importance during your presentation. This is a powerful person and you will need to identify this personality as quick as possible during your presentation and the goal will be for you to treat such a one with the utmost dignity and respect during your time in the boardroom.

The Influencer will thus have the most power in determining what is to be bought, and in fact, may even determine your sales fate in the boardroom and thereafter.

## The Purchaser

We don't need to dig too deep to understand the true role of this individual within the group presentation. This person either has the authority as the owner of the business or the power to purchase on behalf of the company has been bestowed upon him/her by some higher power. Where I come from this power is referred to as an authorized signatory-a written "license" if you will to purchase and sign agreements/proposals/contracts on behalf of the organization to which you are making your presentation.

Within the realm of purchasing/buying, and the group decision making process this person is for all intents and purposes the DECISION MAKER and the buck will stop with this individual. The "YES" answer that we look for will come from the Purchaser. You will hear me say, on many occasions, as we move forward that as a professional salesperson you MUST deal only with decision makers if you can help it at all.

## Conclusion

In the next chapter we shall advance to what we do when coming across these people. You now have been exposed to what I believe are the critical four personalities and persons within the boardroom presentation environment. The idea would be to make your presentation "all inclusive" and what I mean by that is that no matter the position or personality of those in the room that you will be professional enough to include ALL in the room in your presentation. We shall deal with the presentation a little later in the book; however, I do want you to understand already that making constant eye contact, and allowing your head movement and eyes to make everyone feel like you are talking directly to them. The only time your eye contact will change is when you are focusing on a participant who is about to ask you a question. You must handle questions in a dignified and professional manner and the chapter on handling objections should be a great help to you here as the very same principles will apply as you deal with each question. Remember, in order to answer a question you will need to LISTEN (take notes if you have to). PAUSE before answering, make sure that you have understood the question by feeding the question back in less than objectionable terms if you have to, and include ALL in your response using professional eye contact.

The professional entrepreneur salesperson, after finding himself/herself in a group buying situation, will use all available skills and will customize these for each member of the group being presented to. It is quite possible that you will deal with these types of people and positions on an individual basis prior to presenting your solution to the whole. However, people tend to react differently when they are in a group as there is an underlying pressure to perform as the boss may be present and they need a workable solution the their current crisis. Whether you deal with an individual or a group of people assess each situation and person and react accordingly.

# Chapter 6

# Responding to $ales Resistance
## *Controlling your own attitude*

**Introduction**

When you have just closed and asked for the order and when you meet sales resistance within the boardroom presentation I want to be the first to tell you that your reaction will mean the difference between concluding business successfully and failing dismally. Unfortunately, I am also here to tell you that it has been my experience that an unprofessional response to sales resistance has led to the failure of many businesses and the destruction of many a promising sales career.

In fact, and while this example does not come from the sales environment as such a service manager, who could not handle criticism from a client, succeeded in losing a service contract due to his inability to control himself. Mark was a service manager for a well-known services organization. The service team was accosted apparently by the client who was not happy with the level of service being produced by the service team on site. The company's team leader placed a call to the manager who decided to go to the site in order to resolve the impasse between the client and the team leader. It was understood that the client had high standards and was a difficult person to deal with.

The service manager was usually patient and had an attitude of "I have seen it all" and with this knowledge he arrived at the client's premises, again, with the clear and focused attention to resolve all issues and to get the client happy once again. However, on this day the client was extra difficult and tensions high between the team leader and the client. Mark asked the team leader to leave the room and decided that he would focus on the client first. From the outset the client was verbally abusive and continuously threatened to "terminate the contract". After a short while it was clear that the client was not going to cooperate and once again threatened to terminate the contract upon which Mark lost all composure and stormed out leaving the client in the middle of the passage. The last words that Mark remembered coming out his mouth was "if you want to terminate the contract then do so as we are better off without you!" The problem with this uncharacteristic and most unprofessional response from Mark was not only did the client cancel that contract but every other contract in every other branch in the country was also terminated. Mark was fired for his inability to respond to client resistance despite his training received in this regard.

George was a promising salesperson, and despite all of his training, he could not close a sale. George was not making quota and this was affecting the company budgets and his own financial situation. Albert was the sales manager for the division and had decided to spend the day with George with a view to helping him with his closing ratio which was alarmingly low to say the least. Albert shared with George: "I will go with you today as a spectator only so you will not introduce me as your manager but simply as a colleague. At the end of the day you and I will sit in my office to discuss your meetings for the day". George had no problem with this as he wanted and needed the help from his manager. The first presentation came and went as did the rest of the day.

In Albert's office later as was promised he started his personal assessment of what he thought was George's challenge. It was clear to him that George stopped functioning as a salesperson the moment he received his first "NO!" after asking the closing question. The issue then was not as Albert thought which was that George may not be asking the closing question, in fact, George asked the closing question on queue each and every time throughout the day. "However", said Albert, "the problem is that you tend to go into collapse mode when the prospect says 'NO!' and then you freeze with no apparent way to come back from the first "NO!". George agreed with Albert's assessment and knew that he needed help or he would be out of a sales job-yet again. Albert decided that George will need additional training on how to overcome sales resistance. The following pages in this chapter are what Albert taught George which by the way changed his entire career and the way that he responds to sales resistance even up to this very day.

As an entrepreneur salesperson wanting to become a Master Entrepreneur Salesperson you must understand something that most salespeople and/or sales organizations around the world do not even contemplate on a daily basis, and that is, failure to respond professionally to sales resistance is costing all sales related entities millions of Dollars in lost revenue annually. If you and I respond correctly to sales resistance then chances are that we will be successful in professionally closing for the business – ASK FOR THE ORDER!

**Professional tip:** The key to responding to sales resistance lies within your ability to *control your* **OWN** *attitude* at the right moment.

Master Entrepreneur Salespeople have the "perfect" attitude at the right moment in that they actually welcome objections during the sales process. The question is why would they have this attitude? For the professional it is clear, he/she recognizes that in many instances an objecting prospect is expressing interest; an objecting prospect is participating in the presentation process; the prospect is also furnishing valuable feedback. The professional salesperson, according to their own testimony, who expects to make a sale without meeting resistance by way of objections, is likened to a person who expects to live life without experiencing any trouble at all-we all know that this will not happen EVER! My friend, if you want to change the way that you sell for the better then heed my sincere advice to you today. Not wanting, or not expecting sales resistance is an unreasonable and unattainable expectation and even the thought of such an attitude must be considered unacceptable and I want to encourage you to be realistic in your approach and attitude toward sales resistance.

**Professional tip:** Not wanting or expecting sales resistance during the sales cycle is one thing; however, the greater "crime" to me is that more than 90% of salespeople are not ready to deal with sales resistance when it actually happens.

I want to mention once again that the key during this phase of the selling cycle is that you remain calm, positive and focused throughout. The professional salesperson will quickly understand that in order to prepare for handling objections, or meeting sales resistance, you will need to do three things:

1. Maintain a professional mental attitude.
2. Prior preparation for answering objections.
3. Timing the answer to objections.

### Maintain a professional mental attitude

In my previous book I deal extensively with one's attitude from all aspects, and while I don't intend going through another in depth section at this time I would encourage you to read my book called **ENTREPRENEURSHIP (*minus*) 101** (Publisher: Austin Macauley-ISBN 978 1 78455 148 3 Paperback; ISBN: 978 1 78455 150 6 Hardback) in this regard.

In order to maintain a positive mental attitude three key actions and attitudes are required:

1. Maintain an attitude of SERVICE.
2. Always use TACT.
3. Keep CONTROL of the presentation.

Maintaining an attitude of service throughout the presentation is critical (another chapter in my previous book so read it). This attitude should not only prevail during the objection phase of the selling process but throughout your relationship with the prospect that you hope to either refer to as a client or customer in the near future. Part of the definition of the term "service" here has to do with your ability, and mine, to "labor" for the prospect's business. The term labor then refers to actually doing some work and that is exactly what you will be doing during the selling phase known as objections or sales resistance. I am sure that by now you have heard of the saying which goes something like this: "Anything worth achieving is worth working for". Obtaining success at the final close means that you will have to work (labor) for it and sometimes this can be laborious and tiresome and negative but if you want to succeed in sales then get this into your head now and that is that you maintain a service attitude throughout as the victory is so much the sweeter. Your service attitude must then extend to answering a few questions before you walk away with the prize now what is so difficult about that?

Always use tact when answering objections. Why? Not only do you and I want to use tact at this time in order to show how "professional" we are but you are dealing with something a whole lot more precious and volatile at the same time – THE PROSPECT'S EGO! I want to take this a step further then and also inform you that you, the Master Entrepreneur Salesperson, have the prospect's SELF-IMAGE in your hands at that moment and if you do not understand the critical fact that you need to protect the prospect's ego in order to enhance his/her self-image then you will lose, and if you have a great business with great products and/or services, then it stands to reason that the prospect will also lose. Personal pride is what will make you or brake you within the selling environment if you feel that you and your needs are more important to that of the prospect at the moment of objections then you will understand my claim that more than 90% of salespeople fail at the objection phase of the selling process.

You will be given a chance to build the prospect's self-image during the sales resistance phase by stroking their ego as I have shown you in the previous chapter or you will destroy the same due to your own vanity, pride and lack of understanding and professionalism in handling objections in the correct manner. You will lose and you will keep on losing should you not change your attitude. My advice to you, as an entrepreneur or salesperson, if you can't understand the need for change then move along as sales is not for you. You will give your business a bad name and salesperson, you will harm both the business which you work for and you will destroy your own self-esteem and self-image so get out now as true sales is for the professional only.

Keep control of the presentation at all times. Nothing says that you are in control of the selling cycle more than a positive attitude which will be clearly displayed in a professional manner and be made manifest in (1) Controlled positive body language (2) The tone in your voice.

It is absolutely imperative that you never relinquish "control" of the sales environment to the prospect at any time throughout the process. Believe it or not you will be considered the professional, the technical expert, the advisor if you will and the "know it all" as this relates to your product or service. The prospect will admire this about you and will allow you the space to control the entire process right through to the end, UNLESS, you give him or her reason to remove the same control from you due to your own incompetence, which you may display, during the sales process. I can assure you my friend that once the prospect has taken control of you and your presentation process there is only one outcome for you – FAILURE! I have always said that we are all capable of "seeing an attitude coming a mile away". The idea here is that a negative attitude on the inside cannot hide and will show signs of outward manifestations soon after it is felt on the inside so if your prospect picks up on what is going on inside of your psyche then not only will they pick up on this but it will concern them and lead to questioning everything which you say about your product, service and company. The voice is a major barometer of a person's level of confidence and when we start squeaking like a boiling kettle then you will understand that this cannot be good for you or the prospect.

The goal then in maintaining the right mental attitude is to ALWAYS remain non-defensive. The unprofessional salesperson will be often tempted to become combative when a prospect raises a difficult objection which is aimed at testing the salesperson's temperament. Will you pass the test or be like the rest who daily continue to fail the test?

## Prior preparation for answering objections

A professional salesperson will always understand that there are two parts to preparing to answer an objection and both parts seem intertwined:

1. Past experiences in listening to objections raised by prospects and,
2. Overcoming objections through knowledge.

When your business has been going for a while or when you have been selling in a particular industry for quite some time you will find that the same objections are brought up by different prospects more often. At this time something unique will happen to you in that you will start to anticipate the kinds of objections which may arise during your presentations. You will also start to remember the solutions to the challenges faced by your prospects and your level of professionalism in presenting these to the prospect will vastly increase. You will soon see that, within your industry, there will remain very few objections which you will not be able to handle effectively and professionally. The upside of this then has to be that such a change in attitude will most certainly affect your closing ratio in the positive. My advice to you would be to start a catalogue of objections from the very first day in sales as this relates to a particular product or service AND attach the appropriate response next to each one. I can assure you that eventually you will see a pattern with regards to the types of objections which you receive and will then be able to categorize them into a maximum of ten subjects. For instance, a pricing objection may take many forms but it will still be called a "pricing objection". By the time that you have eventually completed this project you will see that objections are really not that complex to handle because there are just not as many as you would have thought. Then think of the answers. If the objections are not that many it means that you will be in more control of the selling environment by virtue of the confidence which you will gain through "coming to grips" with objections. By adding professional answers to the objections raised over time your levels of confidence will be reflected in your personal self-esteem which in turn will make you a force to be reckoned with in sales and your business will grow in leaps and bounds as they say.

The same knowledge which you have now gained as presented above can also be put to good use during the presentation process, in that, if you are convinced of the objections which you will soon face after you ask the closing question, then why not consider "overcoming the objection BEFORE it happens"! The idea here is to start incorporating the learned objections and their answers into your presentation in anticipation of them coming up at the close. What this may do for you is: (1) Limit the amount of objections for you to deal with at the close (2) Remove any objections BEFORE asking the closing question. The benefit of all of this is a vastly improved closing ratio resulting in a more confident you. Wonderful!

## Timing the answer to objections

**Professional tip:** Always remember that an objection may be raised at ANY TIME during the presentation.

1. Be careful of the "side-track swing".
2. Decide when to answer.

Be very careful of prospects that willfully and deliberately "sabotage" your presentation by raising irrelevant objections during the presentation stage. The obvious time that this may happen is during the group presentation introducing your services and/or products and your company. In many instances, when this kind of thing happens it will come from a group presentation participant who suffers from a low self-esteem and low self-image and want and crave attention. You will find these people to be loud and obnoxious in a sense so be wary and don't be surprised when you come across such a person. When dealing with this challenge then apply the following rules when deciding when to answer this or any other serious and more legitimate objection.

The goal here is to give you some rules which will assist you when contemplating when and how to answer objections or sales resistance. The first rule has already been mentioned but I want to raise it yet again so that you are reminded of how easy it is to overcome objections BEFORE they are brought to the fore. (1) Structure your presentation to overcome commonly raised objections prior to them been brought up. (2) Do not raise objections that do not exist. This is a common mistake made by "newbies" and less prevalent amongst the professional. Only deal with the prospect's objections AS THEY ARE RAISED and never think that you should answer any objection that has not as yet been raised-wait for the objection then as opposed to "jumping the gun!" (3) If answering an objection right away will interrupt the presentation process then postpone it until the end. "John, thank you for bringing this to my attention; however, may I request that I deal with this at the end of my presentation as that way I can give it my complete attention?" This will not only keep you in control of proceedings but allow you the time to consider the answer. I have often ignored an objection once it has been raised during the presentation phase (obviously once I have recognized the prospect's right to do so as is stated above) with a view that if it is serious enough then it will be raised again. The other consideration, once again, is that the objection may very well be raised during the rest of the presentation so it will not be raised as a serious objection then.

## Conclusion

Whatever you do remain focused during the presentation phase. You know what you need to do and are working through the presentation phase in order to arrive at the point where you will be asking for the order. This chapter has taught you to anticipate and cover objections BEFORE they are brought up by the prospect. The goal will be to reduce as much sales resistance as is possible so that when the closing question is asked it will leave the prospect with only one decision to make and not any questions for you to answer. Unfortunately, and while this negative action by some immature salespeople still continues today, I will remind you to only answer the objections given by the prospect and this means that you will pay attention when the objection is communicated to you as you may only have one shot at a professional response. Do not read into the prospect's objection neither must you become "suspicious" of his/her reasons for objecting. By doing this you will prove your poor level of sales maturity and lose control of the selling cycle. The worst thing is that you will start "reading into" and anticipating the prospect's objections and motivations which may cause you to raise objections which do not exist. In other words you will become counter-productive and your own worst enemy. The combination of a low self-esteem, a quick mouth and the inability to listen carefully has been the destruction of many a promising business and salesperson so don't let this be you. Opening your mouth at the wrong time with the wrong understanding of the objection will most certainly cost you and your business dearly.

# Chapter 7

# $ales Attitudes
## *People are different NOT complicated!*

**Introduction**

In my opinion we now come to the heart of UNCOMPLICATED sales-the back to basics road which we have embarked on. In my lifetime you will understand that I have read many books when it comes to developing my own sales career. As the selling environment, and the psychological interactions between the parties involved, would be considered by most as "complicated and technical" in nature I want to assure you from where I am sitting this is the furthest thing from the truth. While I have admitted to "drowning" myself in good quality sales books over the years I also want to confess that I was willingly influenced by some of the most technical and complicated books dealing with the psychology within the sales environment. I want to report to you in all honesty today that had I known the impact upon my sales career I would never have wasted my money and time on buying and reading some of the most ridiculous books on the psychology of people and how they react within the sales environment. Hence, my personal philosophy which you and my psychology colleagues may or may not agree with and that is: "People are DIFFERENT not complicated!"

Of course, I am referring directly to the sales environment. It will be my task to bring to your attention, that in my opinion and in my experience (which you may or may not agree with entirely) that when in a selling environment you will come across four groups of prospects. The idea is to get you to understand the four groups and so I have divided them up into four SALES ATTITUDES in keeping with our theme over the last few chapters of the book in your possession. It has been my experience in using and developing the RAID Matrix (Sales Attitude Matrix) over the years that while there has most certainly been the exception to the rule (like everything else in life) I have successfully placed sales attitudes into the following four quadrants: (1) **R**esistance (2) **A**cceptance (3) **I**ndifference (4) **D**oubt. Is there a reason why I decided on the acronym R.A.I.D.? No! This is just to help you to remember the four quadrants without stressing your brain out too much!

While I would love to be able to tell you that ALL people are alike within the sales environment we all know that this is not so. I want to say then that contrary to what some may have you believe we will move forward then based upon our understanding that people are in fact NOT all alike. Personal value systems distinguish each person from the next and therefore make them unique. With this in mind, when you sit in front of a prospect you have got to understand that his/her personal value system will not be the same as "Cheryl" whom you have just come from who is the MD or CEO or President of the company down the road. Do not get confused with the work done so far as we have already established that objections sooner or later, as this relates to a specific company or product or service, take on a similar pattern. We are now talking about the psychological make-up of the prospect as a subject in this chapter. Irrespective of the personal value system of the prospect I want you to consider adopting the RAID Matrix in order to help you to understand who it is that you will be dealing with during the closing process and how to deal with them professionally and efficiently in order to receive more positive responses to your closing questions. The long and short of it all then is that while objections may be similar in nature the people whom you are dealing with are different and may fall into one, or more, of the categories known as sales attitudes.

## The R.A.I.D. Matrix ("RAID")

As a Master Entrepreneur Salesperson you will face sales resistance from the following four types of people:

1. **R**esistance.
2. **A**cceptance.
3. **I**ndifference.
4. **D**oubt.

As we have been dealing with handling resistance up to now let's continue the thread as we come to terms with a prospect who has the sales attitude known as resistance (objection).

## The attitude of RESISTANCE

You will notice in the matrix as presented below that someone who has the sales attitude of resistance will offer two challenges and that is they will have an internal conflict between their own needs and desires. The objections which they raise then are usually coming from an attitude of conflicting desires or needs. A prospect in this state of mind is NOT saying no to your proposal but rather in his or her way is sending out signals for help in possibly three areas:

1. They are in need of additional information before moving forward.

2. They are resisting in an attempt to bargain in some or all related areas (financially, benefits etc.)
3. They may be communicating an inability to make a decision.

It is thus clear by this that this prospect's attitude of conflicting desires or needs (resistance) means that he/she may like one aspect of your proposal but not another. They tend to wrestle so to speak within themselves as to how to resolve this internal conflict and of course this is why you are there. Having now understood the internal conflict with such an attitude you will need to know how to "untangle" the internal confusion which is most certainly not as difficult as it would seem.

**Professional tip:** The good news is that the internal conflict would not exist if there was not something about the situation or your proposal that the prospect did not like.

Sales resistance or an objection must be kept in context of the situation between salesperson and prospect. An objection, as we have already discovered, to the professional, is simply considered an opportunity to conclude a sale. Professional salespeople and Master Entrepreneur Salespeople consider objections so important that they actually become uneasy with quiet buyers. Objections are considered feedback by most professionals and in most cases they would rather have some feedback, in any form I might add, than have no feedback at all. Quiet buyers hold back questions and give few clues as to their inward resistance – this is not good so be happy not to meet such a person. In fact, most professionals go out of their way to encourage the prospect to air their objections/questions/resistance as the only way to effectively deal with them is to listen to and understand them with a view to a resolution. You and I cannot resolve that which we have no knowledge of and as long as it remains hidden we cannot close the sale. The ultimate goal then would be to find what the barriers are which stand in the way of making a sale.

An objection, by the prospect, is also an indirect request for more information. Always remember, the prospective buyer has always used objections as an indirect way to ask questions, and this, many times, due to personal reasons which we shall discuss. The prospect has fears as we do and become embarrassed as we would when we are caught out not listening or paying attention. In order to hear one must listen, and believe it or not, prospects sometimes don't listen to what you are saying until you ask the closing question and then they realize that they have lost you somewhere along the way. OOPS! "What do I do now so that I don't look like a complete idiot? I know! I'll raise an objection to get my answer!" This is not uncommon my friend so don't fear this attitude in prospects as it is far better than you walking out with absolutely nothing to show for all of your work to date.

Prospects usually feel that asking direct questions might give the impression that (1) They are naïve about the selling process or that you may discover that they are new in the position of decision maker (2) That asking direct questions may weaken their bargaining position (3) Create an adversarial position with you and me (4) Give the impression that they are about to buy. However, the shrewd and experienced prospect is able (many times without the knowledge of the untrained salesperson) to use objections to gain assurances without any obligation to the salesperson at all. For instance: "Trevor, in your presentation of the financial proposals I noticed that you included a once-off installation charge. Is this charge really necessary?" They feel risks are reduced by indirectly asking for information without overly encouraging the salesperson.

To the professional salesperson an objection is evidence also of indecision on the part of the prospect. Many times an objection is simply a way in which buyers communicate to a salesperson their inability to make the decision. Prospects with the attitude of resistance usually want the salesperson to tell them what prices and terms are on offer without embarrassing themselves about their indecision. At times this sales attitude needs leadership and guidance as to how to make the final decision. It may be likened to someone running a marathon that has fallen down just before the winning line. A running mate, while she will not be allowed to carry her friend over the line she picks her up and coaxes her to take the last few remaining steps so that she can finally cross the winning line.

## The attitude of ACCEPTANCE

The prospect says: "Where do I sign?" The salesperson does not say a word but points to the spot with reassuring words such as, "right over here". The salesperson gathers the documents, places them in his/her briefcase and gets out of the sight of the prospect now turned client as soon as is possible and saying as little as possible. My friend, I can tell you that I have heard of so many occasions of how salespeople have talked their way out of a successfully concluded sale just because they cannot shut-up. They continue talking to the client who eventually leads back to the sale and then one thing leads to another and before you know it the salesperson has talked him/her right out of the sale. Not good! Learn when enough is enough; close the sale and your mouth thereafter.

The prospect in this attitude has bought and is willing to show and reveal all of the signs needed for a sure close. This attitude therefore shows no resistance whatsoever and is ready to go ahead with the purchase. The prospect obviously feels comfortable with the salesperson and has placed some trust in the product, service, the company represented and the salesperson. Great! A job well done! Do not say "are you sure" as all you need to do right now is sign in order to conclude business and leave before you mess it up!

## The attitude of INDIFFERENCE

This is the most difficult attitude to deal with of all four as is presented in the RAID Matrix. This type of prospect just does not seem to care at all and there is nothing that really concerns this individual whether specific or in general terms. You will notice that there is no strong overriding motivator for this person and nothing that you do or say is making any difference at all. In fact, you would probably be wondering by now what he gave you the meeting date for. As a salesperson you can feel acquitted with this type of attitude as I can tell you with a great deal of confidence that most professionals would more than likely have stood up and left in a professional manner – you should do the same.

## The attitude of DOUBT

Doubt is an attitude of disbelief and skepticism. The time when doubt is most likely to occur is during the pricing presentation stage of your close. If you find yourself saying all the right things to a prospect, but they do not respond, then you were probably experiencing an attitude of doubt. Do not confuse this attitude with that of indifference as all is not lost when dealing with the attitude of doubt. There is interest even if the interest is displayed in a face which says "doubt". "I don't believe what you are telling me as I simply don't believe that your product can do what you claim".

These prospects will not believe that your facts accurately reflect their situation. They also don't believe that their situation is the same as those experienced by your other clients – they, and their challenge, is completely unique to them. Where else does the attitude of doubt come from? This may come about as a result of a misunderstanding which has stuck with the prospect during the presentation phase. You will now understand why I am so adamant that objections are good for you and will help you to close the sale. To avoid plunging your prospect into an attitude of doubt always (1) Tell the truth (2) Build deep and sincere rapport (3) Support ALL of your conclusions with evidence.

**Professional tip:** Remember, even if you offer proof, the prospect might not agree with your evidence. You must find out what sort of facts the prospect would place credibility in and then rather present these facts before closing yet again.

In order to assist you in both understanding and memorizing the discussion on sales attitudes I have developed a matrix, as presented below, depicting the attitude and the actions associated with each one. The acronym R.A.I.D. was chosen in order for you to easily remember what they stand for within the matrix: **R**esistance, **A**cceptance, **I**ndifference and **D**oubt. Please review the following matrix and then we will conclude the chapter thereafter.

**The R.A.I.D. Matrix ("RAID")**

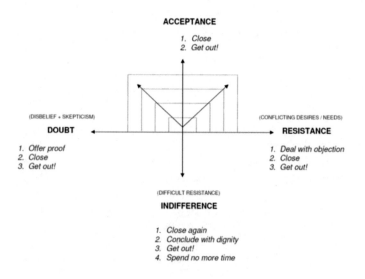

116

## Conclusion

The key to assessing which attitude the prospect is in is to be aware of what the prospect is telling you, both physically and psychologically. Remember, what is on the inside will surface and the quicker you allow this to happen the better you are able to assess the attitude and deal with the prospect accordingly. As a professional Master Entrepreneur Salesperson you would have memorized and practiced identifying the sales attitudes BEFORE seeing the prospect. You and you alone will have to master the technique of identifying and understanding each sales attitude, and when you have done so, the next step is to always remember that not every prospect is in the same sales attitude from one sales call to the next. In fact, it is quite possible for a single prospect to move from one attitude to the next either between sales calls or even during the sales presentation stage – be aware at all times!

It is generally easier said than done while one is learning to be professional; however, many professional salespeople will tell you that the best way to identify the correct sales attitude is for you to remain calm and relaxed – difficult you would say? Yes! It will be difficult in the beginning but let me reassure you that the more you use the system the better you will become at analyzing the prospect and the quicker the response time from your brain. The best way to relax, as we have already alluded to, is to build professional rapport with the prospect. Building rapport will not only relax you but also the prospect and when the prospect is relaxed and finds you easy to talk to then he/she will open up to you and make it easy for you to analyze them. It is a fact, unfortunately, most people don't like to be confronted by a salesperson as the objectives and goals during the sales process are diametrically opposed to one another – we shall deal with this subject in depth as we move forward. However, when the prospect is made to feel relaxed and understands you better then perceived "threats" dissipate as it is far better to deal with a friend than it is to deal with a salesperson. The idea is to build rapport throughout the presentation of your services, products and company. You will only "break the ice" once during the very first part of your meeting but thereafter you will continue to build rapport which will make it easier for you to identify the sales attitude and deal with the prospect according to the matrix.

Understand this, during the presentation phase you (as we discuss further) will go through the following stages if you are a professional-NO SHORTCUTS!

1. Introducing YOU.
2. Presenting your company's history.
3. Understanding the problem/s which your prospect faces.
4. Presenting the solution to the prospect's challenges.
5. Performing an on-site survey of the prospect's needs.
6. Presenting the final proposal which must be filled with solutions.

The idea here is for you to understand that there is no need to "rush" your analysis as this relates to the RAID MATRIX. As you can see by the process above you have plenty of time to come to a professional conclusion before you finally present the quotation or proposal. Body language and psychology will be revealed in the numerous buying signals that are given off by the prospect, and these or the lack of these, will tell you exactly what sales attitude your prospect will be in at any given moment in time. However, once you have arrived at a conclusion as to the sales attitude of your prospect then deal with him/her accordingly and according to the RAID MATRIX.

They say that "practice makes perfect" and so I wonder then what the saying is for when one receives good advice and then chooses to ignore the advice – FOOLISH.

**Professional tip:** Please understand that there are *no shortcuts* in the selling process, and if there were, don't you think we would have found them by now?

# Chapter 8

# The "Old School" Basic $ales Adage
## *Use Empathy!*

**Introduction**

My goal here is to spend some time in unlocking an age old secret when it comes to concluding a sales presentation and/or call successfully. We live in a world today where people are becoming more and more self-centered and less time is being spent on considering other people. In order to be successful in sales you and I will need to change this attitude and do so quickly and without any hesitation whatsoever. Due to the current pervading phenomenon known as selfishness most unprofessional salespeople will approach the prospect with the attitude of "let's see what I can get out of this prospect so that I can achieve my goals so that I can look good at the office and with my family"! This is the wrong attitude and I can tell you without a shadow of a doubt that the fathers of old were more successful at closing the sale than most of their contemporary counterparts of today. Their attitude was different in that instead of being self-centered they projected a caring and selfless attitude when it comes to satisfying the needs of the client, hence, the selling technique known as "need satisfaction selling".

## Empathy-The Meaning

Webster's Collegiate Dictionary gives a rather lengthy definition of the term: *The action of understanding, being aware of, being sensitive to, and vicariously experiencing the feelings, thoughts, and experience of another of either the past or present without having the feelings, thoughts, and experience fully communicated in an objectively explicit manner.*

A simpler, shorter and more understandable definition is presented by the Collins Dictionary which states: *The ability to sense and understand someone's feelings as if they were one's own.*

While I have taken time to expand on this term and its use in **ENTREPRENEURSHIP (*minus*) 101**, and recommend that you read this as a more in depth study, I would like to ensure that you have a working understanding of both the definition of the word and how to use it within a practical sales environment. In my own practical application of empathy I have used it, and applied it to mean for me as having the "gift" or ability to place oneself in the "shoes" or position of the client/prospect to the point where I view the needs, desires and frustrations from the direct perspective of my prospect. I have found that this removes me from being selfishness and self-centered. In a sense then I become the prospect for the duration of the sales process through to the close. Once I have perfected this technique, and while it has been forgotten by most contemporary salespeople the world over, I have found that I am able to do almost everything better and more professional during the sales cycle. I am able to break the ice quicker and easier, and I am able to build and continue to build rapport throughout the sales process as I feel that I understand where the prospect is coming from, I also feel that it is easier to probe for needs and wants and to satisfy these with the benefits of my products and/or services, and all of this, to the complete satisfaction of my client. This is a forgotten art today as we truly believe that the computer will replace the one-on-one relationship building which should take place between humans. To me, this (the use of the computer as a human replacement) is considered a SHORT-CUT and many businesses are falling short on sales quotas/targets and goals because of it. Salespeople have become even lazier than ever before and simply no longer want to move off of their chairs and feel anxiety when separated from the computer. This is not sales my friend this is cyberspace and today's salespeople are caught up in this ridiculous world of make believe. The worst thing of all is that many sales managers and companies around the world are most guilty of fostering this kind of backward thinking when it comes to sales. Buyers don't buy from computers and companies they buy from PEOPLE! Sales are lost because sales people are nowhere to be found and have changed from real people to a name on a screen. How is this progress? To me, this is considered anti-social behavior!

Professional salespeople are successful today only if they are able to match the benefits of their services and/or products to the very specific needs as is expressed by the prospect. Many prospects have specific challenges which they are forced to deal with daily and this causes much frustration on their part I can assure you. The professional entrepreneur salesperson learns quickly that in order to close the sale he/she must solve the problems or challenges faced by the prospect in a swift and economical manner. The key to it all though is that in order to define the problem or challenge from the perspective of the prospect, and to identify the exact needs, the professional salesperson must be able to use an "old school" basic sales technique known to all professionals as EMPATHY.

In understanding our use of empathy in this chapter I propose that we investigate and understand the following four critical factors:

1. Empathetic selling involves three crucial techniques.
2. When the prospect talks the salesperson must not.
3. Prospects usually develop strong egos.
4. Professional salespeople understand the prospect and his/her company.

You and I must always understand that empathetic selling involves the use of three critical techniques namely (1) Listening (2) Concentrating (3) Responding.

## Listening

When attending any form of learning institution one would need to attend a class-at some point. When arriving in the lecture hall the idea is that the lecturer gives the lecture and the student listens. It becomes clear that the student does not listen in class because he/she has not actively listened to the lecture or lesson when they fail to make the grade after an exam. We also fail to listen when we attend church services and somehow cannot repeat the minister's message just after we have left the church premises. The same thing will happen to us then if we fail to ACTIVELY listen with a view to hearing. This is the very reason why I recommend that salespeople take notes when the prospect is doing his/her level best to explain the frustrations and needs currently being experienced. A clear sign in this instance that you have listened is the fact that you and I are able to repeat the words as were spoken by the prospect and that he/she agrees when you repeat the same back to the prospect. Listening means then that you "take notice" and that you "pay attention" when the prospect speaks and both of these entities entail a conscious effort from your side – not a passive activity but a concerted effort. The very notion and action of listening denotes that there will be a concentration on the part of the one doing the listening or the entire message may well be lost – this is not good in the sales cycle.

## Concentration

During the sales process, and in particular, it is vital that you and I not only perform the exercise of actively listening but that we must also place all of our efforts in also performing a critical task called "concentration" at the same time. It is possible to listen and not hear a single thing and the difference then between listening and hearing has to do with *concentration* during this process or the lack thereof. The word concentrate then must be understood to be the conscious effort on your part and mine to "focus", "direct", and, if you will, "aim" all of our efforts on what it is that we are supposed to be hearing. In other words, don't listen with half an ear but really listen! The goal is to "intensify" the listening process through a focused effort called concentration.

## Responding

Please remember; never be too quick to respond. When responding, a subject which you and I have already covered in some depth; however, understand that responding in the sales environment must not be taken to mean "react". Reacting to a negative comment from the prospect is unprofessional. The prospect may have stated one negative comment and you decide not to let go of this and you think that you have a right to destroy all of your work to date because you became defensive. I am not talking about a negative reaction from you in this context but a professional response to the prospect's genuine need and/or challenges.

The response which I am referring to here is in the form of an "answer". This is an answer to an objection which is raised by the prospect; or an answer to a simple question posed by the prospect during the sales environment. Responding accurately is as a result of your ability to listen by means of concentration, and this response comes in the form of an answer as opposed to a reaction to a question, need or objection.

With regards to the three definitions as stated above we will also now understand, using empathy of course, how to phrase our questions to the prospect as our goal has not changed. In need satisfaction selling it is important to identify the needs professionally and using our new found knowledge of using empathy to do so, and our understanding of the communication process, we will need to understand the kinds of questions to formulate during this process. Therefore, the professional entrepreneur salesperson must formulate and ask questions that lead the prospect to discuss problem areas.

**Professional tip:** A closed question (probe) is asked when a "yes" or "no" type answer is required and an open question (probe) is asked when an expanded answer is required from the prospect.

The prospect may have certain concerns, needs and challenges which may be all encompassing. However, we have already discussed that certain objections reoccur on a consistent basis. I can assure you that so do certain needs, challenges and concerns from one prospect to another. For instance, the following examples represent certain constants when needs are spoken of by the prospect, and these, are not exhaustive by any means.

The concerns, needs and questions may involve:

1. Past consistent service complaints.

"John, you have shared with me that you have had consistent service complaints in the past with your current supplier. May I ask you what these are and why they have caused you irritation?"

## 2. Design issues.

"Suzanne, when I spoke with you on the phone recently you mentioned that constant design flaws are the cause of many of your products being returned. May I ask whether your concerns have been ignored by your current supplier or has the damage already been done as far as you are concerned?"

## 3. Source of irritation.

"Mark, I understand that the current situation concerning backorders has been a source of irritation for you. May I ask how this has affected your ability to service your customers?"

## 4. Deadlines.

"Joan, we have discussed the importance of you creating and meeting production deadlines. What kind of lead time would you consider reasonable in order to ensure predetermined delivery dates?"

## 5. Credit Controlling.

"David, I hear that you are not happy with the current arrangement regarding payments to your current supplier. May I ask is it the number of invoices that bother you or the terms of payment?"

## 6. Reliability.

"Wendy, according to you the current supplier never keeps to service arrangements. I am sure that you have addressed this with ABC Company. What was the reason given for your consistent frustration in this regard?"

It has been my experience that with the minimum of encouragement most prospects which I have dealt with have told me a great deal more than I asked for. The idea is to get them talking as you are considering matters from their point of view (empathy) and they sense this in you and begin to trust you and when they trust you and me they will open up to us- exactly what we want! I have often experienced that asking a single question can open up "a can of worms" (after breaking the ice and building initial rapport that is) such as: "Mike, thank you for having me come by! I'm curious, what made you give me the appointment to meet with you today." Frustrated people are ALWAYS willing to talk, just to vent to someone that will pay attention and listen. Venting is welcomed by someone like me and is considered "dumping". I welcome dumping by a prospect as this tells me that I have used empathy professionally to the point where the prospect feels so comfortable with me that he/she is able to let go. When the prospect let's go then I get the needs, wants and challenges revealed. When I identify the needs, wants and challenges I am able to align these with what my business has to offer and if these satisfy the client's needs, wants and challenges, then I have a sale and success. The more I am able to do this with as many prospects as possible the more successful I will be. I see myself helping my prospects as opposed to how much I can get out of them and the prospect senses this in me immediately – empathy!

You must understand that if you want to be successful in selling anything working for anyone (even yourself) then you will also understand that prospects respond favorably to personal warmth and a real and sincere interest in their situation. I am absolutely convinced that once a prospect perceives that the Master Entrepreneur Salesperson has a genuine concern (using empathy) a long standing and fruitful business relationship will develop.

Once the prospect starts talking the salesperson must start the listening process and this means that two things need to happen:

1. SHUT UP!
2. LISTEN for the wants, needs and frustrations and/or challenges.

It stands to reason that your goal is to get the prospect to vent so why would you interrupt this process when you have done so well in getting it all going? Do not interrupt but encourage the prospect to keep going if this is what you feel that you need to do. All you have to do is LISTEN and write as you will need all this information in order to conclude business successfully. The focus will be to identify the wants and the needs so that you are able to satisfy these with the benefits provided by your proposed solutions to the challenges faced by the prospect.

Psychologically, all buying behavior is a complex mixture of reason and emotion, and as you may be aware the two entities are opposed to one another in most instances relating to life and sales for that matter. However, when you understand these two opposing factors you will also understand that they, in the business or sales environment, will result in either corporate gain or personal gain to all parties concerned – in this instance however specifically for the prospect. The prospect will always have an explanation or justification for why he feels the way that he does about a matter relating to his/her needs and wants. The reasons will seem logical to him/her and at times the prospect will not understand why everyone else around him/her does not feel the same way – for instance a salesperson in particular and within the context of our current discussion of course. The idea when reasoning is used by the prospect has more to do with him/her using intellect, facts and persuasion in order to get the salesperson to see their point of view which is always right in their eyes by the way. Think about it then will you? Do you and I not do the same when we are trying to convince the prospect that our solutions are best?

Once again, within the context of our current discussion, emotion would be taken to contain feelings such as passion, warmth, excitement, fervor, sentiment, frustration, anger and definitely intensity. All of these displays are more often than not an outward manifestation of what is actually going on inside as mentioned before, and are prevalent during the sales process. When using empathy then, you and I will understand clearly that both reason and emotion will be a fundamental part of understanding how to use empathy, and also when to do so. The prospect will use both reason and emotion in order to convince you and I to see things their way and their motivation for doing so MUST lead to either corporate gain on behalf of the company which they represent or personal gain allowing them to be a hero within their organizations or amongst their peers. You and I will have to understand then that decision-makers (the very people whom we meet with) are highly motivated to see their companies succeed through every transaction which involves them directly. The question is though how do they achieve this goal?

Decision-makers ensure their success, which is paramount to them by the way, by doing their jobs and doing it well. They do their jobs well, according to them, by having you come and see them with a view to buying your products and/or services from you. They most certainly have a motivation for buying because this is their responsibility and this is why you are sitting in front of them. The question is though that while they are willing to buy are you good enough to convince them to make the inevitable spend with them or should they keep looking for a supplier who understands them better and who can meet their corporate and personal gain goals? In all honesty, and as was stated before, "people are DIFFERENT but most certainly not COMPLICATED! When trying to understand your prospect's motivations through the use of empathy you must ask yourself a question: "If I were the prospect right now what would my motivation be for doing business with me today?" You may come to the same or a similar conclusion to the one that I arrived at namely three things:

1. You must offer lower costs.
2. Lower costs from you must lead to higher sales for the prospect and his/her company.
3. These two critical factors must lead ultimately to an increase in corporate profit for the prospect's company.

Understand this, my friend; decision-makers (prospects) have a desire to move up the corporate ladder toward senior management positions just as much as you want to grow your business and client base. Why? They have families (usually) and have personal needs and wants, goals, dreams and desires just as much as you and I do. Climbing the corporate ladder will mean that they will be in a better position to provide more for their families and achieve their own goals this way. They also have recognition goals and climbing the corporate ladder will make them look good to their siblings and extended family not to mention to their peers. Buyers (decision-makers) have egos that need stroking just like you and I have; so do not view them as any different-not complex! The best way for the decision-maker (prospect) to draw attention to themselves is by making SUCCESSFUL changes and decisions such as the one which you may be proposing at any particular point in time. One big reason that you and I may be having to deal with more objections during the selling process is that we have come across a prospect who likes what he/she hears, and sees all his/her goals being achieved, but wants to be sure that by making a decision to close with you he/she will be SUCCESSFUL when making the change/s. The question for them then will be: "Will this make me achieve my personal and corporate goals – WILL THIS DECISION MAKE ME LOOK GOOD!?"

Prospects also have a serious motivation to make their jobs a lot easier-the convenience factor if you will. Some would consider this motivation a time management essential and would place this need on the top of their list when you try to uncover the needs and wants. This is the kind of prospect who would be interested in saving time by having one service provider supplying a package of services under one company meaning fewer suppliers, one bill/invoice for all the services and one responsible person in the event of quality level failure. Wow! This is a no brainer for some prospects! The goal or motivation here then would be to obtain as much service as is possible from one vendor – convenience and added value. Prospects also want their jobs made easier by having the opportunity to avoid unprofessional, incompetent and unreliable vendors – this makes them look bad, and even worse, if the original poor decision to go with these vendors was made by the prospect. Unprofessional vendors are a great source of frustration to the prospect and this frustration will most certainly show during the needs analysis and sales attitude analysis stages of the selling process.

**Professional tip:** Prospects are severely influenced by the risk of making a bad decision and the cost of any change proposed by the salesperson.

The goal, if you can understand the concept and context of our discussion, may lead you to conclude that your task and mine, before, during and in concluding the sales process will be to do all in our power to make an absolute HERO of our prospect. Guess what? You would be absolutely correct in your conclusion. Just so that you know, and while the prospect may not tell you that he/she wants to be a hero, I can assure you that this is most certainly his/her personal and corporate goal. If you want to succeed in sales over and over again then learn the secret of using empathy as this technique will help you to understand how and what you will need to do in order to make your prospect the hero. Do this and I can assure you that you will succeed over and over again in the close.

You may not know this or you may not even have thought about this and that is why you are not succeeding in sales as you would like to. However, I want to assure you that prospects DEVELOP strong egos. A mature buyer or decision-maker is a seasoned prospect and has been around the block a few times with salespeople that promise the earth and then deliver poor results. You will thus have to forgive the prospect for viewing you and your promises with a certain amount of skepticism when you first meet. However, when using empathy then you will soon get to understand this fact sooner rather than later. In understanding that the ego is strong in these people you will also have to come to terms with two very important needs:

1. They have an innate need to feel IMPORTANT.

2. They also have a need to be RESPECTED.

The prospect is important in the bigger scheme of things in that he realizes that he/she has the ability (power if you will) to also make you and I succeed or fail at our task. Many of these people hold the authority to spend vast sums of money in procuring products and services on behalf of their organization, and while the money is not theirs on a personal level, they feel that it is from a corporate point of view-hence the sense of importance which they feel. They realize that salespeople work on quotas/targets and commission and those salespeople are usually under a certain amount of pressure most of the time and that the salesperson is reliant upon a positive outcome to any sales meeting with a prospect. The prospect also understands that you too have goals, dreams and desires just as he/she does and that they hold your ability to achieve this in a decision which they will eventually have to make. Because of all this perceived power they feel important and you and I will do well to remember this psychological weight in favor of the prospect.

While we understand the prospect's need to feel important and even now agree with the reasons why this happens; the prospect also has a secondary need born out of the first. When one feels important a natural spin-off from this is the need to be respected. We all have knowledge of the old adage claiming that "respect is not demanded it is earned". I am here to tell you to forget this saying as it does not apply to the prospect with obvious power. The prospect will understand that he is respected (maybe "feared" in a sense?) so you and I will have no option but to comply for to treat such a one with contempt because of his/her power or position will be counter-productive for the salesperson.


**Professional tip:** Master Entrepreneur Salespeople NEVER fail to "massage" the prospect's ego and understand that not to perform this task throughout the sales process will most certainly render a certain amount of his/her credibility and effectiveness useless.

What happens then if the prospect/decision maker is not a part of the corporate world and in fact is the owner of the company? Without a doubt his/her motivations for wanting to buy from you will be different. The goals will change as why would he/she "want to climb the corporate ladder"? The business is already owned by this individual who happens to be highly motivated and is a business person or Master Entrepreneur in their own right. The reason that these people buy and their personal motivations for doing so are different to the corporate buyer and you will do well to understand this fact from the outset. This is the very reason why I admonish salespeople to research the company that you plan to approach for business. Personally I enjoy doing business with owners and entrepreneurs as decisions are made at pace and more for convenience than out of pressure as in the case of the corporate buyer. Therefore, we need to understand what the differences are then between the two buying groups. If the decision maker is an entrepreneur or the owner then advancement issues (climbing the corporate ladder) are usually not a priority; however, there are other more personal factors that come into play, such as:

1. Convenience.

This term must be taken to mean that such a prospect will be more interested in saving time, saving on labor, services being done on time and the same with promised deliveries. This prospect will also be pleased and motivated by the fact that your company performs ALL the services, and provides all related products which he/she requires so there is no need to source a second or a third supplier. All the services and products are on ONE bill/invoice so there is less administration which reduces bank costs and charges.

### 2. Comfort.

This prospect is keen on doing business with salespeople who make it easy to do business. The less he/she has to do business with you the more likely they are to close business with you. The old adage applies here: "give before you receive". "I will perform a site survey for you so you don't have to leave your office and then I will compile all data with a view to preparing the proposal/quotation. Once I have completed all the work, and only then, will I give you a call to set up an appointment/meeting for around fifteen minutes of your time for the presentation of the proposal"? Ease of doing business with you is important to this prospect.

### 3. Security.

Of great interest to this prospect would be your ability to fulfil your promises and that of your business. They want to be protected from late deliveries, back orders and poor service. The current supplier's poor stock management is affecting their ability to achieve sales targets which has a direct effect on the cash-flow in the company. The reduction in cash-flow will directly affect his/her ability to pay salaries and other critical overheads so assurances from you that this will not happen are crucial to your success. They will want you to produce tangible proof that their business is protected and will have relative freedom from harm when it comes to poor service delivery.

### 4. Envy.

There are two sides to this term which will present a challenge for you and me. The word envy in this context and as it applies to this type of prospect deals first of all with the competitive nature of this prospect. This prospect wants to succeed ahead of their competitors at all costs and the question is then are you able to help them achieve this goal? They are extremely aware of their competition and make it their business to know everything they need to know in order to stay ahead – are you and the business you represent able to keep them "ahead of the game"? Envy in this sense also has a retribution tone in that should you fail this prospect then you must expect reactions such as bitterness, resentment, deliberate signs of dissatisfaction and ill-will. You will have no cooperation from such a prospect, and should they become your client through a legally binding contract/agreement, then they will do everything in their power to terminate the relationship with you in the most unpleasant of ways and as soon as is possible.

## 5. Fear.

The owner/entrepreneur, as you and I are fully aware, has put all of his/her energy and resources into developing their business. The worst thing that can happen is that some salesperson, with false promises, will come along and threaten this investment with poor and non-service despite all the assurances to the contrary. The idea here is for you to understand that this fear is constant until you create the necessary trust, but will be prevalent and in the mind of the prospect from the outset and from the moment of meeting with you. While they may not show it they will have emotions of trepidation, panic (in certain cases), anxiety, concern, and a strong sense of uneasiness upon meeting you and throughout the presentation and/or sales process. You must remember this emotion and work throughout the process to alleviate this stress.

## 6. Pride.

A business owner/entrepreneur is by his/her very nature a person who takes great pride not only in what they do but also what they achieve. They also take great satisfaction in being the best, having the best staff, the best suppliers, being the best in their industry, having the best vehicles and the best premises, and all this, they believe, makes them look good to all who care. They detest failure in themselves and anyone else and cannot understand people who are not motivated to be same as they are. If you are to succeed with this type of prospect then you had better display the same kind of pride in your dress, your company and your product and/or service. Nothing impresses this prospect more than a person who he/she deems to be PROFESSIONAL as they themselves take pride in all that they do AND it shows. Pride also extends to their great sense of achievement which brings satisfaction, delight, pleasure and comfort. Being successful will affect their own psychology positively in areas such as self-esteem, self-respect, honor and dignity.

**Professional tip:** As a Master Entrepreneur Salesperson you should NEVER underestimate the importance of the six emotional factors as stated above.

Professional salespeople also make it their business to understand both the company and the prospect BEFORE making the approach. There are certain key aspects which you and I will need to understand about people and companies when they are ready to change suppliers or make purchases. The very first key aspect of the buying process that I want you to both understand and to never forget is that it is PEOPLE make buying decisions. The reason that I want you to understand this is so that you don't become confused as to this fact. You see there are salespeople out there who would much rather sit on their computer "working hard" to generate sales, and guess what; companies are allowing this to their detriment. You see computers do not make buying decisions people do and organizations do not make buying decisions people do. The biggest mistake made by salespeople today is to assume that the "modern way" of doing business means that people can be excluded from the selling process. So let me say this again, organizations and computers do not make sales decisions and you will have to, at some point, get off the chair that you seem glued to and go and face the prospect. Facing the prospect seems to be a fear by todays "modern" salesperson and, to me the other word should be "lazy" salesperson. You cannot do EVERYTHING on the computer, and while a lot can be done, we have to face the prospect at some point in time surely? I cannot understand salespeople and businesses who cannot grasp that the selling process, in most cases, remains a face to face activity as people make decisions to buy not computers or organizations.

Another key aspect about FACE TO FACE sales is that we all buy from people we like. If I have never met you then how am I going to like you? Face to face sales meetings with prospects will allow you the space to "break the ice" and build critical "rapport" which is most conducive to building long-term business relationships. The goal for the professional salesperson is to get the prospect to trust them as nothing can happen without the trust factor between parties – ask your wife or husband! Trust can only be achieved when you meet the prospect and once this has been accomplished then making friends is the next step in moving forward in the sales process. Why would you and I buy from someone whom we neither trust nor want to be friends with? We buy from a person we like and that is a fact! Please understand this then will you? We don't buy from people that we usually don't like. When you take time to research and/or make it your business to understand the prospect and the company for which he/she works or owns then you will quickly understand what they are looking for and what it would take to make friends.

## Conclusion

The professional use of empathy in today's selling environment is a lost art. Most companies take the candidate salesperson through an interview process where all promises are made by the salesperson as to how self-motivated they are and how focused they are on achieving targets. They will even tell their employers that they are able to operate without supervision and have no problem with company employment policies. Most companies today do not do reference checks of new salespeople with the sole purpose of checking their ability to achieve sales targets. I am willing to lay my reputation on the line when I tell you that when a salesperson is looking for a new job the odds are that they are currently underperforming where they are. I have found salespeople of today to be self-centered and many are untrained in the art of true sales. A key to effective sales is that salespeople are able to perfect the art of using empathy with prospects and it has been my experience that they do not even know what the word means. The professional use of empathy will allow the salesperson to see that he/she is not the hero but the prospect is and must be made to feel this way right from the outset. The professional salesperson, right from the first meeting, will make the prospect feel important and respected. In order to successfully close the sale the salesperson must first sell him/her to the prospect. The prospect must first buy what he sees sitting in front of him/her before he/she will buy what you are selling. You sell yourself first and if the prospect buys who you are as a person then the prospect will listen to you, and if not, it would be like you are talking to the wall. The prospect will simply go through the motions with you (some will not even do this and simply ask you to leave their office) and at the end tell you that they are not interested – THANK YOU!

However, once the prospect has learned that you can be trusted then a foundation will exist for a successful conclusion to the sales cycle. Your prospects will buy from YOU and not your company or for any other reason for that matter. Understand the concept of this chapter and you will understand the importance of using EMPATHY in the early part of your meeting with the prospect, and who knows, you may be fortunate enough to turn him/her into a client or customer.

# Chapter 9

# Basic $ales Negotiation
## *Is this a lost art?*

**Introduction**

"Trevor, I am ready to move forward however I find both your monthly pricing structure and your initial installation costs high. We will need to 'talk' about this."

Does this sound familiar to you, and if not, get ready as this type of objection may pop up more often that you would like it to. You may say, and you would be correct, "I suppose that I will now need to 'negotiate' with the prospect in order to secure the sale?" However, for most salespeople their ability to negotiate is limited by the sales manager and him/her in turn by the senior management team of the business. Even as an entrepreneur you will have limits as to what you can do, and please do me a favor will you, don't be like so many fools who sell "below cost" as you will not be in business for too much longer. We all have limits as to what we are prepared to negotiate on to begin with and then how much would be considered a reasonable amount to come down on the pricing structure or any other objection for that matter. This chapter deals with the negotiation process (this will come along at some stage) and the goal is to equip you to deal with your prospect professionally during the negotiation process. There are very few sales activities that will ensure your level of professionalism before the prospect than your ability to negotiate both parties to a win-win situation.

In order to answer objections and close the sale, the Master Entrepreneur Salesperson will understand and practice the art of negotiation. A successful negotiation is one in which the prospect feels that he/she has won and the salesperson walks away satisfied. This may not ALWAYS mean a win-win situation but the idea is always to get as close as is possible to an amicable conclusion. In order for you and me to more fully understand the critical activity of negotiation we will need to define the activity. While there are many varying definitions of the term negotiation (some brief and some lengthy) our goal has always been to reduce any complications by the so called "intellectuals" of the sales world.

Collins Dictionary: *To talk with others in order to reach (an agreement); to succeed in passing round or over (a place or a problem).*

Webster's Dictionary: *To confer with another so as to arrive at the settlement of some matter; to deal with (some matter or affair that requires ability for its successful handling).*

The idea or goal then is that we have to negotiate with another and that some successful conclusion should happen for both parties. This is similar then to what I have already stated above. I want you to see though that the notion of negotiation does exist and that it happens between parties that are desirous of reaching a successful conclusion to a matter. In our case we would be negotiating in a sales environment and the goal will be for both parties to get what they want. Is this even possible? Yes, but not all of the time as you will see.

Summarizing the process named *negotiation* then, and using the abovementioned definitions, we shall conclude that it is the give and take action between two interested parties and by which the prospect who tries to obtain desired products and/or services at the best possible price and/or terms of payment. This will include negotiating the terms and conditions of the sale. The negotiating process is to bring the parties closer to a successful conclusion to a transaction and to minimize the difference of opinions between the buyer and seller as this relates to price, delivery, and the terms and conditions in order to conclude a transaction.

Once again, I must point out to you that there are many sophisticated books on the book shelves dealing with the art of negotiating, and I will admit, the intensity of negotiations will be largely determined upon what is being negotiated. The sales process is vastly different to the world of hostage negotiation or a negotiation for peace. These are considered criminal and political negotiations which most certainly become complex and are not within the scope of our current discussion. I shall however refuse to believe that the sales negotiation, no matter the product and/or service, is ever going to be that complex that one would need a university degree to decipher the steps to follow for a successful conclusion. While I am sure that there are many ways to negotiate we must go back to basics and present you with the following five ways which I have used in order to successfully conclude business. At times I have simply walked away from a sales situation due to unreasonable expectations by the prospect and so I want to inform you that there is not always a win-win situation; however, at the right time you will need to make the choice to walk away rather than gain the sale to unreasonable demands.

The five types of negotiating alternatives are:


1. Making a trade-off.

The idea here is to give up one thing in return for another. For instance, when a prospect, raises an objection regarding pricing during the sales close, and presses for a five percent reduction in the overall cost, then the salesperson may respond as follows: "Mary, thank you for allowing me to make a call to my sales manager regarding your request for a reduction in price. I was given authority to agree to your request for a five percent price reduction on the overall cost based upon a written commitment from you to settle the invoice within seven days from date on the bill/invoice."

## 2. Adding an enhancement.

To enhance something means to improve it. When a restaurant owner was concerned about the traffic passing through washrooms he requested more soap dispensers than was quoted for. The salesperson, knowing that he/she was not in a position to add product at no charge decided to offer an enhancement. "John, unfortunately I am not in a position to add product at no charge; however, as the owner of my business I am in a position to add an additional service for the same amount of money."

## 3. Splitting the difference.

When there is disparity between what the prospect wants to achieve and what you are able to offer we must revert to a technique we call "splitting the difference" and this means just that-split the difference between where the prospect wants to be and what you want to achieve. Your goal is ALWAYS to achieve more sales surely so when the prospect wants a large price reduction you may want to consider the following win-win outcome: "Natasha, ABC Hospital would be a great addition to our client base; however, while I am not in a position to give you the price reduction of ten percent as you requested I am able to reduce the monthly cost by at least five percent should you include the pest elimination agreement as a part of the services package on offer?" If you feel that this offer is too "cheeky" and you feel that making it will be detrimental to your closing for business then simply offer a five percent reduction as opposed to the ten percent requested by the prospect.

4. Making a concession.

In a sense this is the act of giving up something small in order to achieve the whole. Your focus is on closing the sale however the prospect has unexpectedly made it clear that, to him/her your company is largely unknown and now wants to use this perceived "weakness" to his/her advantage. Making a concession in this case may be all it takes in order to close the sale. "Peter, I can understand that you may be nervous to try our services based upon the fact that you consider us an unknown quantity in the workplace services industry and I want to assure you that you have nothing to be concerned about. However, my goal is to prove this to you so I will offer you something which I have never had a need to offer before. I will request that my sales manager forward you a letter of guarantee which will state that should you not be happy with the services for any reason within the first ninety (90) days of the agreement then you shall have full right to terminate the same with immediate effect without recourse at all."

5. Simply walking away.

A prospect, who owns a gas station, wanted the pavement skimmed (removal of oil, grease and grime) and would not enter into a service agreement because the salesperson was not in a position to offer skimming the entire surface as a demonstration. The salesperson correctly offered to skim a small area as a sample but the prospect refused this as well. When a prospect is adamant about the entire area being skimmed and refuses to enter into the service agreement it is better to remove yourself from the situation and simply walk away. This is business not worth pursuing.

Believe it or not but it would seem that small companies prefer to do their buying from larger companies and they also like to sell to larger businesses as well. Buyers for larger organizations are well trained in the art of negotiation so never forget this and if you think that negotiating will not come up at your close then think again. They may employ "strong arm tactics" in your dealings with them which may include, but are not limited to, some of the following threats or objections. I have set up the objection and the responses for you so you will quickly learn how to respond professionally:

1. Intimidated by a high-pressure prospect.

**Objection:** "Take it or leave it!"

**Reaction:** Sidestep (review) the demand and decide what is taken and what is left.

**Reasoning:** By side stepping the demand you and I must rather (1) focus on the value offered to the prospect and (2) the potential loss to the prospect if the business is not concluded on the day.

2. A prospect wants to move ahead with you but …

**Objection:** "… no money available!"

**Reaction:** Express concern and understanding and prorate their proposal downward to meet whatever money IS available.

**Reasoning:** The prospect insists that he/she is keen to use your product and/or service; however, he/she cannot decide on going with you or continuing to use the competitor company currently on site. While the services or products do not overlap the prospect expresses the unwillingness to go over budget in order to include the much needed additional services being proposed by you.

You should suggest to the prospect that he/she consider reducing some of the unessential services or products with the current supplier in order to make room for the more essential services offered by you. The idea would be to find the money to take on part of the services this year with a view to ensuring full service inclusion in next year's budget. This way the prospect feels a sense of victory as at least half of the essential services will be installed and a phase one of two is thus concluded. This way the prospect would cover some of the health and hygiene concerns as mentioned during the needs analysis stage of the sales presentation.

3. The salesperson presents the proposal/quotation (in the closing stage) and the prospect reacts by ...

**Objection:** ... the prospect says nothing at all ("strategic silence").

**Reaction:** HE/SHE WHO SPEAKS FIRST LOSES!

It is preferable at this stage (if your nerves can hold out) that you say nothing but that you wait for a response, to remain positively focused, and not to show any self-doubt and/or any discomfort – SIT STILL!

**Reasoning:** Take the attitude that an agreement has been reached (an "assumption close") and continue to close: "I'm glad that you see the value of our services; we could install by next Monday or would Tuesday be better for you?"

4. A prospect appeals to a higher power or authority.

**Objection:** "My boss will only authorize the agreement if you can install at the end of the month!"

**Reaction:** "May I meet with your boss?"

**Reasoning:** The goal here will be (and should always be your goal from the first call to the company) to get to the INFLUENCER or the PURCHASER in order to cut out an indecisive GATEKEEPER.

5. A prospect is not happy with the price (now where have you heard that before?).

**Objection:** "You've got to do better than that, Trevor" or "Trevor; it would seem that there is fat in your price".

**Reaction:** Refocus attention on the VALUE aspects of your product and/or service.

**Reasoning:** Price is relative and is only one factor in the buying decision. "Paul, I'm sorry I may have forgotten to include all of the value of our product and service so I will just summarize these for you".


6. The prospect plays your proposal off against one from your competitor.

**Objection:** The prospect wants some form of concession. "Trevor, I am willing to pay 50% of the shipping costs if your company will subsidize the remaining 50%."

**Reaction:** Know or find out what the competitor is offering. "David, would you mind showing me what our competitor is offering in this regard as I will have to discuss this with my partner (or sales manager). To my knowledge we have not made the same exception to any of our current clients as the cost of shipping is a deductible business expense from a tax point of view."

**Reasoning:** While once again, reminding the prospect of the fact that shipping costs are also a business expense and therefore tax deductible it would not be wise to take your frustration out on your competitor. A Master Entrepreneur Salesperson will rather spend time focusing on the benefits versus those of the competitor.


7. One prospect in a group presentation is taking an aggressive stand.

**Objection:** You are facing an aggressive GATEKEEPER who is attacking some aspect of your proposal. "Trevor, we have been through your company's proposal before, and we have had bad experiences when dealing with your company, why should we believe a word you say?"

**Reaction:** Don't fall victim to the aggressive tactic or let this person distract you-deal with this person in the following manner and then move on without hesitation.

**Reasoning:** Rather acknowledge the concern but immediately re-focus on how these attacks actually address each point. For instance: "Mary, from my side, having had nothing to do with your experiences to date, I am truly sorry to hear that you have had bad experiences with our company. However, may I ask that despite your past difficulties you would consider giving me the opportunity to prove to you that not all salespeople are alike and that some of us do care about what you think?"

8. A prospect makes a phony demand on your company.

**Objection:** The prospect says that he/she will give up a phony demand in exchange for a meaningful concession on the part of your company – "the bargaining chip". "Trevor based upon our previous bad experiences with suppliers for washroom product rentals and services we are not prepared to enter into an agreement for at least the first ninety days."

**Reaction:** You must immediately present alternatives that supersede these presented by the prospect.

**Reasoning:** The above would be considered by most salespeople and companies to be an unreasonable guarantee request as the cost to install the units must be protected at all times. However, there is nothing stopping you from preparing a letter of guarantee outlining that if there is not complete client satisfaction within the ninety day period then the client shall have the right to terminate the agreement without having to justify the decision.

You must always be aware that during the strategic negotiation phase (objection phase?) prospects may want to fragment your proposal (break it down to their benefit) to gain concessions in each area. Should you be professional enough to pick-up on the prospect's strategic maneuvers then you will also be professional enough to know, that in order to remain in control of the selling environment, you will have to continue to present your proposal in its entirety and subtly refuse to have your proposal fragmented. You will be smart enough to discuss any proposed concessions only in relation to the total package. "Hamish, unfortunately the discounts offered has been calculated with you taking all four services as was originally discussed with you and unfortunately we will be forced to revise the pricing structure should you now wish to remove some of the services from the original offering."

**Professional tip:** When prospects offer to "split the difference" or say "let's bargain", you must always remember that this action will only benefit the prospect.

With this in mind you must always give concessions reluctantly as you will be limited in this regard. Business, when operating in a competitive environment, will calculate a selling price in order to make inroads into the market and these selling prices are many times done so with little room to negotiate on pricing or benefits. Some companies are irresponsible in their costing's, get the business based upon a ridiculous price, and then go out of business because the prices negotiated with the client are too low to make a profit-RIDICULOUS! Remember, the prospect will also have to understand that he/she has a vested interest in your business being profitable or you will not be able to provide the great service which they will become accustomed to. What is the use of promising the prospect the world and in a few months (or weeks for that matter) if you are out of business because you are not able to make a reasonable profit? PROFIT will keep the doors open and PROFIT is why you are in business in the first place. NEVER apologize for making a profit as this is why you are in business and this is why businesses exist all over the world. Why should your business be any different?

Make the prospect believe that he/she has received the best proposal/quotation that you have to offer. I have shared this with you before, and it is imperative that you remember that if you have sold all the features and benefits of both your product and your business then it reduces the impact of the price no matter what you are offering. The prospect needs to see the difference between what he/she is paying for your product and the features and benefits of the same and this, to him/her must clearly represent the net value between all of these components.

As a Master Entrepreneur Salesperson you MUST be aware that any and all concessions agreed upon are irreversible. Once you have made a commitment to a concession, no matter how unreasonable, and whether it is in writing or a verbal commitment, it is permanent and cannot be reversed. Think carefully and consider what you are able to do and what will cost you your business (or your job as a salesperson). Making concessions simply because you want to "spite" the competition is not prudent and will ensure that you become a business statistic as opposed to a business model. I have seen salespeople and competitors alike making the most ridiculous concessions just to get the sale and to ensure that no one else gets the sale – this is how salespeople and business gets a bad reputation as expectations are usually not met by these same irresponsible people and entities. Once a commitment has been made to a concession then this does not mean that the proposal/quotation can be changed or the prices or terms can be revised – an agreed upon concession means that it is over and matters have been finalized so think BEFORE concessions are made.

The best way to prevent making business-threatening decisions as this relates to making concessions is for you to have a CLEAR understanding of what your "bottom-line" offer is. Be sure, BEFORE you present your proposal, and BEFORE you close for the business, and in anticipation of prospect objections and requests for concessions, what your proposal pricing and terms will allow and what it will not allow as a professional business person and salesperson. If the prospect asks for concessions beyond your limit then what should you do? Exactly! Well done! You will get up and professionally pack your bag/s so to speak and GET OUT! BRILLIANT! Make sure then that you have a clear cut-off point for any negotiation and then implement this knowledge at all times if you want to remain in business doing profitable business. I want to help you in one other area as this relates to negotiating concessions. Please understand who you are negotiating with! There is no point at all in negotiating with a personal assistant or a gatekeeper. You also need to realize that negotiating with the janitor or housekeeper is not the way to go as none of the aforementioned has the authority to close the sale with you. The goal then is to get you to realize that when it comes to any form of negotiation and/or concession that such actions be done in the presence of and with the DECSION MAKER only. Should you refuse to heed my advice here then get ready for some serious disappointment and frustration? Remember, the negotiation process will lead up to another opportunity to close and you cannot close the sale with anyone other than the decision maker.

## Conclusion

The core feature and/or function of any business then must be to ensure that it is profitable at all times – a positive "bottom line". Most prospects and clients will be more than happy to share their disappointment in their suppliers in the event that a business is less than profitable. A profitable business is a healthy business and clients and prospects prefer dealing with successful companies. Unprofitable suppliers become a threat to a client as this threatens their ability to provide the client with a secure line of product or services.

While the sole focus for the Master Entrepreneur Salesperson will be to close the sale successfully it is also your responsibility to do so profitably on behalf of your business. Proposals must be packaged and structured in order to produce not only the greatest benefit to the client but also to your business. Many successful businesses are packaged this way because they have clearly understood this principle and they practice the same. Maintaining the level of profitable integrity is vital if we are to sustain company growth. A growing business is healthy for all concerned and this most certainly includes both the prospect and the client. This chapter has been presented to assist you to understand that while negotiations are an integral part of successful selling you cannot negotiate to the point of destroying your business.

# Part 2

# Basic $ales in Practice

# Chapter 10

# T.O.T. Management
*Time, Organization and Territory*
*Section 1*

**Introduction**

TIME, is an expression of the limited span of life. Time exists
on this planet only and in the lives of its inhabitants only. You
and I are a part of the inhabitants of this earth so we are
subject to a thing called time. We came into the world not
understanding nor caring about the concept of time, and yet,
as we mature it would seem that a concept which meant so
little to us in the early stages of life now consumes and/or
permeates every aspect of our lives. In fact, it would now
seem that we have a limited amount of this entity called time.
The universe, if it could in fact talk to us would reveal that it
knows no time as a concept at all as everything we see in
outer space has no time and time has no effect on the activities
of outer space it would seem for earth. However, you and I do
not live in outer space and the very next moment of our lives
where time will mean nothing to us will be when we die. If

you believe like I do then there is life after death, and what will matter then is where eternity will be spent. For now though we are winding down time on earth.

Back on earth and with the living then, we understand that time is always of the essence and many valuable actions and activities are all measured in time. In order though to remain within the context of this book we shall not be interested in all of your time only the part of your time which will allow you to either become successful in your endeavors or will see you fail in your attempts. I can assure you that I know of no other aspect in your working life that will make you fail more rapidly than a lack of understanding of professional time management. We sleep much of our lives so we can assume that close to half of our lives are spent sleeping. We eat, we drink and we watch television (lots of it). We shave (yes even women have now indulged), brush our teeth and we comb our hair. We trim our nails, polish our shoes (at least some of us) spend time with our children and spent time in making our children. We spend time in raising and clothing our children and then we see our children have children and we then spend time with our children's children and the cycle of spending more time with our children's children starts all over again. We buy, build and furnish houses to protect and provide shelter for our families and we spend time repairing or maintaining these shelters of protection.

However, in the bigger scheme of things we perform another activity using our time which allows us to make all of the abovementioned items possible – WE WORK! Most of the population of the world, male and female alike is hard at work, using up valuable time performing daily activities which we call work in order to earn a thing called MONEY! We all understand that we can do very little without money as this is how the world system allows us to buy the necessities of life. Because of the world system being this way we all understand that without money it becomes very difficult to live. The amount of money which you and I earn will, according to world standards, determine how well off or how poor your family is and money will most certainly determine your family's standard of living. We all say then that we have to work! However, may I put it to you that the idea of work is surely to work smarter not harder? We have heard this saying before, and yet, many choose to simply ignore the concept. The idea that if you plan your time and activities better one can earn more money using less effort is too much to contemplate and enact for some. I do understand that money is not everything to everyone. I do believe that there are some people out there who are more interested in a better quality of life, and are happy to get along with less, which mean to them that they do not have to participate in what we have come to call "the rat race". However, I am not talking about these fortunate individuals! I am talking about the rest of us who are most certainly caught up in the rat race and who have set a standard by which we would like to live for at least the time which we refer to as the active years of our lives. This attitude will more than likely change as we get older and our energy seems to wane and our focus changes from earning a living to taking care of our health. I am talking though about you and I right here and right now.

Generally, unless you are what we have come to label as a "workaholic" the amount of time which we allot for a normal working day is around nine hours. Where I am from people are generally at work and on the job for nine hours per day; however, one of the nine hours is set aside for a lunch time. Effectively then, and using this example of working hours, we should all be "at the grindstone" for at least eight hours per day. On a weekly basis then, assuming that your week consists of a Monday to a Friday, you and I are handed around forty hours per week in order to make a difference in the lives of our families. We have at least twenty-two working days in a month on average throughout the year meaning then that we have at least one hundred and seventy – six hours per month in order to change our lives financially – we are talking about work and not the health club at this point right? Let's take this working time aspect a little further shall we? Notwithstanding that we are aware that throughout the world we are given non-productive days in the form of public holidays, celebrations (Federal and National Holidays such as independence days and the like), and bank holidays, the amount of hours which we generally then (give and take a few here and there) have for income production annually is two thousand one hundred and twelve hours.

Should you retire at the age of sixty then the average amount of hours, using all of the examples as stated above, which you will spend working to accumulate things which you cannot take with you when you die, but which are needed (some would argue) in order to live would be one hundred and twenty-six thousand seven hundred and twenty hours. Considering that at the age of sixty you would have lived (if I have this right) five hundred and twenty-five thousand and nine hundred and forty-eight hours we could take a guess that we work approximately twenty-five percent of our working lives up to the age of sixty. Getting back to reality then we have eight hours in a day to make a difference for our families.

I hear you younger generation – I HAVE PLENTY OF TIME!

Please allow me to share this with you will you? I can remember the days when I was eighteen, twenty-three and I can most certainly remember when I finally turned thirty, and guess what, it all seemed like it was yesterday. I am now three years from the age of sixty ( considering that we are talking so much about the age of sixty) and I can tell you with all the confidence in the world that I have in me that if you think that you "have all the time in the world then think again! The biggest lie that you can tell yourself is that you have all the time in the world as I can assure you that you do NOT have all the time in the world and considering how we squander our time on non-productive activities during working hours it is no wonder there is such a gap between the rich and the poor. Only fools believe that they have all the time in the world and it would seem that these same fools are the ones complaining about how poor they are and how their families are suffering and these are also the people that plead poverty at every opportunity.

## YOU DO NOT HAVE ALL THE TIME IN THE WORLD!

The time which you and I have been given is all we are going to get as we most certainly cannot go to the ATM and buy some more. There is in fact no place or no person on earth that you can go to in order to add more time to your life – THIS IS IT! Your life will be over before you know it! My goal here is not to push you into a state of panic (although for some people this would be a perfect result) but to get you to "catch a wake-up"! I have assisted and counselled many "entrepreneurs" and "salespeople" who have issues with productivity and lack of success moments in their lives and I can assure you that while there are always more than one area of their business lives that need attention the greatest by far is their inability to plan their time professionally. I am interested in your success and this is why this chapter has been included in this book and this is also why this chapter STARTS Part 2 of this book – yes, it is that important!

As an experiment, I decided one day that I was going to go have a cup of coffee with a friend; however, my motivation for going was not discussed with my friend as I am sure that he would not have gone with me had he known what I was about to do. I checked the time and it was around 11h20. We ordered our coffee and I asked my friend to excuse me for about fifteen minutes and all I saw was a question mark on his face. I got up from my chair and decided to start at the back of the coffee shop and started asking selected people one question: "Hi, my name is Trevor and I'm doing a one question survey. May I ask you a question?" The answer usually came back as "yes"! My question went something like this: "What do you do for a living?" While the answers may surprise you they most certainly did not surprise me. I got what I was looking for and that my suspicions were confirmed. One after the other gave me an answer which went something like this: "I own my own business" or "I am an entrepreneur" or I am a sales manager" or "I am a salesperson". In all honesty, I did speak to a few people who were retired and housewives and the like-the point is that these people could afford to be sitting in a coffee shop at this time of the day.

Can you imagine! How is it possible to achieve goals and sales quotas/targets if these people are sitting in a coffee shop at 11h20? This is the very reason why I have the opinion that I do of salespeople who report to their sales manager on a Friday that they have not made quota/target and then give one excuse after the other as to why they feel they had "a tough time this week". Sales managers are swallowing this rubbish and companies are losing production because of the laziness and lies. Entrepreneurs have "a thing"! "I do business in the coffee shop and on the golf course" – RUBBISH! I talk to the guilty here! While there may be a moment in time when this actually happens I can assure you that professional business is not done on the golf course or in a coffee shop. Not everybody wastes time like you do! There are successful people out there that will not set foot into a coffee shop during normal productive working hours and neither will they play golf during this time. If you want to have a cup of coffee then by all means make it in your office while you are setting up business appointments to close sales or have it with a prospect. Having a cup of coffee at the coffee shop can cost you around one and a half hours at least depending on where you go and in particular should you go to the local mall you will have to park, walk and window shop before you even sit down-this is stealing time! If you have coffee, at a coffee shop, during normal working hours then I tell you that you are stealing time from both your employer and your family. If you are an entrepreneur, and you steal time, then you are nothing more than a fool as you will only have yourself to blame when you fail. Should you constantly be having coffee in a coffee shop and performing like activities called time wasters then you are only making a fool of yourself as the inevitable result is that you will fail – not IF but WILL!

By now you will understand that I am pretty passionate about time management and less enthusiastic about people who act as though they have all the time in the world. However, I am more upset with people who deliberately choose to waste time every day doing all the wrong things and then use their time wasters (created by the guilty party to begin with) as excuses for not performing and/or not succeeding at what they do. Here is the crux of it all for me. Did you know that someone somewhere will eventually pay for the time YOU waste every day (family or employer or business, etc.)? I am sure then, now that you understand my passion for time management that you will forgive me for spending a great deal of time on the subject. I want to warn you that this chapter is long for a reason. I also want to warn you that while this chapter will give you all the direction you need you will absolutely hate the contents if you are a perpetual time waster.

It is understood that you and I have twenty-four hours in each day and this goes on for just over three hundred and sixty-five (365.242) days per year. However, I will not be interested in discussing all of your time only the time which is expended in income producing activities which we have now worked out is at least eight hours per day from Monday to Friday. You will have to plan your financial production time for forty hours per week and for an average of twenty-two days per month. The idea is that you and I understand time management and that each minute of production time is accounted for and that our activities should be focused on financial production only.

**Professional tip:** When you work you work and when you play you play!

My youngest daughter would be considered smart mentally, and yet, she started developing the wrong attitude about prioritizing her time. She started confusing the lines in her time management at school and at home. For instance, when she started school in the mornings her friends and her played on the playground to their heart's content. The problem that my daughter had (a few of her friends had the same problem) was that when the bell rang for the commencement of classes she, and a few of her friends, did not understand that it was now time to focus on the teacher and the lesson. While you and I understand that attending school generally leads to two benefits: academic preparation for future studies and life and the growth of the child socially. This is the challenge of most parents when the child is young and struggles to distinguish between work and play – to a child life is all about play. The problem with this is that many times parents allow this attitude to continue on throughout the school years to the point where the line between work and play is so blurred that as an adult there is no line at all and all time seems to be allocated to that of play.

For instance, in case you think that I don't know what I am talking about, through an acquaintance I know of grown men who sit in front of their computer for hours playing war games. These individuals shall remain nameless, but I can confidently share with you that they play this cyber war game from the morning till the night in some cases. I have seen with my own eyes how involved they get with playing games, and this, to the point where it is quite possible for them to sit through the night not realizing or even considering the fact that they soon need to get to work. They arrive at work like "cyber zombies" and they laze around unproductive trying to get through the day. One would think that the goal would be, after a sleepless night, to catch up on some sleep when they get home; however, this is not the case and is the furthest thing from their minds as the only thing occupying some of the empty space in their heads is to get back into the game. Wow! How stupid! These grown men have never understood that there is a time to play and a time to work and if you play too hard you will not have the energy to work, and then, they wonder why they never achieve in life and start blaming everything and everyone around them for their failure. Marriages become affected and children grow up just like their fathers – all play and no work. Let me say this again: WHEN YOU WORK YOU WORK AND WHEN YOU PLAY YOU PLAY!

## The Practical Application of Time Management

We will deal with time management only as it relates to when you work. All other non-related time will be handed to you for management purposes. I am interested in you being financially productive and this is going to be my focus in this chapter. I would like to start the discussion on time management with a statement clearly depicting the basis of the road ahead: ***Organizing your time and geographic territory is not an option but is an absolute MUST!***

In our understanding of time and time management we will assume (in most cases anyway and we know that this statistic is improving in some parts of the world) that we have an average lifespan (male or female) of around seventy years. However, if you think about it we tend to spend most of this time in time spaces which I have come to term as "non-income producing time". On average then, and again you and I can work this out, we spend around fifty-five years of our lives on so called non-income producing activities and these include but are not limited to the following: sleeping, eating, personal grooming, cyber time, newspaper time, television time, daily commute, personal, being sick and time wasted. We could, as this time is spent largely in non-productive activities, claim that this time be allocated to the "play time" in our statement of "when you work you work and when you play you play". The time that you and I will be more interested in is the "work time" which by my simple method of calculation may add up to around eleven to fifteen years (dependent upon ones work ethic and planning) of your life and mine.

As a Master Entrepreneur Salesperson you must understand that most people can't grasp the fact that if they manage their time, they are better able to manage their lives. You need to manage your time as you have so very little of it each day and when you are organized then you gear your activities in the most productive direction. When you are organized as a salesperson then everything else seems more organized and you begin to manage productive tasks and not chaos on a daily basis. You will also be wise in coming to an understanding that if you plan your time you will organize your personal life into a wonderful and exiting space to be in. No one like's chaos so you must not operate in this space at all if you can avoid it. Seeing the advantage of making the most of every moment comes with age. The older one gets the more we realize that that there is not much time left and this makes us more aware of how we use time and manage it. The older we get the more we understand that time spent can be done so with quality in mind and we start using phrases such as "quality time" as opposed to wasting time. The emphasis changes from wasting time to careful planning of the use of whatever time it is that we have left before we meet our Maker. The younger generation has a different view of time but this will only last until they realize that time is running out and running out fast. They feel, at a young age, that they have so much time left so there is no need to plan and time can be wasted without consequence. The best way to become motivated to manage your time effectively is to realize as soon as is possible that you are going to eventually die and your life will be over on this planet – you may want to also start thinking about what you will do in the next life as you cannot stop this moment either.

## The Objectives of Time Management

To give us all greater control over CHAOS! We need a greater sense of (1) control over our businesses (2) control over our sales activities (3) control over our lives as an ultimate goal.

Chaos, in the business environment and sales in particular, is a characteristic ascribed to the unprofessional and to those that fail in business. Chaos represents everything a professional salesperson and Master Entrepreneur should not be such as:

confused, disorganized, uncontrolled, and disorderly and a severe lack of focus. When you and I are in this state we fail as we simply have no direction in sales whatsoever and we lose valuable time when all we do is "put out the fires" each day. Many salespeople sit at home on a Sunday evening contemplating the week. These same unprofessional arrive at the office on Monday morning not knowing what they will be doing for the week let alone what their activities will be for the month-they are totally directionless. Sales activities MUST be planned or they will not happen as simple as that! If you don't plan to act then you won't act! Your mind will do what needs to be done but even it needs the correct instruction or it will carry out what your flesh tells it to do like go to the golf course for a day and coffee shop for an hour and a half. Time management gives direction and direction ensures that we succeed and nothing makes us succeed more than when we gain control over our business, our sales activities and ultimately our lives. The best part of achieving all of this is that planning will help a great deal in reducing stress. For instance, when a salesperson arrives at the office on a Monday morning having set up calls/appointments for the entire week he/she will have clear direction for that week so how does this impact on stress levels for this professional? On the opposite side when a salesperson arrives at the office not knowing what to do for the week and not having face to face meetings/appointments with prospects what kind of stress levels do you believe this type of person would be experiencing every Monday morning?

Another objective or goal of effective time management is to give us more income as a result of more effective time usage. If you understand that not having pre-set appointments/meetings or calls for the week is not good then effective time management will reveal this weakness and time will be allotted for this activity. Setting up more appointments will allow you to be where salespeople ought to be and that is in front of the prospect presenting your product and/or services. The more you present the more proposals/quotations you will be required to hand out. It stands to reason then that if you believe that "sales is a numbers game" then the more proposals you present to prospects the more chance you and I will have of these being converted into business through professional closing – how do you do this from the golf course or coffee shop? With this in mind then, do you think that you would start enjoying life just a little more and in particular your Sunday evenings? For once and always thereafter you would be happy to get up on a Monday morning so that you can do what you do best and that is to sell, sell and sell! Your life will change as it usually changes for the better when we are successful at what we do and planning our time is this important I can assure you.

The goal of managing our time must also be to make us more selective in what we do. For the first time we may think twice about going for coffee or playing that game of golf as it has not been planned for and to participate in these non-productive activities will create chaos with your sales goals and targets. Professional time management will also assist us to eliminate the pressures of too little time and increase our creativity. Instead of finding ways to get to the golf course and the coffee shop we will find ways and reasons why not to go. Instead of spending all night on a violent war game as a "cyber dummy", your planning will remind you that when you work you work and when you play you play and playing for too long will severely affect your ability to focus on the next day's action plan. Managing your time and mine professionally will help us in establishing meaningful priorities in our life and our work-particularly in our sales activities.

### Why do the unprofessional fail to manage their time?

While it is not the idea you may see yourself in this paragraph and the goal is for you to be truthful enough to recognize your own weaknesses with a view to changing them.

There is a misconception by the unprofessional that planning a course of action limits our freedom. In other words they do not want to plan as this makes them responsible for a set of actions which they feel "are etched in stone"! These people want freedom to "roam" like the Buffalo of old-free to come and go as they please with no sense of accountability whatsoever. Set plans make them accountable by its very nature and this is not in their nature. Most people find it difficult to plan because there is also an overemphasis on day to day "activity" which inevitably pushes professional planning into the background. These are the same people that will rather spend their time "shuffling paper" and perform firefighting tasks as opposed to fire prevention activities. Sir Winston Churchill summed it up when he stated: "It is difficult to look further ahead than we can see." Some people don't actually want to see what is coming and would much rather wait for things to happen, and then deal with them, as opposed to making things happen. Unprofessional entrepreneurs and salespeople generally find time planning so time consuming that they rather focus on getting back to the chaos in their working lives. Believe it or not, and whether they would admit to it or not but most unprofessional salespeople secretly enjoy living their lives in chaos and disorganization. These are the "busy" people of the working society. The "busy" people are always "busy" and you will see them frantically running around the office with nowhere to go, they never seem to achieve anything at all and are largely dissatisfied with life and themselves. These people never have enough time in a day and go home feeling both depleted and dissatisfied with their accomplishments for the day, week and the month – THEY HAVE NO PLAN AT ALL! Many salespeople do not have written goals. They have no specific short-term goals and neither do they aspire to any achievement in the long-term. When one has goals there is no room for messing about and goals will motivate you and me to plan for the achievement of these – THIS IS WHY WE PLAN! Procrastination also comes easy to those with no clear written goals, and because of this, no time management planning.

Certain people have an aversion to change and lack the commitment to stick with time planning until it becomes habit. In order to change a habit you have to move away from the non-productive activities in sales and REPLACE these with productive activities. For instance, if you are not calling to set up meetings/appointments then you will start to do this. If you present the proposal and have not been closing for the sale then you will stop not closing for the sale and start closing for the sale. When we replace a bad habit with a good one it means that you and I have altered course, so to speak, in that we move away from a destructive course, to a more productive course. Thus we modify our behavior for the sake of professional time planning and achieving our goals not simply for the sake of it. When we change course we reshape the course. Reshaping means that we change our attitude and actions for the sake of achieving our goals and targets and nothing shows our intention to change course more than professional time management. Therefore, as a professional salesperson, you cannot have or develop an aversion to change as a time management program is the very epitome of change with positive consequences. When you and I commit to a course of action which has obvious positive consequences then we promise, pledge and undertake to complete the change and we do so for those around us that we admire most and respect and we do all of this for the ones that we love. These are the people at home who are longing for you to break free of your unprofessional self and your self-centered self so that you and they are able to finally live the kinds of lives which you had promised in the first place. The word commitment must also be taken to mean that you "guarantee" the positive change and nothing secured this guarantee more than a workable and sustainable time management program. Breaking a bad habit is never easy – ask the smoker, alcoholic or drug-addict. It has been said that it takes only three weeks to change a habit whether good or bad and then the action will become a part of you. I have no idea if this is true or not but I have no reason to refute this statement as it makes a great deal of sense to someone like me.

We have bad habits such as not having goals, targets and a workable time management program but the good habits are what you do. The connotation regarding the word habit means to practice the good habit or the bad habit if you desire negative results, you become accustomed to a routine and in our case we need this to be a positive routine if we are to attain a positive outcome. We develop a pattern; a tendency if you will which ultimately becomes a way of life in sales. The word habit within the context of taking some or other form of drug implies an addiction as we all know. This addiction becomes a compulsion, a craving, an obsession and a fixation, and while I do not want to dehumanize the terms in this negative context, I do want to ask you to contemplate the contents of the sentence within the role of time and territory management. If only entrepreneurs and salespeople would be as committed to time management then we would most certainly have no need for this chapter.

## Realities of time and time management

The reality of time is that you have all the time that you will ever get as long as you are living on this planet and that is why, it is imperative that we take time management seriously.

Whether you are rich or poor or whether you are uneducated or a genius the one thing that we all need to understand is that time makes us all equal. The question is rather what you and I will do with the time that we have? We need to understand that we have all the time which we are going to get and none of us knows when the final hour will come. Some die early in life and others die later; however, it is a certain thing that we will all die eventually. The time that has been allotted to you and me then is the time that has been allotted. Time is the most unique and valuable resource upon the face of the earth, and yet it cannot be "mined" manufactured or stored. Being this unique means that time, for you and me, will and must be spent sooner rather than later. Napoleon was once quoted as saying: "There is one kind of robber whom the law does not strike at, and who steals what is most precious to men – TIME".

**Time wasters**

There are eight characteristics of time wasters:

1. If you consider an activity to be a time waster then it probably is.

If you and I perceive that an intended activity will be a time waster then the chances are that it probably will be – FOR YOU! For example, if you think that calling your mom when you should be working will waste your time because she will keep you on the phone for longer than you plan for then you are probably going to be right. If you think that meeting your brother for coffee will waste your time then it probably will so don't do it during work hours.

2. All time wasters cause negative reactions.

Reactions will include physical and emotional and positive and negative. When we waste time deliberately then we apply pressure to ourselves and this pressure will affect us physically. It is common knowledge that while a certain amount of pressure is good for you and me an abnormal amount of pressure affects our immune system which is responsible for defending us against disease such as flus and colds. Many times we have to take time to recover which only adds more pressure in the long run. Time wasters also affect our ability to achieve as we are spending time on doing all the wrong things and when we place effort and energy into doing non-productive activities then we do not succeed. I can tell you that if you do not succeed in life you will find this failure affecting your emotional state known as self-esteem and self-worth. A low self-esteem is the worst thing that can happen to an entrepreneur and/or salesperson. The idea here then is to take into account that when you and I react to time wasters in a positive manner we increase our chances of controlling them as opposed to them controlling us.


3. Wasting time will waste more time.

Please think about this carefully with me as I claim that all time wasters have the ability to become a time waster compounder. For instance, I have already given you the example of playing cyber war games. As long as playing the game in your own time is controlled and ended at the appropriate time you should have no consequences. However, should you play the game on Sunday afternoon as an example and you find yourself out of control then one thing will lead to the next. The night will come and go and the early hours of Monday morning will be at hand before you know it. The alarm will wake you before you are ready to and the rest of the day, your productive income earning time, will be negatively impacted simply because you could not determine that time wasters have a potential built-in time waster multiplier.


4. Time wasters are an unprofessional use of your time.

Every time waster is an unprofessional use of your time by definition. The goal is (1) to change it (2) to eliminate it (3) to re-negotiate it. We have discussed this previously so you will now understand that you must not continue on with making poor time wasting decisions-substitute bad time wasters with good time wasters and do this sooner rather than later. Instead of playing war games that never end participate in time sensitive games so that they have a start and an ending or better still, don't play the games at all and rather spend time reading this book and **ENTREPRENEURSHIP (*minus*) 101**. You will find everything you will need to know about goal setting and quotas/targets in this book. If you cannot play the game within a certain amount of hours then renegotiate and substitute the hours for when you can make it.

5. They are caused by three things.

All time wasters are caused by YOU, OTHERS and/or a combination of YOU AND OTHERS. You need to recognize that time wasters are caused by people. On many occasions the people guiltiest of wasting your time will be the ones that you love. Because you are a salesperson Mom thinks that you are free and available to run errands for her during working hours. Children have a terrible habit of distracting you when you are in the middle of financial production activities and this will not only distract you but will also ensure that you fail when aiming at a pre-set goal. Your spouse will feel that you should be available and at her beck and call at a moment's notice and that you should drop what you are doing because she needs you to buy some milk for the house and bread for the kids. Not on! Don't let this happen to you! You will have to teach those affecting you negatively and ensure that they understand that when you work you work and when you play you play.


6. Time wasters produce negative consequences.

All time wasters ensure negative returns and the unprofessional will have no trouble in rationalizing these at a moment's notice. The unprofessional will blame other entities and actions, circumstances and even other people as the cause of failure instead of the real cause being the actual time waster. To you and me having coffee is not the problem; however, having coffee at a coffee shop in the middle of the working day is the problem. It will not be a problem for this action to be rationalized as "I was between prospects and had some time". You and I might ask them if they had this time available could they not have performed some income producing activity (prospecting?) rather than wasting the time?


7. They reflect who you are.

You and I must understand that we are being watched by those around us on a daily basis including those that love us. That is why it is important to be aware, at all times that all time wasters make statements about us and the way we run and manage our lives. We all say that respect is earned and so is trust, and yet, the entity creating the most chaos in our lives is our own inability to manage our time and who we are. How is it possible for your wife to respect you if your life is in a constant state of chaos and disorganization? You must agree that it is hard to trust someone who shows clear signs of chaos in their lives and the disorganization, as a result the chaos is palpable and an air of unprofessionalism persists. Who wants to deal with an unprofessional entrepreneur salesperson as this also reflects upon your business and the way that you manage this part of your life. You and I cannot blame the outside world if they have poor perceptions of whom and what we are if we live our lives in a chaotic, disorganized and unmanageable state. I want to make it clear then that you are being watched and the more organized you are the more confidence you will instill in others. People want to do business with successful people and companies. You would do well to contemplate this thought and become organized and the best place to start is to manage your time professionally. My advice to you at this point will include admonishing you to "listen" to what time wasters are saying about you and this can be achieved by understanding what people think about your level of professionalism. However, the question is more: "What do YOU think about your level of professionalism in managing your time and your life?" If you feel that you are not capable of answering this question honestly then ask your spouse, or your best friend, for an honest opinion as to your ability with regards to our subject at hand.

8. Time wasters can be substituted.

The wonderful news is that if you are disorganized and chaotic due to your constant time wasting you will always have the freedom and the ability to replace these negative activities with more productive activities. You are the only one preventing the change but first you will have to identify the negative return activities which seriously affect your ability to be more productive. Once you have identified the negative result activity the simple answer then will be to remove this from your daily business activity and replace this with high yield actions. Get used to using the HIPO and LOPO method of time management in order to produce better personal and business results. In other words, substitute high priority – high payoff activities ("HIPO") for low priority – low pay off actions ("LOPO").

## Types, causes and solutions to time wasters

The following table has been developed to help you to determine the type, cause and solution to your time management challenges. While I have cited but a few examples for you I have only done so in order to get you on the track (or into the habit if you will) of identifying types, causes and solutions in your own life. Some of the examples presented may apply directly to you or none of them may apply to you at all. The goal then is for you to take some time out (I know some of you will say that I don't have the time to take time out so I will say to you that this is exactly why you should take the time out to assess and apply this to your working life) and contemplate where you stand regarding professional time management. You must be able to get to the point where you know what works for you and will not work for you. You must not only be able to identify the bad influencers in your life but you must also have the ability to change them so please review the table below and get started – DO NOT PUT THIS ACTION OFF! By the way, this activity is not a once off contemplation of your time management activity state but rather a constant assessment to get to where you are most effective and professional.

Types, causes and solutions to time wasters:

| TYPE | CAUSE | SOLUTION |
|---|---|---|
| Lack of planning | Failure to see the benefit, action oriented, see success without it | Recognize and experience how much time it saves |
| Lack of priorities | Lack of quotas/targets and objectives, does not see time as valuable or see time as a limited commodity | Write down goals, discuss with others, keep goals visible |
| Over commitment | Too broad and time consuming interests, chaos in priorities, no set priorities | Learn to say NO, prioritize activities, develop a personal philosophy of time and understand spending it |
| Telephone | Lack of self-discipline, distracted by non-working "essentials" | Develop a plan for making and taking calls |
| Meetings | Fear of responsibility for decisions, Indecision, rampant communication, poor leadership in setting clear agendas | Make decisions without meetings, attend only necessary meetings, always have an agenda and time frame |
| Haste | Impatience, always "putting out fires", lack of future vision, procrastination of tasks adding pressure to complete | Do it right the first time, planning before acting, delegate more |
| Disorganized work area | Insufficient work area, lack of adequate filing system, being a pack rat and saving everything | Modify work area, establish filing procedures, use the waste bin more often |
| Detail work | Paperwork is "safe", Makes you look "busy", more satisfaction from paperwork than people work, perfectionist | Streamline, hire a PA, be imperfect once in a while |
| Fatigue | Excess stress, overweight, no exercise, too much "play", sleep deprivation | Exercise regularly, activity in moderation, less play more drive |

## "Back to basics" laws of time management

You may not agree with me but there are certain "old school" laws and principles which still apply in time management today. Notwithstanding the fact that time management as a thought and concept no longer receives the attention which it deserves we shall however be smart enough to consider the notion. Time management, within the worldly human parameter, must be based on some foundation surely? However, just so that you understand, time management principles are as numerous as the laws guiding professional time management. As stated before, many have even managed to complicate this simple planning phenomenon and I refuse to do this as a principle. My goal will be to at least give you a foundation to work from so that you are able to understand the old school thought processes on the subject and also see the application. Having a foundation for effective time management while we are alive and are operating a business or a sales territory is imperative to us developing our own plans and ideas. The ability to understand where the concept of time management came from will help you to understand how it was developed and then how to implement these into your very own plan and life.

As I have stated, there are many ideas, theories and principles out there. Many are so complicated that one cannot apply these to one's life as they are written by "theorists" (people that love theory as opposed to the practical implementation) who have no concept of the practical side of time management – we are not interested in such complications. On the other hand we do not want to be guilty of overcomplicating our lives but we do need a foundation so I have taken it upon myself to share my own foundation with you. Over the years, having understood the need for effective time management and the implementation of a program that actually works, I have selected four principles which have been developed by men who are well known in their respective fields. The four principles and laws are:


1. The Pareto Principle.

Vilfredo Pareto, an Italian economist, according to Wikipedia, observed two interesting phenomena (1) 80% of the land in Italy was owned by 20% of the population around 1906 (2) he observed that 20% of the pea pods in his garden contained 80% of the peas (The first principle mentioned was developed by Pareto based upon this observation in his garden).

This principle is commonly and still used in business and around the world today. We all have come to know this principle as the "80-20 rule". In theory this is a cause and effect principle and what we all claim is that should you and I apply ourselves diligently to a 20% effort we shall produce 80% of the desired result. I am sure that you have heard of "only twenty percent of the people in the group are actually working and yet they are producing eighty percent of the result"? In business we have heard the same principle – "20% effort produces 80% of the result. In sales we refer to the very same principle focusing 20% of your effort effectively will produce 80% of the sales target. Of course then, the same principle will apply in time management in that you and I will then be "working smarter not harder".

In short then, the Pareto Principle may be summarized, and be applied as follows for our application: Eighty percent (80%) of your time expended (if you are not smart) will yield only twenty (20%) of the result. The goal will be though to spend twenty percent (20%) of your time in yielding an eighty percent (80%) result. This phenomenon then clearly shows the effectiveness of concentrating and focusing our attention and efforts instead of using a "shot gun" approach to getting things done. Effective time planning and thereafter time management is critical in assisting us all to reach this level of professionalism.

2. Mackenzie's planning vs. Execution Time

This principle of time management is attributed to Melody and Dr. Alec Mackenzie (*Investing in Time for Maximum Return*. American Media Publishing 1977). We deal with two very interesting entities here and you will soon see why this principle is critical to effective time management (1) "Every moment spent in planning saves three or four in execution" (2) "The planning time added to the execution time is less than the execution time without planning".

This is particularly geared toward lazy people who say that they don't have time to plan. When planning an action or activity it must surely stand to reason that the planning of the action will give clear direction as to the execution of the action? Recently, we all had the option of watching the Commonwealth Games which were held in Scotland. It was great to watch although it was most certainly not the Olympics which are considered the pinnacle of summer and/or winter sport. Have you ever considered what would have happened if the organizers had exclaimed: "Great job to one and all, we have selected the next venue, which will be Scotland, see you there in five years from now!" The absolute chaos that would ensue is indescribable. No! The Commonwealth Games as an organization has a PLANNING committee whose responsibility it was to plan the entire event from start to finish. I most certainly don't have the time in this forum to present the hundreds of activities that would have been planned but I am sure that with a bit of thought you can work this much out for yourself.

As time planning goes we can in fact refer to the Olympic Games and contemplate the disastrous results of such a mega international event if no planning was done prior to hosting such an event. We can also refer then to the soccer world cup, the Super bowl, the World Series, the Rugby World Cup and so on. What would happen if the organizers refused to do planning "because we don't have the time to plan?" Disaster! We all agree I'm sure so please tell me why you think that by not planning you will develop and nurture absolute chaos and disorganization in both your business and your life? The benefits of Mackenzie's principle here then becomes clear and that is that it will allow the Master Entrepreneur Salesperson, the Entrepreneur and the businessperson to work at a less hectic, pace and achieve more and produce a better quality result. Once again, I must therefore refer back to the old adage namely "work smarter not harder".

3. Parkinson's First Law

"Work expands so as to fill the time available for its completion"

In a nutshell, and applying this to our discussion, what we understand this law to mean is that if you need to do time planning and that you have to have it completed by next week, the planning will take the whole of next week to finish. However, should the goal be to complete the time management planning within the next thirty days then it will take the next thirty days to complete the task. In my book **ENTREPRENEURSHIP (*minus*) 101** I specifically refer to the fact that people operate better under pressure – some kind of pressure at least. I am not talking about the kind of pressure which leads to stress which leads to physical illness (as in when you refuse to do time planning) and is negative in context. When you and I set a time goal to complete time management planning then we most probably feel some kind of pressure to get it done, and until it's done we develop a nagging feeling until the project is complete. It is common sense then that if you decide not to give yourself a time line for completion then you will take as long as you like and if you do this then there will be no pressure at all. This scenario is the time waster's ideal environment – NO PRESSURE! The goal as you and I contemplate and apply this law is to schedule tightly everyday (when planning your time), always set deadlines (you operate better under a certain amount of pressure) whether these are real or imaginary; in other words, yes, I am going to say it – BECOME A CLOCK WATCHER!

4. Drucker's Law

Peter Drucker has written numerous books starting in 1939 and culminating in 2008. Most of us that know his works have a love hate relationship with the man in that he has been able to blast traditional business and management thinking to kingdom come. Love him, hate him, the fact is that many of his ideas have changed the way business is viewed and conducted. As a management consultant and business educator he presented a principle which many corporates still adhere to today: "Most people incorrectly concentrate on the efficient use of time – DOING THE JOB RIGHT". According to this principle, and as an explanation within our context, "efficiency" according to Drucker, "although important, only contributes 15% to one's overall productivity". Drucker goes on to expound that: "People should be concentrating on the effective use of time – DOING THE RIGHT JOB". Meaning, "Doing the job of the highest priority contributes 85% to your overall productivity".

Most people, and particularly when performing time planning would rather focus on the efficient (15% contribution to a goal) use of their time than the effective (85% contribution to a goal) use of their time. No wonder, in many cases time planning and time management fails. Not performing time planning will lead to poor time management and poor time management will inevitably lead to frustration and failure. Planning the EFFECTIVE use of your time is our goal not the EFFICIENT use of the time at our disposal. As per Peter Drucker we want to spend our time in the 85% time zone in high priority activities producing great results. In other words, instead of "doing the job right" we want to be guilty of "doing the right job" and performing this task correctly. I can tell you that planning your time for the most effective use must be your goal if you are to avoid chaos on a daily basis.

What then, in final clarification, is the difference between the two key words as mentioned above namely "efficient" and "effective"?

## Efficient

"Doing the job right" – The meaning of the word describes the actions of one being methodical, mostly systematic in performing a task (time consuming?) and well organized for a specific task but not in general. We are told that being this way and having these attributes in the working environment only contributes 15% to one's overall productivity. So while efficiency then is important within the working environment it will take up more time and produce far less.

## Effective

"Doing the right job" – Doing the right job as opposed to choosing to do the wrong job. Choosing the right job will help you to find workable solutions as opposed to time consuming solutions. The solutions presented will be workable, successful in implementation and worthwhile. The word also denotes that solutions will be productive, effectual and potent and will get the job done at maximum levels of productivity.

## Practical application of time management principles

Time management principles are important because they give us an understanding of the foundation needed to build our time planning master schedule. Daily activities are critical if we are to achieve our overall time management strategy but they need to be efficient and they need to ensure that we do the right job right. In my opinion, any plan must have a "master plan schedule" where all activities are visible on a single page either for weekly, monthly, quarterly and annual activities. However, the way to ensure that time management plans succeed is to break these down even further – DAILY ACTIVITY PLANS. If you need to then reduce the daily plan down even further to the eight hours per day that you are in lifetime production time. When you and I plan activities for each day of the working week there are certain critical aspects that need to be included in order to ensure achievement of tasks and the ultimate goal. While I am sure that there are many activities that a time management specialist would like to see either added or removed from my list as stated below, I do feel that the following items are basic to your success. I have chosen eleven pillars for you to use as an initial foundation in time planning. Again, you are more than welcome to change these to suit your own personal life and working environment.

1. Become "hooked" to your calendar (diary or Day-Timer for some) and make sure that the layout suits your personal application.

2. Do planning the "night" before (just before you leave the office) or very early the next morning but ALWAYS before you start a new day.

3. Daily planning is placed on to a prioritized TO DO LIST and don't begin a day without completing this time management tool – your road map for the day.

4. Unprofessional time managers confuse ACTIVITY with PRODUCTIVITY – don't be so busy "doing" that you produce no or very little result at the end of each day.

5. Deadlines apply subtle pressure so set a deadline for each activity and undertake to complete tasks EARLY each day.

6. Do climax block planning.

7. Begin each day with the actions you dislike most – if you have such a syndrome.

8. Assess your task and evaluate time throughout the day.

9. SPEEDING up the pace DAILY will increase your overall effectiveness and productivity.

10. Discover hidden moments in every day.

11. Effective filing systems still work.

**Become hooked to your calendar and make sure that the layout suits your personal application.**

You are unique in some aspects and so is your business so ensure that you have a time management planning system that works for you. There are many elaborate systems available in the marketplace and you may feel that such a system will work best for you; however, like me you may feel that the system freely available on your computer will suit your application. In order to decide upon an effective system for you it would be good to ensure that your chosen system is able to meet the following requirements:

1. Be able to list prospects, clients, customers and associated transactions.

2. Must have a daily "to do" section – daily activities.

3. A yearly planner at a glance is imperative.

4. It must accommodate at least a five year planner (I am not too keen on ten year goal setting as in my opinion the "arrival time" is too far into the future).

5. You must be able to break the annual plan down to a clearly visible MONTHLY and WEEKLY planner.

6. It must accommodate a telephone directory.

7. Expense/budget spreadsheet.

8. Long range projects section (six to eight months) – not to be confused with one/five year time planning schedules.

9. Personal and business goals section – it must be visible on a daily basis.

**Do planning the "night" before (just before you leave the office) or very early the next morning but ALWAYS before you start a new day.**

The idea here will be to group your daily activities into certain key sections of your to do list. Please also remember, using a master planning calendar/diary will ensure that both your work and your life will start to come together. The to do list becomes your road map for the day and so it must be clear and precise as you will not have the time during the day to decipher the contents if you have overcomplicated this single sheet. The "to do" list is just that a SINGLE SHEET! You must be able to view the sheet in a minute and be able to see every activity for the day without complication. Make it easy to read and to monitor throughout the day. Categories may include, but may not be limited to some of the following K.P.A.'s (Key Performance Areas):

1. Priority actions for the day.
2. Proposals/Quotations to be presented today.
3. Site surveys to be performed today.
4. New presentations set for the day.
5. Block out times allotted for travel between prospects /clients.
6. Follow-up calls to be made – WITH CONTACT NUMBERS.
7. Urgent matters to be dealt with tomorrow.

**Daily planning is placed on to a prioritized TO DO LIST and don't begin a day without completing this time management tool – your road map for the day.**

Never start a working day without first prioritizing your to do list. You may use any method to prioritize and this will not really make a big difference to your day; however, what will make a serious difference to your ability to be productive in any given day is if you don't prioritize the things which you have planned for the day. It stands to reason that some activities will be more important than others so these need special attention and we will need to prioritize these so that we focus more attention on the completion of these tasks. The following is an example of what I am talking about:

1. "A's" – MUST DO (Imperative action to start or complete that day)
2. "B's" – SHOULD DO (Important to complete but may not be imperative)
3. "C's" – COULD DO (These actions are never imperative, are seldom important, so should be delayed, or even eliminated, until "A's" and "B's" have been accomplished.

**Unprofessional time managers confuse ACTIVITY with PRODUCTIVITY – don't be so busy "doing" that you produce no or very little result at the end of each day.**

During my career I have had dealings with many salespeople. The lazy ones and I never become friends and I tend to spend more time with professionals who clearly succeed. Having a choice I would most certainly spend more time with someone who is succeeding than waste my time on lazy unprofessional salespeople. The reasoning behind this for me is simple. Professional salespeople can be helped to become more professional and thereby more productive. Businesses, and in particular entrepreneurs, need more productive salespeople, and yet they hire and fail to effectively train people who will not make it or at the least will just "tick over" each month with no motivation whatsoever to better themselves – these people are tolerated. Why? I have often, when mentoring or consulting with companies, decided to do a random walk through the sales department unannounced and you will be amazed as to the unproductive activities that go on in such a place. I have seen many, many "busy" people performing tasks frantically with no focus at all on production. Actions and activities are centered on "shifting paper" from one side of the desk or office to the next. This is NOT the function of a professional salesperson. I have noticed many of the unprofessional playing games on their computers during normal productive hours or they are "researching" whatever on the web. I find this behavior irresponsible and repulsive as someone will land up paying for this slothfulness.

The word "activity" defines a person's direct actions and not a result. A sales manager or Master Entrepreneur Salesperson must be more concerned with the result than undirected futile activity. In many sales offices I have seen two things that bother me: (1) what are they all doing in the office in the first place as surely their prospects our out in the field? (2) The constant "hustle and bustle" that takes place in the office without getting anything accomplished. I want to tell you that a sales office that is "lively" or that has "life" or "commotion" does not necessarily represent a productive sales team. Here is some more news for you! A sales office that is "animated", seems "excited" and is full of "movement" does not represent a sales office that is productive. When the "bell rings" constantly then that is what I call production. When contracts/agreements are authorized for new business and the service or production department cannot keep up with the orders coming in then this is what I call a professional and productive sales department – anything else is simply hot air my friend and you should NEVER be guilty of these futile characteristics. If you find it difficult in sales then leave and go do something where you will not waste your time but more importantly where you will not be guilty of draining the resources of your business or your employer. If you don't know the difference between activity and production then this is your first clue to get out now. Productivity within the sales environment means that you are producing results and results within this context means that you are producing new business for your business or employer – nothing else matters during your production hours each day NOTHING!

**Professional tip:** It is not the QUANTITY of activities checked off a "to do" list that matters; it is rather the QUALITY of the items produced.

**Deadlines apply subtle pressure so set a deadline for each activity and undertake to complete tasks EARLY each day.**

As discussed before, there is "good" pressure and there is pressure that leads to stress which may have all kinds of physical repercussions. I am not asking you to set time lines and/or deadlines in a deliberate attempt to place stress upon you. The idea of time lines and time goals is to ensure that you are on track and that you hold yourself personally (not blame others or "things" around you for your failure) responsible for your production levels. Continue to participate in these good practices and you will most certainly become more proficient in time planning and time management.

### Do climax block planning.

It will be important to know, when developing a time planning schedule, what your workload capacity is in any given day but also when you will operate at peak performance at any given time throughout the day. Some people are "morning people" and others are not. Many people will tell you that they operate better in the morning and others in the afternoon or mid-morning. Whatever the situation for you it is important for you to know when you are operating at optimum capacity, physically, emotionally and psychologically. The idea then is to organize you daily workload and life to carry out critical actions when you are most apt at succeeding at each task. You have to be ready and motivated on a daily basis and some tasks are best performed during your peak performance times of the day. Block out peak performance times of the day and fill them with "A" category activities if this is what it will take for you to achieve.

**Begin each day with the actions you dislike most.**

Difficult and disliked tasks tend to drain one of energy and affect motivation levels in different ways for different people. For instance, I have always set mornings aside to be in front of the prospect, and this, not because I don't want to sell but rather because it drains me of energy. When you are putting one hundred percent into a presentation, or when you are closing the sale more often than not because you are a productive (and not just sitting in the office making as though you are BUSY) professional salesperson and when you are concentrating in the answering the objections stage of the selling process, then this can become telling on you emotionally, psychologically and physically. The idea then is for you to recognize this in your own selling career and adapt to these pressure moments when you are full of energy and are able to concentrate and focus on the prospect – he/she deserves your undivided attention. You may want to consider the following:

1. If you are a person who becomes bored easily, or who has lower energy levels as the day goes on, then you may want to consider changing tasks on or about every hour.

2. It may also help to alternate difficult and easy tasks on a daily basis.

3. Save up on activities that may require a minimum of concentration and perform these when you are at your lowest capacity levels.

**Assess each task and evaluate your time throughout the day.**

At the very least you and I have eight hours of production time each day (if you push for more that is up to you) and this time is easily divided into four portions if you will. With this in mind then the goal will be to classify these hours in order of priority. The reason that I recommend this to you is simply so that you will take time to analyze what portion of your day you are spending in each category. Please consider the following example as a way forward for you:

1. Category "A" – Main priority.
2. Category "B" – Preparing and planning sessions which lead to "A" category time.
3. Category "C" – Limited detail and other low energy output work time.
4. Category "D" – Personal time (usually a break for the day and some refer to this as lunch-time)

It will become imperative for you to monitor both the time used and the task in order to determine whether certain tasks have been postponed to other days more than other activities. It will be good for you to understand that if they are mundane then you may be able to catch up, but what you don't want to do is to develop a reputation for procrastination – even to yourself. If you constantly find yourself putting actions off for another day then beware as the procrastination trap is the undoing of many a well-meaning salesperson and entrepreneur. However, if you develop a clear pattern for certain actions then you must change your time planning to incorporate and accommodate these at the appropriate time for you throughout each day of the week. One other thought as this relates to you categorizing your time every day is that you become better at plotting your potential and real income against the amount of time spent in each of the four categories. Once you have this information the logical thing to do is to shift activities which maximize your ability to earn more money with doing less work. Reduce spending time on activities that have a poor return as far as production is concerned. In time planning and time management everything is proactive so you will need to get used to having a hands-on approach to your time at all times.

**SPEEDING up the pace will increase your overall effectiveness and productivity.**

When you and I watch any athletics meeting one of the most exciting parts of the meet is when the fastest runners in the world compare their pace against one another. These runners are called sprinters. They usually don't do well when it comes to running long distance as both their build and air supply limits them to the shorter distance usually. However, when the long-distance runner, the football player and the soccer player want to increase fitness levels they all turn to the sprint in order to achieve this. When one sprints we all understand this to mean run fast, dash at speed, tear down the road and dart to the finish line. Sprinting, in the athletic sense happens for two reasons one would conclude (1) a one hundred meter race (2) in order to gain fitness.

In applying this to time management we must understand that short bursts of energy discharged from time to time will help us to gain time (as in gaining fitness). Hence, become a SPRINTER to increase your overall effectiveness. How is this accomplished within the context of our discussion on time management? For four days out of the month you may want to consider:

1. Starting very early.
2. Work very late.
3. Having a written plan to complete as much during this allotted time.

Once you have completed these four days then return to your normal schedule on the fifth day. The ultimate goal is to get you to be able to accomplish more work in less time. You will free up much needed face to face time in order to see more prospects. The more prospects you see the more presentations and proposals you will put out. This will allow more closing for more business which is ultimately the function of a salesperson.

**Discover hidden moments in every day.**

The hidden hour here refers to those times of the day when you find time when no one else is around. People are a distraction, they are great, but a distraction most times at best. You do not want a lot of people around during these times and if you are trying to find the hidden hour in each day and you still have people bother you then tell them to leave or your idea will fall flat and you will build frustration, resentment and will not accomplish your goals. In order to accomplish the task of finding the hidden hours in every day consider the following actions and make adjustments according to your own unique situation:

1. Arrive at the office an hour early-perform tasks that take concentration.

2. Remain at work an hour after people leave – (1) tie up all loose ends (2) prepare your "to do list" for tomorrow.

3. Have an "I" basket for all matters that are not that important – when you finally complete these throw the notes/contents in the trash can and never refer to these again.

4. Constantly have your name removed from unwanted mailings lists – UNSUBSCRIBE!

5. Review memos, letters and mail near your trash can (waste bin) – discard junk mail WITHOUT OPENING.

6. Keep your "to do list" visible and in the same place for easy access – use a stand-out color.

7. Maintain a clean desk – clean your desk at night to arrive at a clean desk in the morning.

**Effective filing systems still work.**

I remember the days when the "computer world" (today referred to as IT probably wanting to get away from misleading the public many years ago) promised that we were moving to a "paperless society" and that we would also move toward "working less" – something like a four day week we were promised if I remember correctly? Well we all know that this did not work as we generate more paper now than ever before and we work longer hours than ever before by virtue of the fact that computers now exist in the workplace and at home-we cannot escape! The creation of more paperwork is a problem for a salesperson in that he/she has to deal with this distraction on a daily basis. The challenge here is what to do with all the paperwork? As we deal with this issue I want you to know that there is always room to develop an effective "old fashioned" filing system. Can you believe that the computer wizards have not been able to replace the generation of paper (as was promised) to the point where we can go without a filing system?

However, in stating the above it is a fact, that it is estimated that eighty to ninety percent of filed paperwork is never referred to again. In my particular case I can assure you that my statistics are even higher and that is that ninety to ninety-nine percent of paperwork received and generated by me which is filed by me is never referred to or used again. When creating a filing system then I would advise you to consider creating broad and/or general categories under which you file (archive) your correspondence. In fact, I would recommend that you consider using six files to start with – what you do after this and as the years move on is up to you.

1. Activity File.
    a. Save all "To Do" lists-for goals consolidation and action assessments.
    b. Time sensitive tasks.
    c. Business and personal accounts that need to be settled.

1. Planning File.

    a. Add in one file per project-place all related paperwork per file.

    b. File these into the Time File-file under appropriate date.

1. Study File.
2. Sales Study File.

    a. Place all reference material related to sales techniques.

    b. Also add related (not rubbish) newspaper ideas.

1. Prospect File.

    a. Prospect and Buyer lists.

    b. Client base spreadsheets.

    c. Insert a territory file-all related matters with regards to development within a given territory for which you are responsible to develop.

1. General File.

    a. A to Z file-when necessary items don't fit in any other file category.

It is advisable to set up expiry dates as to how long paperwork will be retained so I suggest that you mark each document with an expiry date BEFORE filing the same. General files tend to swell a whole lot quicker than most so as the day approaches for you to review this file for "thinning out" purposes then it becomes a simple task to look for the date and discard without even having to review the document. Whatever you do, don't try and look "busy" by creating more files than is needed for you to be effective. Before you create a file first find out if a file already exists somewhere in the office. You would think that this next point is self-explanatory? Not so! I would like to suggest that you LABEL each file clearly so as to make it quick and easy for you to identify at a moment's notice.

### The technique for handling paperwork

Depending on how you look at it you may be happy to deal with paperwork on a constant basis or you may be like the rest of us who view paperwork as a necessary evil so to speak but most certainly an impediment to you and me managing our time. The idea with paperwork coming across our desks then is for you and me to get into the habit of handling the paperwork once only and then move on with life. Procrastination when it comes to handling paperwork is your worst enemy as not handling paperwork quickly and efficiently will ensure that the same will pile up on your desk and the bigger the pile the more propensity there will be to procrastinate.

I want to introduce you to five rules which I have used for years when it comes to handling the dreaded but necessary paperwork:

1. Organize your paperwork.
2. Handle paperwork once.
3. Handle emails/letters professionally.
4. Save your best correspondence.
5. Use the "Deadline Technique".

**Organize your paperwork**

Understand that important paperwork needs an important place. You must be able to access important paperwork at a moment's notice. I cannot tell you how many times I have seen people become frustrated when it comes to finding important documents at a moment's notice. One reason that I believe this happens is because most people have way too many files and too many places to "hide" files and documents all over their desks. Keep important paperwork and matters close to you such as in a drawer located at your desk.

Use three categories as a way to organize paperwork:

1. "Vital/Essentials" file-vital matters in one file placed into the desk filing cabinet.

2. "Important/Limited" file-important but of less importance matters in one file placed into desk filing cabinet.

3. "Insignificant Matters" file-file away into a remote but accessible part of your office.

There is no need, as a salesperson that is, for you to develop a complicated filing system. More often than not you and I struggle to find the important things that we need at a moment's notice and this is due to overcomplicated filing systems-what a time waster! The longer it takes you to find paperwork which you may need the more time we waste and the greater the impact upon our time management program. When we use time unnecessarily throughout the day then this adds pressure, and this pressure is not of the good kind, this pressure will lead to unnecessary stress caused through frustration – not good for you or me!

## Limit the handling of paperwork

The trash can (fondly known to me and others as "file 13") must be close and become your best friend when going through paperwork. You should never be in a position where you are going through "mountains" of paperwork as this must be done daily. Piling up paperwork is for the unprofessional and time wasters so don't get into bad habits in this regard. You MUST do at least one of four things with paperwork when you have set time aside to perform this task (1) trash immediately (2) delegate immediately (3) file immediately and (3) always do SOMETHING with all paperwork. Never procrastinate, never put working on reducing your paper load off to the next day and never pile paperwork up on your desk – get rid of it one way or the other. Keep a clean desk. The idea that a messy desk is the sign of a busy person is absolute rubbish but a clean desk is most certainly a sign of an organized, time conscious professional. Which one are you?

## Handle emails and letters professionally

There is no need at all to write a book each time you answer a letter or an email. There is a tendency, for those that must always explain themselves fully to go on and on when responding to incoming correspondence. This is wasting time! Say only what you need to and be brief – this saves time and money. I have noticed, and I understand that we are not dealing with telephone techniques at this point; however, that same unprofessional, who also writes way too much when answering correspondence, is also guilty of talking way too much on the telephone. This is all unnecessary and is a major time waster when one adds the two time wasters together. No wonder the unprofessional are always complaining about "not enough hours in the day". When responding to emails use single sentences and send the response. When answering a letter use one page only – no more. I know of certain sales professionals who also consider calling the sender when receiving an email or letter – this may be a quicker way to respond? They also keep the call short and to the point. The focus of the call is simply to give an answer to the sender's question and nothing more.

## Save your best correspondence for re-use

The longer one goes on in the same industry the more certain actions are repeated and this includes emails and letters. Save good emails which make an impact and save emails which can be used to respond over and over again (may need some minor alterations with each use). The idea is to use the email again and again but obviously you would change the contact details and the like. Even consider saving good emails which you receive from others and re-use them as and when needed. Letters, marketing emails, letters of reference that can be used again must be placed in a folder directly on your computer for easy access. You may want to name the folder

"Correspondence". The professional time manager will always be on the look-out when it comes to saving time and re-using emails and letters is a great way to start.

## Use the "Deadline Technique"

When managing paperwork always give yourself timelines for every action that is required. For instance:

1. *Decide by:* (fill in a time and date)
2. *Collect by:* (fill in a time and date)
3. *Act by:* (fill in a time and date)
4. *Evaluate by:* (fill in a time and date)
5. *Clarify by:* (fill in a time and date)

As a reminder, and on the above-mentioned timelines, always ask yourself a question when it comes to managing paperwork: "What is the absolute worst thing that can happen if you throw it out?" This is why I recommend that you have "file 13" right beside you at all times-GET RID OF USELESS PAPERWORK!

## Use the phone in a professional manner

The telephone is the professional salesperson's best friend as it opens so many doors to new business. However, the same tool can be used as a "weapon" of personal destruction if the sales tool is not controlled professionally. You and I are quite aware that there are the unprofessional who simply don't understand when enough is enough and they will keep on talking no matter what. In fact, these people do not even consider the time being wasted on the telephone and both the opportunities and money being missed while they "blabber" on the phone. One simply cannot have personal goals, and expect to achieve these, and then waste time in all different kinds of ways including spending time and money on the telephone talking about the most unrelated issues in the world. Time is money and I say that if this is an indication of how people waste time then there is no wonder that they cannot achieve their sales quotas/targets and personal life goals.

As a professional entrepreneur and salesperson it is imperative that you learn to make effective use of the telephone. In order to save time and manage your use of the telephone professionally I have compiled an action list which will help you to get into good habits before you apply the bad ones.

1. Always write down a phone number next to a name.

Believe it or not some professional salespeople continue to use a physical day timer (diary) despite the many time management tools available to us all. From my side, I applaud people who are willing to use the business tools that make time work for them. The computer, and other "smart" devices have also been developed with the time manager in mind and these offer the most modern ways of controlling one's time. My goal here is not to get you to choose a means of controlling your time but rather to ensure that whatever the management tool employed that you are able to apply personalized additional information. For many years I used a Day-Timer or diary to control my time. I forced myself into certain time management habits such as I would make sure that once an appointment has been set to meet with a prospect that I included ALL relevant information directly into the diary and next to the first name and last name of the person I call a prospect. In other words, in order to save time, I would include the physical street address of the prospect together with the name of the company for which he/she worked, the contact numbers, his/her title/position, email details, fax number, birthday date, website details and whatever other pertinent information I thought that I might need. I cannot tell you how this habit helped me over the years to save time and frustration so whether you prefer the computer, a tablet or the use of your mobile phone my suggestion is for you to follow my example. Once you have set-up this information in the place suggested you will always have it at hand and this saves so much time I can assure you.

2. Prepare yourself BEFORE making the call.

The idea is to understand that you are about to make a call to a prospect which could potentially assist you with achieving your personal and family goals. What reason could you and I possibly have for not being ready to make such a call? The thought process here is that you must ensure that you are both ready to make the call and also organized enough to make the call. CLEAR YOU'RE DESK! Make sure that you have your script memorized and that it comes across professional, friendly and polite. Understand the goal of the call so ask yourself is this a call for new business, to an existing customer or a service related call? Make sure you understand the reason for the call so that you can keep the call focused upon the goal of why you are making the call in the first place. Have paper ready for taking critical notes such as needs and wants that may be revealed during the call.

3. Make your calls early each day.

While we will be dealing extensively with the professional use of the telephone later in this book I believe that a good time to block out time for sales calls is early in the morning – before you start one-on-one sales calls with clients and prospects. However, you may feel that you are not at your best at making calls first thing in the morning. However, whatever the time blocked out for your calls I do believe that you will also need a quick and easy way to track what happens during each call. You may choose to develop your own system but I have used (1) a checkmark (√) which represents " call made and person contacted" (2) a cross (X) which represents "call made, no contact & unable to leave a message, must call back" (3) a circle (O) which represents "call made, message left for person to return call".

4. Make prospecting calls in blocks and avoid distractions.

While it may be that today's office design and layout may find you sitting in an open plan office you may have to find a way to make your calls without distraction. As a Master Entrepreneur Salesperson you will be able to control both the space and the peace and quiet which you will need to make your sales calls and to focus on the task at hand. When starting the "telephone block" (special time set aside for calling) you must be free of interruptions so if you have an office then place a "do not disturb" sign on the door and make sure that all calls to you are held back – messages should be taken on your behalf. You will also want to ensure that you have total privacy and ensure that you will receive no interruptions during this activity at all. Some people can't read and they will burst into your office while you are in the middle of a conversation with a prospect that has the potential to help you reach your goals so lock your door if you have to.

5. Call back (messages) in blocks.

As you block out time for outgoing calls so you will block out time for returning calls which have come through via voice messages, emails or written messages through the front office. Unless the message has an "urgent" written on it do not succumb to the temptation to return calls on a random basis- one at a time throughout the day. Set time aside to return calls and do them in batches so that once these calls have been made then you know that you will not impede the rest of your planned activities for the day.

6. Teach clients, prospects and other callers when the best time it is to reach you.

People have a nasty habit; largely through "Murphy" I may add, of calling you at all the wrong times, like in the middle of a meeting with a prospect. The advent of mobile technology can help us in so many ways. When you are busy with your sales block make sure that your mobile phone is on "silent" or "vibrate". Better still leave your phone in your vehicle! Why salespeople take their mobiles in to see a client is beyond me- maybe a personal security and confidence issue? In the good old days taking a telephone in with you to see a client was not even considered and would be viewed as preposterous to say the least, and of course comical. However, the point here is that many "old school" salespeople never had the opportunity to take phones of any sort into a presentation situation so why the need to do it today? I have had salespeople present their products and services to me many times and on some occasions the phone rings. I cannot tell you how I feel when that happens so all I do is stare at the salesperson IN SILENCE until he/she feels so uncomfortable that they decide to leave their mobiles in the car when they visit again.

Ensure that your voice mail message is professional and gives the caller options. The caller should have the option to call your office in the event that you are unable to answer the phone, they must also have the option to leave a voice message and/or send you an email noting the reason for the communication. The message could also state the block when you return your calls on a daily basis but that urgent calls will be returned the moment you are free.

7. Program critical numbers into your mobile phone.

Program every client's contact details into your mobile phone. If you were a client calling you what would impress you more? "Trevor Whittaker speaking!" or "Good morning Mr. Jones, how are you today?!" Programing client numbers into your phone and responding in the appropriate way will add so much value to your desire to portray professionalism and develop client loyalty. Your client will feel that you care and this goes a long way to building what we call client loyalty. You should program any critical number into your phone but also those which you feel will save you time. There is nothing more time wasting that looking for telephone numbers when a call must be made.

8. Summarize major points of a conversation.

When you are making calls be ready to record pertinent details of each call. When making sales calls you may find out all of the needs and wants before you see the prospect – write these down so that you have a record of each prospect's conversation. It will be impossible for you to remember each call and the gist of the conversation so listen carefully for important facts and record these on your computer or CRM system under the prospect's name. The same thing applies when you return calls at the end of the day – make notes so that you will know how to resolve the challenge. Even Einstein needed help remembering and you and I will admit that we are not Einstein's. Please listen to me then when I admonish you to take notes of the important facts of a conversation so that when you deal with the person again it will seem like you actually listened – this is usually considered impressive!

9. Understand how to handle talkative callers.

Certain callers are "talkers" and take a long time to get to the point – this can become a major time waster. Be ready when you answer the phone. No matter who calls, you should introduce yourself but then add a "get to the point sentence" which is professional and non-offensive. When I answer the phone I have taught myself to pre-empt the caller (no matter who it is, yes, even family!) when the call comes through during working hours. I answer the call and say: "Good afternoon! This is Trevor Whittaker speaking; how may I help you?" This prompts the caller to get right to the point without wasting time. Be careful, as this has to be done in a friendly and professional manner and must not come across like you are a drill sergeant.

10. Always have a reason why the call must be concluded sooner rather than later.

Despite the fact that you have used the above technique (point 9) it may go right over the head of the caller who is them self a perpetual time waster and who uses the telephone to accomplish this in his/her life. This type of blabber has no regard for your time or his/her employer's time and money. Be very careful of this time waster, and understand this, I am also talking about well-meaning family members who have nothing to do on a daily basis and they would prefer to do this with you. The professional way to get around such a time waster is to always have a reason why you need to terminate the call. I have used various things in my day but one that I use more often than not, simply because it also gets a laugh is:

"Joey, I am sorry but if I don't get to the washroom right now then I won't have to!" Other appropriate reasons for cutting the conversation short are: "Suzanne, I am told that I have an urgent call holding so I will have to hang up" or "Jack, I am sorry but I have to attend a meeting in about five minutes and I have to get going". Make sure that the reason you give is both appropriate and the truth.

## Developing effective reading skills can save you time

Can you imagine!? Acquiring effective reading skills will help you and me to save time. Fantastic! Where do we start?

The idea is to read faster so that you can absorb quicker and learn more-sounds almost impossible. Not true! When I attended university a wonderful man of God asked me the following question. "Trevor, do you want to do well while at university and in life?" I immediately sensed a moment of wisdom coming along so I quickly said "yes". He replied with: "Take the university's speed reading class the moment it is offered". I listened! The class was offered during my freshman year and I can honestly say that it was one of the best things that I could have done. After completing the course my ability to discern what to read changed as did my ability to retain that which I read. At university one is under constant pressure to produce good grades, a decent GPA and to maintain these and I was no different and this is why attending this class "saved my bacon" on many occasions. Today, I still use the techniques as these have now become a part of how I save time and manage my time more professionally. It is important to read and we do so daily – reading can take up a lot of our time and reading the wrong material in the wrong way can cost you and me precious time. I want to save you time and give you the same advice that I was given so many years ago. *Learn to acquire effective reading skills as a means to help you save time.*

Start speed reading your way to success by considering three critical actions (1) read the table of contents first (2) read the first sentences in a paragraph (3) read for concepts and not for words. The table of contents will give you an overview of what subject matter the book contains. It is always easy to understand whether the book will be worthwhile reading at all and if so what chapters you may want to focus on. I have often bought a book simply because there are two or three chapters that appeal to me and which I feel could help me and teach me more than what I know on a particular subject. Read only the chapters that you feel will support your success – says me from the side-line: "You must read every chapter in my books because each one was designed with you and your future in mind".

The first sentence in a paragraph should tell you what the paragraph is about in most cases. When you have selected a chapter and have decided to read the contents then understand that one chapter will contain many paragraphs and the question is do you really need to read every paragraph to understand what the author is trying to say? No! By reading the first paragraph, as per your consideration of the outline, you will understand the gist of what the author will be saying so if you understand what is coming then move on to paragraphs containing material which you are not yet familiar with. Why would you and I waste time on reading content with which we are already knowledgeable about-this is wasting time and keeps us "busy" and "busy" people are usually not the epitome of success. These people are just busy doing all the wrong things which produce no tangible results as far as their daily production is concerned.

Reading for concepts and not for words may be a new concept to you, and in that case, then you will be reading this next paragraph I hope. Reading to discover the concept as opposed to reading for words only simply means that you will be training your mind to seek the IDEAS in each paragraph. The word "concept" may also be taken to mean, for the sake of clarifying our goal that you will be looking for notions, for principles maybe, in some cases even theories and the deeper meaning. Words are "surface" and you and I will have to dig a little deeper. Once you have understood the author's concept then you will retain the meaning rather than the words and it is always easier to remember a concept than it is to remember words.

Be very discerning as to your choice of reading material. Reading the wrong article or book can cost you time and money and as we all know by now that both of these items are in short supply, and even more so as we get older. Ask yourself a simple question when you are ready to decide on what to read: "How will I benefit by reading this article or book and how will it contribute to me achieving my life goals?" I know that everyone has their own view on what they read; however, my view is that I don't read anything that will not promote my knowledge in my spiritual life and my business life. For example, I am a big fan of Sci-Fi, but I have never read a single Sci-Fi book in my life as I would rather read a book that will help me to grow spiritually and in my knowledge of business. You will not get a bigger fan when it comes to The Lord of the Rings and the Hobbits. However, I will not waste my time reading such novels as it does not promote the two key areas in my life. You must understand that I have seen the movie version of these books. Why? Well the reason is quite simple! The movie version is a lot shorter than the book! It would take forever to get through the book versions of Sci-Fi and the likes of The Lord of the Rings – time management. These fictitious aspects are simply entertainment so how will it help me in promoting my personal goals? They entertain me but they don't educate me!

When deciding on what books to read consider developing a "buddy system"? Join forces with like-minded professional people who are more interested in developing their intellect with a view to using the information to develop themselves than for entertainment (a waste of time) purposes. The idea here is to get to point where, as reading buddies, you develop a circle of "referral buddies". Referral buddies constantly refer good books to one another which will serve the purpose of promoting the goal of saving time and knowledge. For instance, let's use the book which you are now reading (**ENTREPRENEURSHIP $ALES 101**), and let's assume that you are impressed with what you are learning. You have a friend/s and you feel that they too should get a copy because the contents of this book will most certainly promote the achievement of their personal life goals and business knowledge, the referral buddy system means that you would introduce the book to them as a gesture of your friendship and common goals in the sales and business environments. This saves time in that the book that is recommended comes from someone who cares and has a common goal of saving time as it may have been a while before the book was discovered by your acquaintance. Having other people be on the lookout for the types of reading material you are interested in and recommending these to you and vice versa is a good idea. Don't waste time reading books that will not promote your personal goals.

Discern carefully and quickly what to read and consider reading "steaks and not stacks". Understand that it is better for you, if you are serious about your sales and business career, to focus on reading quality works that will build your person and your knowledge with a view to success. I have met some people in my lifetime that have boasted about the amount of books which they have read. I have gone into their homes and much of what they read has to do with every topic other than the one which they desperately need to move their lives forward. Some would not but I view this as a total waste of time as while he/she is "entertained" one cannot do anything in life with books that entertain you. These are designed to relax one and to "take one to another world" and to "get away from it all". I can tell you, as can billions before you and me, that there will come a day that you will be relaxed permanently – it is called the grave. When I am faced with a choice of reading material I would rather choose quality reading over quantity of reading any day of the week.

May I suggest that you stock up with industry, sales, business and personal growth articles and place these in your briefcase? There will be those times that the prospect is running late and his/her personal assistant has just informed you that he/she will be busy for another ten to fifteen minutes. You are sitting in the reception area waiting. Waiting is time wasting! Take out an article as mentioned above and read these in order to utilize the potential time loss and turn it into a net gain of time. This is what professionals do and this is what time conscious salespeople and business people do – they never waste time but are ready to fill the gap at every opportunity. Furthermore, also save reading material for those other times at which you are not able to do anything else.

## How organized is your mobile office?

What is a mobile office you may ask? Your vehicle is your mobile office! Much of our time as salespeople and entrepreneurs is spent in travel and generally this is accomplished by making use of an automobile (for some of you it is also called a car or motor car). I am sure that you will agree with me that the state and use of one's vehicle is a reflection of the owner. One may be correct then in assuming that a dirty car belongs to someone who is disorganized or just too lazy to wash it. Arriving at a prospect's premises with a dirty vehicle may not be the smartest thing to do because many people are judged by the state of their vehicles. While the maintenance of your vehicle is your own business I do want you to understand that this mobile office can be used wisely as this relates to time management and is most certainly a reflection of who you are as a salesperson. I would like to mention a few items that may help you to understand that the time spent in your vehicle could be better utilized. The reason that I would like to point this out to you is simple. Organizing your vehicle is a good time management technique and you should consider implementing the forthcoming ideas as a recommendation from me.

Firstly, never operate your vehicle under a quarter tank of gas (petrol). Getting stuck on the highway will cost you valuable time and cause mayhem with your program for the day. You may have to cancel or postpone appointments which are critical – not ensuring that you have enough gas is simply not worth taking the risk as the cost is too high. Ensure that you always have the necessary roadside tools, first aid kit and equipment, and this in particular, if you plan to travel long distances. Replacing a damaged or punctured tire yourself will most certainly save you time as opposed to you waiting an hour plus for roadside assistance. Ladies, if you have not as yet changed a flat and/or damaged tire then I would suggest that you practice this as a matter of urgency. It has become extremely dangerous for a woman, on her own, to have a flat on the side of the road. Waiting for road side assistance places you in a precarious situation so get the tire changed as quickly as you can and move on. I always give the same advice to my wife and daughters.

It is very dangerous to use your mobile phone while driving and please listen to me; you could die when doing so. I have heard of so many instances of drivers who die using their mobile phones to text and die with the phone in their hands showing the unfinished text message. Don't become a statistic! This is not saving time it is pure suicide! Invest in a hands free mobile phone kit for your vehicle if it was not fitted during the manufacturing stages. Talking on the phone has proved to be fatal; however, should you absolutely have to perform this task while driving it will be better for both you and other road users that you do so hands free or pull over. NEVER text while driving! Focus on the road at all times! You may feel that talking on the phone while driving is saving time but it may also cost you your life and you may even be responsible for killing or seriously injuring an innocent third party which may or may not include infants and children – NOT WORTH IT I TELL YOU!

A more positive time saving technique is when you utilize the time on the road to listen to CD's containing motivational and other material which would enhance your ability to perform positively and to achieve your goals. Listening to music if you are an entrepreneur salesperson is a waste of valuable time as this time is better utilized in audio that promotes healthy and positive living and this includes any item that will promote you achieving your life goals. Smoking in your car does not promote healthy living; the choice to smoke is yours, but don't perform this nasty and life-threatening habit while driving in your car. You never know when you are required to have a prospect or a client travel with you in your vehicle and it will smell like a chimney. For non-smokers, the stench on the smoker is repugnant so never forget this. Having someone that does not smoke sit in your smoke-stained vehicle is torture and the first thing that they will do is have their clothes dry cleaned once they get dropped off. You want your prospect or client focused on what you are saying and not on the stench in your vehicle. Should you choose not to heed my advice here then it will cost you time and money to remove the smell from your vehicle should you need to have a prospect or client ride along to visit a site.

I would also advise that you ensure that you keep a quality camera in your vehicle if you have a need to take high resolution photographs of installations and various sites. Most mobiles have this facility and if this is all you require then you are set. Consider it a fact that your automobile may become a free advertising board for your company, product and/or service. There are so many ingenious ways to make this happen and almost all of the ideas out there will not damage or deface your vehicle in the least. For many years I used magnetic signs which I attached to my car and removed when I needed to for some reason. No damage was ever done to my car when using this method. Using your vehicle to advertise is smart and free. Please check the laws in your state, province and country before applying any advertising to your vehicle. Finally, a major time-saving tool is to ensure that you have a stock of essentials for transacting business. Arriving at a prospect in order to do a presentation without the correct material is not only embarrassing but unprofessional.

BEFORE you leave the office for any meetings/appointments always make sure that you have confirmed the meeting and that the prospect is still available to meet and then make sure that you have the essentials for conducting business. I have always, over the years, ensured that I have a container in my trunk containing any and all business essentials, and this includes, but is not limited to pens, brochures, catalogues, samples, business cards, presentation folders and agreements needed for signature. Going back to the office because you either forgot a crucial item or you have run out is a major unprofessional time waster.

## Use people and services that free up your time

You cannot do everything on your own. What is critical time for you and me? Critical time must be you and I being able to sit one on one with the prospect and our current clients. This has got to be our most productive time as without face to face meetings with the prospect how do we close the sale? Therefore you and I will have to do all we can to delegate some of our time-consuming activities to those around us. For instance, delegate and train someone else in your office to transmit marketing emails on your behalf or hire a company to do this for you. There are many supporting businesses whose entire function it is to support men and women like you and me who are way too busy with face to face calls with clients and prospects to be able to perform these tasks ourselves. Monthly or quarterly newsletters can be sourced to specialist businesses who deal with developing and sending these out to a list of prospects – why do this yourself? Your goal is to sell and if you and I are not actively performing this task then we simply become "busy" people with no results where it counts most – SALES. While there are many more ideas and people out there who can assist you the idea is that you consider any and all ways of sourcing out an activity, no matter how big or how small, to people who can deal with them rather than you. Your time and talents are valuable so use them wisely.

**The way forward**

The most successful salespeople, entrepreneurs and business people on the planet all seem to have one critical characteristic (you can check me on this if you like) and that is that they have a REASONABLE and WRITTEN plan for each working day of their lives. This gives them direction, focus and purpose. When you and I have purpose for each day then we are able to set personal and business goals with the understanding that these will be achieved. Managing time is the key though. We have been through many time management principles and tips in the first part of this chapter but I can assure you that there are so many more for you to discover.

So you may now be convinced that you will need to develop your own time management program for prosperity but what then? My admonition is that you work this plan like you would work any other plan – ONE DAY AT A TIME! The goal is to get things done but the question is how? I want to close off this first section of time management principles by ensuring that you understand the way to making your plan work. Trust me when I say that it will take both hard work and DAILY dedication but if you want the plan to work then you must consider implementing the following six K.P.A.'s.

1. Keep accurate record of all time used – DAILY.
2. Do not tolerate "back sliding" – DAILY.
3. Exaggerate the habit change actions – DAILY.
4. Make use of affirmations – DAILY.
5. Asses your actions and reward yourself – DAILY.
6. Be persistent in practice and in psychology – DAILY.

If you never were then you must now become time conscious. Be aware of every moment you put into one of two categories. "I have spent my time wisely today" or "I have wasted time unnecessarily today". You must be aware of how you are spending your time and change bad habits but cling to the actions which avoid this waste. As professionals you and I will need to track and treat time as we do our money. Some people do not respect money and so they will not respect time but as they say "time is money!"

Back sliding has always had a bad connotation so if you understand the concept then apply this to your daily time management habits. Once you start a good habit then don't go back to the bad habit/s EVER. Stay away from influences that may encourage you to waste your time and thereby force you into doing all the wrong things. Remember, those that you love may be just as guilty of wasting your time as anyone else so always be aware of these actions and deal with this gently but decisively. The concept here is that you allow no slippage into bad habits whatsoever so don't tolerate it from anyone else but more importantly don't allow it from yourself. Whenever you see yourself falling back into your old bad time management habits then stop whatever you are doing, consider where you are and what you are doing wrong, and then get back on track immediately.

When you and I are ill we visit the doctor who prescribes us medication. We take the medication as we trust the doctor to know better and we thus believe that by taking what he/she prescribes we will get well. I have spent a great deal of time, and will spend even more time, on giving you a "prescription" for your time management woes. You have the option to take it or leave it. However, I want to encourage you to exaggerate the cure that I have given you. In other words, if you have been disorganized then become a fanatic at organization. Go above and beyond what I have suggested to you within your own environment. If you have been a late comer at the office, and feel that you have a license to come and go as you please then stop this today. If you have in fact been coming into the office late every day and leaving early this is considered theft of company time and your family's time. I want you to come in extra early to make up the time which you have stolen from yourself, your employer (if you are a salesperson working in a business other than your own) and your family. I also want you to leave extra late. You will need to spend this time in catching up so that you will become productive and that you will finally earn a professional's wage so that you can make your family happy when they see yours and their goals being achieved. As stated before in this chapter, practice the correct habits for at least three weeks and these will become a part of you in no time at all.

Make use of affirmations on a daily basis. The word "affirm" means to state something in a positive manner. You need to state something positive about you and your goals for the day every day that God gives you when you wake up. The fact that you have woken up is surely already a positive affirmation so why not carry on with clear and concise one-sentence affirmations about how organized you are as a new found time management professional. The goal each day will be for you to write down at least five positive affirmations about how organized you have become and how organized you are today. Do this even before you start organizing yourself for each new day. Keep the affirmations short, written down and visible for you to affirm at a moment's notice (like when you are sitting in a reception area waiting for your prospect who is running late) throughout the day. The more you affirm the more it will remind you of how organized you are and the more organized you keep telling yourself you are the more you will believe that you are an organized professional.

Asses your actions and reward yourself daily. Emphasize or stress the positive aspects of your daily program, and in particular, the successes achieved each day. Focus on these and understand what you are doing better than you have ever done before – identify these and affirm these before you start each day. Don't be afraid to self-praise and while we all understand that "self-praise is no recommendation" I am not saying that you should do this in public. For instance, I had a habit for many years. I had a certain affirmation that would motivate me from one successful sale close to the next. I used to say, and still do when I get the opportunity, and particularly when I have closed a sale successfully and "rung the bell": "Trevor, you are a mean, lean money making machine!" This was what I used to give myself as the proverbial "pat on the back". Take your family out for a meal the very evening that you closed a big deal as a reward for you and them – after all they put up with the likes of you and me right?

Be persistent in practice and psychology. Your mind is a powerful tool and can help you overcome some of the greatest and insurmountable obstacles in life by offering you solutions to your challenges. The best thing that your mind is capable of helping you and me with is preparing a professional time management plan in order to achieve our daily goals. We are also capable of understanding that we need to work our plan one step and one day at a time. The more we stick to our plan in practice the more positive our psychology and the more positive we remain the more likely we are to overcome the negative time management influences in our lives. This is good news!

**Conclusion**

I am led to believe that Benjamin Franklin was quoted as saying: "Time is a capital asset. You cannot borrow time, you cannot hoard time, you cannot work exceptionally hard and earn more of it, and all you can do is spend it". The phrase is not as yet complete as to me the best part is yet to come: "How you spend it is the difference between success and failure".

Managing one's time has been the theme of this section of the chapter on time management. The statement by Mr. Benjamin Franklin is apt and timeous even today. When you waste time you will fail but if you manage time professionally you greatly increase your chances of success. Being organized on a daily basis will make the world of difference to your life and that of your family. Everyone loves to do business with successful people so be successful! Managing your time will mean that you will manage your business and your client base professionally. Prospects will hear of you by word of mouth and will want to do business with you. You will learn that there is a big difference between work and play time and these do not cross over ever. When you learn when to work you will also learn when to play and when people see this difference in you they will also understand that you will be serious when you need to be but when you need to relax you are also capable of this activity.

Successful people are taken seriously but the unsuccessful are not. Which one are you?

# T.O.T. Management
## *Time, Organization and Territory*
## *Section 2*

**Introduction**

We have just completed Section 1 of our focus on time management and as you know it deals largely with the principles of time management during your productive hours of each day. We have covered the foundation and now need to build upon this. At this point you may be asking why we have such an in depth focus on time management and I would say to you that this is a relevant question. My answer to you then is simple! If you have read the first section and still have to ask that question then I am afraid that I have done something wrong. However, the focus has one goal and that is to get you to understand that if you think you have all the time in the world to the point where you feel that you have license to squander your productive hours in each day then I can assure you that no matter how many goals you have and the fact that you even have them written down you will not achieve them. Goals are achieved by managing your time effectively. You will be successful in business only if you manage your time effectively. You will be an effective entrepreneur salesperson only if you manage your time effectively. I will go as far to say that unless you manage your time effectively you will not achieve anything you set out to achieve and the reason I say this is because you have to spend time in order to achieve and wasting time is a luxury which neither you nor I can afford.

As you are fresher in the mornings of each day so you have more energy in the younger years of your life. Use the younger years to establish yourself for your more mature years where one usually tries to find energy. The problem is that most people have no clue as to how to professionally manage their time. While I am a mature individual at this point in my life I can assure you that my feeling is that if I was given the advice contained in both of the books available to you (1) **ENTREPRENEURSHIP (*minus*) 101** and (2) **ENTREPRENEURSHIP $ALES 101** when I was a young man I would have been so much further ahead as far as my life goals are concerned. I learned life lessons the hard way and I want you to understand that I am acutely aware of the time which I have wasted. The idea then is to learn from me but don't repeat my stupidity!

We have concluded that we now have the basic principles in order to move forward. The question is then how we put all of what we have learned to date into practice in order to achieve success in the real world. While the time management principles can be applied to each occupation and to any occupation in life our interest shall remain in you and your success. The context going forward then, as this is a book about sales, is to "convert" the principles (theory) into actions which will assure sales success. Remember, "Nothing happens without a sale" so we will not move away from this knowledge but rather spend time in enhancing our understanding of how to achieve sales professionally.

Whether you are an entrepreneur salesperson (who will one day grow an effective sales force), a salesperson or a sales manager, you must understand that the cost of generating sales leads and turning them into real business is very high. Why not consider the cost to you and/or your business for a while? Add up all of the associated costs and you will be amazed as to how quickly the costs add up just to generate a single sales lead and/or sales close. You and I must understand then that if these costs are as high as we think then these same high costs will emphasize the importance of professional planning and organization surely? In my view, planning should be done in two crucial areas:

1. Directly relating to the salesperson's production activities.
2. Activity related to a geographical territory or area.

The goal will be to get you to see the need to make more effective calls on the best prospects and the most QUALIFIED prospects and existing clients possible. When calculating the cost to company as this relates to generating sales leads and/or business one has to consider things such as (1) Compensation packages over a full year – basic salary, commission and relevant bonuses (2) Company paid selling expenses such as travel, vehicle, entertainment, telephone, samples, presentation manuals, brochures and other relevant printed materials (3) Fringe benefits such as retirement plan, medical insurance, life insurance and any other direct benefit to the salesperson. The total of these expenses would then represent the annual cost of keeping a salesperson in business. Please note, we have not as yet mentioned things such as, office space, training, annual sales conference and seminars throughout the year and the cost of furniture and the like. In order to work out the cost of getting the salesperson in front of the client is high and one cannot simply use the direct monthly compensation to the salesperson as a way to arrive at the overall cost – there is so much more involved. The one thing that we are able to deduce, even at a guess, is that the cost is high. The next time you sit in front of a prospect you should maybe consider this if you are an entrepreneur salesperson or any other kind of salesperson for that matter. I can assure you that you will view the entire selling cycle in a different light if you were actually paying the money for the lead out of your own pocket. By the way, the cost will also apply if you are generating the leads on your own without the help of a company lead generation system.

As an entrepreneur salesperson, a salesperson or a sales manager you will have to highlight to all in your business and/or sales team, in the strongest possible terms the following critical considerations:

1. Their actual cost to the company each day of the week.
2. The cost per hour to employ the staff member.
3. The cost per call on the prospect.
4. The cost to the company in order to achieve the sale.
5. The cost to retain and develop a new client.

Everyone in the organization should be aware of these costs as I can assure you that in most instances these costs are never given a second thought by employees. This is the reason why so much waste exists in businesses today and that is why the bottom line profit in many instances comes out as poor as they do. Once a salesperson has come to an understanding of the tremendous cost to generate sales it may be easier to take matters a little more seriously. It may well be that the realization of the cost to sale ratio may make the difference between success and failure and the ability to move away from not performing time management exercises and to ensuring professional time management planning from that moment on. "Time is money"!

Many years ago I read an article containing the results of a Dartnell survey. I cannot remember the entire article but I was astounded as to the results of the survey to the point that this has stuck with me till today. The study had to do with how salespeople spend their productive selling hours of each day. The startling facts about salespeople that I am referring to go something like this:

1. 32% – Time spent on face to face selling.
2. 19% – Time spent selling using the telephone.

3. 21% – Time spent travelling and waiting in reception areas.
4. 15% – Time spent on administrative tasks and non-selling activities.
5. 13% – Time spent on collections, expediting orders, complaints and other service related issues.

If the above is in fact true and if we were able to apply these statistics to the contemporary sales environment (I don't think things have changed that much, do you?) you will soon see why the sales/selling world is in such trouble today. Now do you still want to ask why we spend so much time on ensuring that we actually manage our time? I want to submit to you that planning our time, organizing ourselves and our territories is the only way to obtain maximum output from a business's most important asset-the entrepreneur salesperson, the salesperson and the sales manager. I am hoping that this introduction has prepared you then for what follows and that you will enter into this most practical session with me keeping an open mind to an exercise which will change your entire working life.

In section 2 of time management we will deal with four critical practical areas:

1. Geographic territory management – "Geographic Farming".
2. Territory and time management – "Size is not everything".
3. Structuring territories – Current and potential sales.
4. Time management – Territory time utilization.

**Geographic territory management**

What is the meaning of geographic farming? In the sales environment this represents an active method of increasing company and the entrepreneur salesperson's income by concentrating all sales efforts on a "narrowly" defined geographic area of pre-qualified prospects and/or an existing client base. The word geography according to Collins Dictionary helps us define this term within our context: "The physical features of a region". In our case we will use everything within this region to teach us not only about the region but also how to best utilize these "features" to our advantage. As an entrepreneur you have to consider that where you develop sales will also affect the way that you service, but more importantly, the cost of the services. Farming depends largely on the farmer's ability to understand agriculture and while one would think that the two mean the same farming has to do with agriculture and agriculture has more to do with the science or ability of the farmer to plan the right crops to plant and nurture. So the success of the farmer is reliant upon his/her ability to understand the fine art of agriculture.

The farmer then has chosen a piece of land usually referred to as a farm. The piece of land is just that – a piece of land. This particular piece of land is situated in one or other farming district so it is a parcel of land specifically set aside in a specific area and is used to produce a specific kind of crop through careful planning which we now know as agriculture. The key here is to understand that the farmer has a specific piece of land and this belongs to him/her and the success of the enterprise has a great deal to do with how the land is managed. Failure to understand every aspect of his/her land will lead to crop failure and this in turn will affect the farmer's ability to produce a sustainable crop and thus income, and if this happens, the farmer's family will not realize the much needed income goals which will affect the family negatively, and in some cases permanently.

I use the above analogy because the unprofessional salesperson, when given a territory, will inevitably complain about either the location of the territory or the size of the territory but more often than not they will complain about both. For some reason the unprofessional resents the fact that they are allocated an area and feel "restricted". When the professional salesperson is handed a territory he/she immediately kicks into gear and starts the "agriculture process". The professional sees the benefits of having a restricted area to cultivate in the scope of time management. This means less driving and more time on face to face calls with the prospect – the way sales are closed and income is generated and dreams are realized.

As a Master Entrepreneur you will see your business grow and a sales force develop. Once this happens you will need to understand that by defining geographic territories your business can ensure that salespeople who you employ will succeed in the following crucial areas:

1. Cultivate local markets more intensely.
2. Become more familiar with local conditions.
3. Better understanding of local challenges.
4. More knowledgeable of local business.

There are four reasons why I promote geographical farming:

5. Build a prospect and a client base – all efforts are focused and concentrated and this is so much more effective when the goal is to build a prosperous client base.
6. Assists the salesperson to become an expert – what we want to create is an "area specialist" and we achieve this by concentrating all effort into a "narrow" geographical area. Knowledge of the area and the prospects grows quickly when the salesperson spends more and more time in understanding the overall potential.
7. It will increase income for the company and the salesperson – The goal is to gain a reputation as an expert, and once this has been accomplished, the salesperson will develop a demand for his/her services. The more well-known the salesperson becomes the greater the chance of

the salesperson being called upon for things such as "advice", presentations, introductions, referrals, proposals and sales closes, all of which, will ultimately lead to an increase in income for one and all. The best thing is that the prospect is turned into a client who should receive the ultimate benefit.

8. Generate an income stream-referrals are the best form of business for any salesperson and stand a 2:3 chance of being turned into business on the "closing ratio scale". A consistent stream of referrals is far better than knocking on doors I can assure you. It takes a while, and a great deal of patience, to develop a territory to this point; however, it becomes easier to be more successful when all the salesperson is working on is a steady stream of high quality referrals.

There is a right way and a wrong way to "farm" a geographic territory. We are not interested in the wrong way so we shall focus our valuable time on discovering the right way to farm. It seems obvious, but I will mention it any way and that is that the salesperson will need to study an in depth map of the allocated territory. Discover the main features of the area and note these. Understand the target market mix by dividing your search for businesses up into at least three areas (more if you feel that the territory calls for this) namely (1) Mega-AAA (2) Large-AA (3) Medium-A, and discover the numbers in each so that you have a clear idea of the potential of the territory. Taking a look at the abovementioned target market mix you will now have to determine which of these is a fit as this relates to your company's parameters and expectations. Do yourself a favor; don't do business with companies who don't fit the "mould". Have a clear picture as to whom you see making up your client portfolio and go after these. For instance, the ability to pay is vital for a new entrepreneur so ensure that this forms a part of your criteria for new clients and if you have a suspicion that the prospect's ability to pay is in question then walk away! This is your time to build your business, and if you are a salesperson, your territory. Set your business up the way you see it develop from day one and that includes the kinds of clients that you would like to develop a long-term business relationship with. When you find great prospects you will develop great clients, and of course, the opposite is also true. Develop an "approach roster" meaning that you will have a list of businesses to approach but the question is which ones do you approach first? The higher up on the approach roster are the prospects that you see yourself visiting as a priority. The idea then is to develop a qualified list from your list and determine who is approached as a high priority, a medium priority and a low priority.

No matter if you have been allocated a large or small territory you need to be smart in managing it. You and I cannot (generally speaking of course) eat an entire cake in one sitting – we eat a cake one slice at a time. If we cannot eat the entire cake in one sitting then we place it in the refrigerator and have another slice the next day and so on and so forth. The same principle applies to one's territory. Even a "small" territory in certain countries can have a large foot print. The idea is not to panic when getting a territory but to break it down into bite-sized junks ("slices"?) so that each piece becomes manageable. The way that I have always divided my territory up into bite-sized chunks is not rocket science but "Trevor science" – the simplest way possible! Divide the entire area as is allocated to you into four quadrants-one for each day Monday to Thursday. Why from Monday to Thursday? We will come back to this I promise and it will make perfect sense at a later stage. Once you have achieved this goal then you want to position yourself geographically. For instance, you will need to locate not only the center point of your entire territory but once you have four quadrants you will need to discover the center point for each of the four quadrants as discussed above.

Each quadrant represents a day of the week from Monday to Thursday and the square represents your territory.

The next step is to discover the distance between the center points of the area and quadrants and then to determine how far these are away from your office. Then do the same thing in order to discover the distances (in miles/kilometers) from your home to both the office and all the relevant center points. The idea here is to plan for contingencies and travel between prospects, the office and your home. My feeling is that one can work toward the office from home and then work back to the center point of a quadrant and then home again later on in the day. Why is it necessary to get to the office each and every day if you can save time going directly to a new prospect after leaving home in the morning? Given the traffic conditions and weather, estimate the time (not the distance as discussed above) it would take you to reach the central point of the quadrants under discussion: (1) from the office (2) from your home.

As you and I are professionals, we will not be happy with only dividing the entire territory into only four quadrants as this will still not get us the concentrated focus which we would like to achieve in order to build knowledge and a good reputation so that we start receiving the much sought after referrals. The idea now will be to have you divide EACH QUADRANT into a further four quadrants from Monday to Thursday.

The original Monday to Thursday quadrants have now been sub-divided in order to produce four additional quadrants of Monday to Thursday.

While in certain areas it may be necessary to sub-divide one more time I do believe that the sub-division as presented above will allow you to focus your attention on smaller area with a view to becoming known in each secondary quadrant sooner rather than later. We are not done with the planning phase as yet and will continue now but please remember the goal is to become well known in your territory and a "household name" so that should the prospect require any of your product and/or services then you must be the FIRST person that comes to mind. When you are that present in everyone's mind the results will be that you will receive one referral after the other and the need for cold calling becomes a sales activity of the past.

Once you have set up the quadrants on paper, and over an actual territory map, then you would have completed the paper planning stage. The goal now is to get you into the area/territory for a visual reconnaissance of the boundaries and the inside of the territory which has been allocated to you. I want to remind you again that territories can be vast in some cases (countries and continents are also managed using geographical farming) and if you do not manage them carefully they will confuse you and even overwhelm you so do your planning correctly and professionally – NO SHORTCUTS AS THERE AREN'T ANY! As an entrepreneur, if you are a service-based business then the very same system will apply when setting up servicing rosters with your service department. However, once the planning has been done may I now suggest that you take a weekend or after hour trip into your territory for a visual. The idea is to take your time, without the hustle and bustle of traffic, when the roads are quiet and all you want to do is drive. Don't worry about taking notes at this point unless you really feel the need to. The idea is just to familiarize yourself with the "contents" between your boundaries. While driving through take a look at the segmented quadrants on your map and envisage how these will come together for you. If you have been allocated one of those "large" territories then visit the quadrants one at a time with a goal to being able to see the size of the quadrant for planning and execution purposes.

As a professional entrepreneur salesperson you should notice some key characteristics in each quadrant and in the entire geographical area placed under your care. You will need to take careful stock of the following:

1. All commercial areas in each quadrant (Mega, Large and Medium).

2. All industrial areas (Mega, Large and medium enterprises).

3. Residential areas – if your business focuses on homeowners then this area will be important to you; however, if your company's focus is business to business then residential areas will be avoided as the focus must remain on your target market.

4. Ensure that you are familiar with the major roads in and out of your territory and the central roads ("arteries") which will assist you in gaining easy access to both your clients and your prospects within the area.

5. Again, take note of the prospective businesses and the enormous potential which you have as you drive through the territory and understand the target market and the mix according to your planning and goals.

6. The other smart thing to do is to clearly identify the businesses which you will not be interested in as they are not a part of the target market as identified by you – stay away from these as they will simply take up unnecessary time. Remember, the reason that this planning is done in this manner is to save you time and to ensure that the productive time available each day is spent cultivating great business for your company, business and you.

7. ALWAYS be on the look-out for buildings under construction as a good time to meet with the decision maker is during the planning and/or construction phase-their time is spent meeting with people of all types of businesses.

8. As a reminder, don't be tempted to stop to write anything down during this initial trip as it is merely a survey of what you are going to have to work with. Rather, be aware of the key characteristics only at this time. I can assure you that you will have more than enough time to dig deeper and to make all the notes that your heart desires – the goal right now is to simply observe.

9. When in your territory locate the center point and move outward from there into each quadrant's furthest point and back again until you are familiar with the distances both in time and miles/kilometers.

10. The second trip into your territory (also at a quiet time if at all possible to avoid traffic) has an alternate goal in that this will be set aside for information gathering. You will be surprised as to how much you will remember of the first survey trip made in your territory but you will be equally surprised as to all the new discoveries and the things which you have missed during the first trip so be patient as it will all come together soon enough.

11. During the information gathering trip you will need to record the information so use whatever makes you comfortable. For instance, I have used a pen and paper and/or a recording device to ensure that I don't miss anything or that I don't forget anything important.

12. While a great deal of information will be available to you from the internet and local government offices they are not able to paint the visual picture which you need of your territory and the target market which you are aiming at. By all means use whatever means you have at your disposal in order to gather pertinent information regarding commerce in the territory allocated to you but you will still need to "eye ball" the opportunity and potential for yourself sooner rather than later. Once you have identified a business which fits the target market which you have chosen (or the one you have been handed) then you will need to gather some critical information such as: The business name, street address, telephone number if stated

(if not this can be obtained from the website), fax number (if stated), website details (if stated) and email address (if stated).

13. The goal for this trip is for visual and information gathering only. If all you get is the name of the company and the street address then that is great as you can source the rest from the internet as you are by now aware.

14. Depending on the size of your territory the exercise of gathering information may take a while so prepare for this. However, you will be surprised as to how much information can be gathered in one day and in a single week. If the exercise takes too long then utilize weekends to complete this task as the selling cycle must be started immediately in order to achieve goals and targets.

15. What to do with all the information which you gathered? Spend time (after hours if necessary as extra work is required in the beginning to set up your territory professionally and you should be prepared for this and understand this) in transferring the information onto spreadsheets under the title of Prospect List-include ALL relevant information which will be needed to make contact with the prospect. As you develop these lists you ought to consider that each name you add will represent an immense financial value to you and your company as you move forward as these lists were "hand developed" and as such represent a QUALIFIED list of prospects which now need to be turned into business.

16. When developing a prospect list/s you will need to consider including the following critical information so that you have it all at the "touch of a button". These lists become more valuable so protect them at all times or you will lose many hours of work and effort:

a. Give each prospect a number (1, 2, 3 etc.).
b. Company name.
c. Decision Maker's title (position within the company)
d. Decision Maker's mobile number.
e. Decision Maker's email address

f. Street address.

g. P O Box details.

h. Telephone and fax numbers.

I. Company email (for example: trevor@trevorkwhittaker.com)

1. The research and finger work now begins in earnest so if you have an assistant or extra help now would be the time to make use of such a person. If not, then hire someone on a temporary basis if you have to in order to get the "slog" work done and the schedules prepared for you professionally, and more importantly, ACCURATELY.

2. Some of the work may include making calls in order to get complete, more accurate and/or up to date details as there is nothing worse than lists which are outdated and contain the incorrect details. Whatever you do ensure that ALL details on your prospect lists are ACCURATE and relevant at all times.

3. Once you have your first set of lists completed then get started immediately. Allow your "help" to complete other lists while you are making an approach to the prospect.

You may feel that this is all a great deal of work but I can assure you that this should only happen once and then you will reap the rewards of up to date prospect lists which will propel you forward, save you time and ensure success as you aim at attaining your personal life goals. Laziness never helped anyone and has caused failure in those that subscribe to this inaction. However, I can assure you that putting in the time and effort into developing prospect lists, while you may feel it a lot of work, I want you to be patient and perform in this area as I can assure you that you will receive your just reward. Why bother driving around in your territory? May I say for the same reasons already stated above? Of course, it goes without saying, should the prospect lists be handed to you by your company, or any other source for that matter then get going and don't hold back! You may also have sourced another way to achieve your goal with less work but do not compromise the drive through the territory, but again, use what you are given as this is most certainly a bonus. The goal then has not changed, the quicker you can get to having face to face calls with the prospect the better so use whatever means you have at your disposal but ensure that you do geographic farming for effectiveness and area coverage on a professional level.

## Territory and time management

In order to be effective in any given territory it should be large enough to financially support the entrepreneur and/or the salesperson. An area too large on the other hand is costly to maintain and to organize for effective geographic farming. The closer the sales call the closer the service calls and/or deliveries thereafter. Remember, areas too large minimize the effectiveness of salespeople and thus also minimize profitability. In order to determine the size of any given territory for overall effectiveness the entrepreneur salesperson or salesperson will have to consider some key aspects. For example, (1) Examine the maximum overall call capacity (2) Understand the current market "clusters" in the area (3) Examine potential and current sales level statistics (4) Examine potential prospects in the area and the current clients if any (5) Examine the road network and transportation systems available in the area allowing the salesperson access to every part of the territory.

The entrepreneur salesperson must now take the next step which is to schedule and organize his/her time effectively. The idea is to follow the local client cluster routes (if clients already exist in a given area) and the prospect clusters of each formulated quadrant. If there are no pre-existing client clusters then ensure that prospect calls are clustered close together each production day of the week. This will help you to spend less time on travelling between an existing client and prospect. As stated before, we need to do time management so effectively that it allows us maximum time on face to face calls with the prospect. After all, we are only able to generate sales by sitting in front of the person who is going to give you the "go ahead" on any proposal which you present. I cannot understand entrepreneurs and salespeople who want to spend as much time as they can on non-income producing activities as is possible at the clear expense of producing sales. Sales production is where businesses start and this may also be where they fail and the same thing will apply in the personal life of any salesperson. Listen to me! Your function, RIGHT NOW, is to understand the concept that you need to be in front of the prospect SELLING your product and/or service. Nothing else matters!

If you are fortunate enough to already have an existing client portfolio then you should save time by knowing some critical time saving parameters. Make sure that you are always aware of the following "time impacts" such as: (1) How often you should make calls on Mega, Large and Medium-sized clients/prospects – these visits are usually service related calls but the opportunity to add services and/or product is always present (2) What time is allocated to spending face to face time with prospects – most of a salesperson's time should be spent in this area and if the portfolio becomes too large for you to handle then it is time to take on a second salesperson for the territory as the situation represents you growing the area correctly and professionally as suggested above (3) If service related calls are a part of the sales function then this will need to be planned for and time allotted accordingly – territories will develop two sales challenges as it is grown and that is servicing existing clients (those who were turned into clients after first being a prospect) and continuous new business opportunities. As the sales grow in the territory you must plan to separate the two functions and appoint a major accounts executive to handle any existing business and a new business sales consultant for the continued development of the territory (4) In all likelihood you will have multiple services and/or multiple products on offer for clients and prospects. In many cases certain services and certain products take priority based upon expected levels of profit and cost of sales. Identify these priority sales items and ensure that you or the salesperson is aware of this priority and how much time must be allotted to promoting these in the geographical territory each day. Plan, plan and plan again! Don't leave anything to chance and understand that you will need to account for every single minute of each production day Monday to Friday – NO EXEPTIONS!

I have seen, when being asked to consult, how businesses can increase their revenues (and the salesperson) by simply implementing better time management techniques as stated above. Without increasing costs at all you will be able to see annual revenue increases by between ten and twenty percent. This is a revenue increase without doing anything except you and salespeople implementing professional time management into their daily production hours. We have discussed theories and principles of time management and I have seen Drucker's Law in practice on many occasions in that it has been my experience that in many smaller business enterprises seventy percent of the revenue (sales) is produced by around thirty percent of the sales team. I have also found that the thirty percent referred to previously have all implemented professional and written time management principles into their daily income producing hours and the emphasis is on not wasting a moment and clear time management structure.

When allocating territories, and BEFORE time management is performed, ensure that territories are equally aligned. Salespeople, particularly after developing their area, become extremely protective of their territories. The one thing that you will find them doing is comparing with one another and they do this because they are competitive in nature and many of the professional salespeople are also high achievers which makes matters worse. Always level the playing field when you develop a sales force. While you, as an entrepreneur, are on your own you will not have that challenge; however, may I suggest that you break out areas now and develop these areas now with a view to someday handing the same over to a professional salesperson to manage and develop further. Plan now and develop areas now so that you have less "pain" later on in your business.

Yet another very interesting observation is that, from what I have seen, the average salesperson spends less than forty percent of his income producing hours each day with clients or prospects. This fact needs to change and it can be changed through instituting professional time management written plan for all daily activity. This will identify clearly activities that are redundant and expose all time wasters which need to be replaced by activities promoting more selling time. Therefore one will understand that professional territory time and territory management increases the number of face to face calls that a salesperson can make-is this not the goal? I can assure you that such planning will also lower the cost per call ratio which improves the "bottom line". The ultimate goal then, although this has been mentioned many times now, but I feel that I need to repeat it yet again, is that time management for the entrepreneur salesperson and the salesperson must be to change the time spent from non-income producing activities to income producing activities. If time management cannot produce this change then it should be considered useless and if your plan does not do this for you then throw it away right now and start again.

**Structuring territories**

At this advanced stage of time planning we will need to consider the impact that structuring territories will have on three critical influences upon production in the sales environment.

1. Influence upon current and potential *sales*.
2. Current and potential *clients and prospects*.
3. Influence upon the *salesperson* as a whole.

Understanding current and potential sales in any given territory is critical to future time planning. What is the point of establishing a territory, appointing a salesperson to develop business in the same, and yet, the potential for business is very low due to the lack of available opportunities. When setting up territories as an entrepreneur, an established business, a salesperson or a sales manager, it will be imperative that a review is done firstly of the sales territory by territory. The second recommendation will be to determine what statistics are available which best indicate the market potential for any service and/or product. There are many business resources today which track every aspect of business including statistics which show the level of potential in any particular area-use these if you have access to them. You will understand that there is no point whatsoever in assigning a territory to a salesperson which contains a majority of residential buildings and very little opportunity for business contacts if what you are selling has nothing to do with the residential market. The third imperative then would be for you to locate all the sources available to you, your business and salespeople which can assist in providing key information and business statistics prior to developing or identifying each geographic territory. The more pertinent information which you have at your disposal the less the risk of making mistakes when planning areas which are allocated to salespeople.

Once the information, as stated above has been obtained, you will need to consider how to use it. The information must now be used in order to ensure that the territories are conceived with an equal amount of potential to develop a client base and even more importantly the ability to grow the territory with a constant stream of prospects. Also, the information must be used to establish territories with better potential to meet the company's marketing objectives. Marketing is a division of any business (not covered in this book) which develops the way in which services and products are brought to market. The idea here then is to ensure that whatever territory and territories are developed and "broke-out" so to speak that these fit into the company's plan for the support of the territory and salesperson. If not, the support levels and market focus will not combine for a successful conclusion to the selling cycle as the service and product may be aimed at the wrong market right from the very start. Again, sources for this type of critical information can be found all over the internet but also from entities such as, industry related trade associations, trade publications, from national, provincial/state and city governments and local Chambers of Commerce. Let's face facts, entrepreneurs, while multi-talented, cannot be considered the resident economist; however, general market statistics should be used to create equitable territories containing the greatest potential for their product and/or service.

A second level of structuring is needed in each territory in order to set final boundaries-current and potential clients. The first level saw us focus on SALES so we shall now shift our discussion to that of CLIENT potential. As a master entrepreneur who is keen to expand the business and get to a positive cash-flow situation as soon as is possible (or a sales manager wanting to ensure success for his/her employer) it would be good to know the number and type of prospects in each territory. In other words how many businesses are located in the territory and do these businesses fit into a predetermined benchmark for your products or services? We need to discover these facts for very good reasons.

While you may not agree as salespeople very seldom agree with me on this but I want to inform you that salespeople have limits despite the fact that their time planning may be impeccable. For instance, they are limited in the amount of QUALITY calls which they can make in any given day. They are also limited to the calls that they can make, weekly, monthly and per year and we need to admit to this fact, and as salespeople, not to fight this but to be realistic as to your ability and capability. Salespeople and you as the entrepreneur will also be limited by the different types and sizes of clients which you can handle at any given point in time. There is a big difference when managing a mega client as opposed to managing a medium client-the larger is more demanding and so you will spend more of your time with them and this will impact on your time severely. The point that I want to make here is that usually the maximum number of clients a salesperson can handle will limit a specific territories size. There is no point at all in allotting a territory with 2000 prospects and 750 of these are converted into business but the salesperson or entrepreneur can only manage 500 clients at any given point in time.

As an entrepreneur or sales manager you should be analyzing some critical areas on a consistent basis using the following suggested formula. For instance, you must first of all be able to clearly identify the number of clients currently on the portfolio and the potential of each territory as this relates to the number of prospects. Secondly, one must now consider the sales potential in monetary terms. For instance, understand the sales value for the current client portfolio and the projected prospects as was identified and that are located in the territory. Finally, understand the time it would take to either service the existing client together with the approach and time spent on the prospect. For example, you will want to know the call frequency for all mega clients and prospects-maybe a call every three weeks? The large client and prospect may only require a call every month and the medium client and prospect a call every six weeks? The one may take more time than the other but right now this is not the point as your goal will be to calculate the total time available to the salesperson, or to you as the entrepreneur, in order to determine his/her capability with a view to setting reasonable territories. Otherwise, you will not get all areas covered and this will be detrimental to your goal of covering ALL territories with a view to becoming well known as soon as is possible. In fact, this exercise will also help you to develop and to "break-out" what we know to be the target market.

Information on the current client base or portfolio should be readily available in any business so this part of the abovementioned formula should not be a challenge. However, while it may seem like an impossible task, it is also not difficult to gather the necessary information in order to determine the size of a territory as this relates to future prospects and the potential of an area. The great thing about the information age is that one can source just about any information relating to business at a touch of a button. The statisticians take great pride in ensuring that we have all they we need in order to achieve our goals, and while in the good old days, there was a lot of hard work needed in order to gather information this is no longer the case. However, on a local level there are still sources that one could approach if the need arises. For instance, company compliment slips, reference books, trade publications, trade and business associations, the yellow pages, local telephone directories and company websites.

As an entrepreneur salesperson, salesperson and sales manager it will also be critical to calculate the amount of hours which you will have each year in order to focus on selling and face to face time. In order to come to the correct conclusion the idea would be to determine how many selling days there are in a year, and by this, I mean that you will need to remove all vacation time, public holiday time, bank holidays sick leave and any other day that will represent a pre-determined absenteeism from production time throughout the year. Once this has been accomplished, and that you now understand the amount of calls and the time it will take to service each call you will be able to extrapolate this information in order to conclude that any particular salesperson will only be able to service a certain amount of clients and prospects annually thereby determining the actual size of the territory allocated. Should you achieve accurate results using the formulas described above then you will arrive at a very important statistic called the entrepreneur salesperson's SALES CEILING. This will clearly then indicate that salespeople will have some serious limits and in order to achieve your goal of covering the entire target market you may have consider your options one of which may be to hire more salespeople or make use of professional telemarketers or both. The entrepreneur salesperson's ceiling will be influenced by the "business density" in a given area, the type of businesses associated within a given area and a salesperson's work and time management habits.

Once the sales ceiling has been established then the only way for this to vary at all will be if the salesperson is supported on a daily basis with telemarketing, a customer service agent and a sales administrator. These functions are purely set up in order to ensure that the salesperson is spending more time on face to face meetings with the client and the prospect. In any event, notwithstanding that he/she receives this great support you will have to understand, and plan for the fact that the salesperson's call rate will most likely not change more than an additional ten percent. You will then have to decide if the extra cost is worth the results which may ensue.

As an entrepreneur salesperson or sales manager it would be wise to travel with the salesperson into the territory, read activity sheets and scrutinize orders, contracts and agreements. The idea here will be to give you a better idea and confirmation as to the total calls that can be made in a single day and project the outcome over a year. You will then also experience first-hand the varying time per call and frequency necessary for each type of client or prospect. When you factor all of this information together in comparison to the planned market share the boundaries of a specific territory becomes very clear. For a clearer understanding of all which we have discussed above I feel it important to once again summarize this section.

Territories thus become defined by:

1. Classifying current accounts as to order of importance.
2. Prospective sales potential in any given territory.
3. The required and necessary sales call frequency.
4. Compare current client base and prospective clients with your desired market share.
5. Understand the physical and time limits of the territory manager (salesperson).
6. Work out the average production days in a year by:
   a. Deducting weekends.
   b. Annual holidays/vacation.
   c. Deduct public/bank holidays.
   d. All sick days and family responsibility days.
   e. Sales meetings.
   f. Non-income producing activity days/hours (i.e., administration etc.).
7. A further goal will be for you to arrive at a Dollar value as a financial ceiling for each salesperson. For instance, in certain cases, this will depend upon the product and/or services on offer and the monetary potential of each. Some industries and salespeople are only capable of producing an annual value of one million Dollars and others three or five million Dollars and so on.
8. Ensure effective use of the time management planner by:
   a. Providing the salesperson with a list of active and current clients.
   b. A list of all past clients but those that are now considered inactive.
   c. List the current expenditure with the company-existing clients.
   d. Provide any agreement/contract expiry dates.
   e. Make sure that clients are divided in categories of frequency of calls:
      1) Mega ("AAA")-four calls per year?

2) Large ("AA")-three calls per year?
3) Medium ("A")-two calls per year?

9. The formula to follow now is:
   a. Note the necessary numbers for each client and record this in the time management planner.
   b. Now you must multiply each client category by the number of required calls per year.
   c. You have now achieved the number of annual client retention calls which you or the salesperson should make.
   d. You will now have the freedom to add in any target for achieving NEW BUSINESS.
   e. The total of the above will equal the number of sales calls to be achieved each year, each month, each week and daily.
   f. Add in all non-income producing time in order to make up the total daily production time on the time management planner.
   g. Monitor all progress DAILY and WEEKLY through the "W.A.R." (Weekly Activity Report) and align with master time planning schedule.

10. It is also important to determine your sales closing ratio in order to plan more effectively. For instance if it takes you ten face to face calls in order to achieve one sale then we consider your closing ratio to be 10:1. You then need to calculate the calls needed (with the closing ratio of 10:1) in order to achieve the planned sales goal as this will impact upon your master time planning schedule. For example, Let's assume forty-eight working weeks per year multiplied by ten prospecting calls in order to secure one new client should be equal to four hundred and eighty prospecting calls for the year, and considering the closing ration of 10:1, you should be able to produce forty-eight new clients from prospects as was planned for.

11. One last consideration should be made in order to project and achieve sales targets. At times calls

made to a client or prospect are more service related than sales oriented. In order not to confuse the one with the other these calls need to be established as a number per year. These are not to be considered sales calls with a view to generating NEW BUSINESS but rather necessary (in some cases not so) for productive sales time planning purposes. For example, it could be that you discover that the salesperson will make as much as twenty calls per week which we call "non-selling" calls. If this is the case these will (using forty-eight weeks in a year) add up to nine-hundred and sixty non-selling calls each year. You will thus see the impact that such calls will have on selling and production time each day and this will need to be taken into account during the time management planning stages. While these calls are necessary they will impact upon selling time and therefore should be accounted for on a yearly basis.

We have looked at structuring territories from the perspective of current and potential sales, current and potential clients and prospects, and now, we will need to understand the influence of allocating territories upon the salesperson as a whole-we refer to this as the 'human element" in this part of our discussion.

Territories must also be set with the salesperson in mind. You will need to seriously consider the level of competency (and yours if you are an entrepreneur salesperson) and psychology of the individual. The level of maturity must also be a serious consideration as is the salesperson's ability to reach and achieve sales targets as per the annual time planning schedule and master time planning schedule. Critical considerations are:

1. Where does he/she live in relation to the territory-there is no point placing a salesperson in a territory

and it takes him/her an hour to get there from any given point (time-waster).

2. Does the "territory culture" match that of the salesperson's personality?

3. Consider the salesperson's needs; goals and personal desires-will the territory meet expectations which may prevail?

4. Understand the salesperson's likes and dislikes-for instance, if the salesperson has a fear of heights and many of the prospects and clients associated with the territory happen to be in sky scrapers then you will have a problem for sure.

5. A crucial consideration is what current "contacts" does the salesperson have and how does this apply to their territory under consideration? I have seen sales managers and entrepreneurs place salespeople in territory "B" when the salesperson has, many personal and past professional contacts in area "A". Placing salespeople in the correct area in this case may mean the difference between immediate sales or future failure.

6. Some salespeople do not like to travel as much and therefore prefer a smaller territory and to place such a one in a large territory may be counter-productive and produce a negative attitude towards the territory allocated. Some salespeople then prefer a smaller territory so find out what the reason is and if legitimate then consider the preference.

7. On the other hand, some salespeople love the idea of being kept productive and understand the concept of geographical farming to its fullest. This understanding allows them to be kept busy being productive with all K.P.A.'s associated with a large territory. The more accounts the better! The more prospects the better!

8. Consider the home life of a salesperson. Some have total support from home and others not. Marital challenges exist with one and all and if the

salesperson is out of town too often then you must expect some backlash from an unhappy spouse. Make allowances for this before you judge and before you lose a good salesperson. The worst thing to have on your conscience is a broken marriage due to your inflexibility.

Salespeople are not immune to boredom and a territory can easily become a source of daily boredom for a salesperson. Of course, I am assuming that you (or the salesperson) have worked the territory professionally and thoroughly and without compromise. I am also assuming that targets are being met and that the territory is not being used as an excuse for failure over a long period of time. If you or any of your salespeople become bored with a specific territory then make a change if this is practically possible. In most cases, professional entrepreneur sales managers and sales managers in general, have a strict policy of rotating sales people into different territories after every few years. However, in some cases this is not always as easy as it seems to achieve. The reasons why it may be good to adopt this policy is because it is believed that a change would prevent the salesperson from becoming lethargic, daily tasks from becoming mundane and developing and continuing on in bad habits. There is also "a new broom sweeps clean" mentality amongst professional managers of salespeople in that a point will be reached when the incumbent salesperson feels that the territory has now been saturated after spending the last five years farming it. "I have no more business or prospects in my area!" This is a common come back from poor producing sales staff, and so, there is no better way of testing the waters than to move this salesperson into a fresh territory with a fresh start-a "new lease on life" so to speak. On many occasions I have seen that when a new salesperson gets moved into the negative salesperson's territory ("I have no more business or prospects in my area!") that they actually achieve better results and are able to continue to produce sales.

It is not always easy to sell the prospect of a territory change or a reduction in territory size to the professional and well established salesperson. This is particularly difficult to achieve with a top producer as the territory has been managed well, "cultivated" professionally and has produced consistency in sales results. Should you move such a productive salesperson without his/her cooperation then it would be tantamount to committing "production suicide". The idea is to reduce the territory size and even changing a territory, with the consent and cooperation of the salesperson and this can be achieved by outlining the perceived benefits for doing so. For instance, there may be less travel and the possibility of more family and/or leisure time and even the prospect of developing more time for important clients. The change could even produce more time to further develop new business by prospecting. Should the salesperson need some persuading then there are ways and means to make him/her an offer that they simply cannot refuse, such as:

1. A temporary allowance to compensate for perceived losses that may result in a move.
2. Offer and override commission on the lost client base.
3. Offer an advance draw on future commission earned-he/she may want to renovate or remodel his/her home.
4. Massage the salesperson's ego with a new title if you feel that this may be a "hot button".
5. Offer to have the salesperson have lunch with the company owners and sales manager-let him bring the wife and let her bring the husband and stroke both egos.

The goal, when making changes in territory is to make the salesperson feel important. Stroking the ego in as many ways as you can think is a good way to achieve this and while I have stated a few suggestions there are many more ways to accomplish this goal successfully. Remember, the idea is to make the changes without personal damage to the salesperson and financial damage to your business. The one thing that will help you as you move forward is to place a clause in the employment contract of each salesperson clearly outlining both the need to rotate territories and the inevitability of territory changes, and that the salesperson will comply at the appropriate time to the change without undue resistance. The other fair thing to do is to explain the policy to the prospective salesperson from the outset so that you do not make yourself guilty of not sharing this vital policy at the appropriate time. It must be understood by the salesperson and the sales manager that making territory changes from time to time "comes with the territory" if you will excuse the pun. However, when making changes try to change territories at the edges and not in the very heart of the territory as most salespeople will start developing and farming territory at the very center. This will assist in reducing resistance as the loss of territory may cover an area currently not being worked by the incumbent. Another suggestion which I would like to make at this point is that you make a change of large and small accounts to "even things out" to everyone's satisfaction.

**Time management**

We have arrived at the last piece to our puzzle as far as time management principles and implementation is concerned. In this section we dealt with geographic territory management, territory and time planning of and in the territory and also structuring territories. As we close our study of time management as a concept and practice we will now deal with how to plan and use time effectively for maximum results within a given territory.

As an entrepreneur salesperson and/or sales manager, after establishing territories that help you to clearly define your target market then you must understand and help your sales staff to plan their time for effective use within the assigned territory. It is imperative, for the sake of profitability, that salespeople learn how to best utilize a limited amount of time within their territories. They must understand that there are negative consequences for poor time management and that they will need to consider some very important aspects in order to avoid failure. They will need to understand that they have to calculate and follow logical client cluster routes or zones. Clustering client visits and prospect face to face calls will save a great deal of time and the services or deliveries will follow the same logical sequence thereby compounding the time saving. The salesperson will need to contemplate that spending too much time on the road will take away from the time allocated in order to be face to face with the client and prospect and the consequences may lead to quotas/targets not being met and ensuing failure. Consider how often to call on major clients and how much, if any to spend on smaller clients. The question is who is spending the most money with you and spend more time with that company and the opposite applies to companies who do not fully commit to a long-term business relationship. There is a fine balance between servicing existing clients and a focus on developing the new business side of a territory. Both are equally important and neglecting either will have negative consequences on achieving sales goals and targets. The salesperson must also consider the sales focus in a new territory. For instance, how much time will be devoted to each of the service and product offerings? In many instances companies have a habit of developing commission structures which favor one service and/or product over another for very obvious reasons and they may change this from time to time. The idea is to develop the commission structure so that maximum benefit will go to the salesperson when selling high profit services and/or product. The salesperson, which is not unusual, will consider the financial benefits and focus on the high commission producing items as this is naturally how he/she is driven internally. Whatever the reason or the choice the idea is that this focus must be planned for as the area is farmed. While we have been through this before the salesperson must not only understand the meaning of the term "time waster" but must also be able to identify the same within his/her life and territory and reduce the negative influences that this will have on their ability to produce sales targets. The daily call limits as discussed above must be clearly seen in the time management plan as is developed by the salesperson. It is vital that a WRITTEN master time management schedule be completed BEFORE work is done in the territory so the salesperson has got to complete all the tasks as have been discussed in this chapter. There is no point in allowing a disorganized salesperson to begin selling in a disorganized territory as the result will be "disorganized". As admonished before the salesperson must give a clear account of how he/she spends every minute of every day. He/she must be very careful as to how time is spent in order to produce maximum results out of the territory which he/she is the manager thereof.

The entrepreneur sales manager must make it his/her business to know exactly what amount of time the salesperson is spending on face to face appointments with clients and the same applies to prospects. This, in my opinion can be achieved by instructing the salesperson to log all of their activity for at least one whole month. The log may be used as a basis for a first discussion on time management and future planning. The activities which should be logged must be drawn from the job description of the particular salesperson. For instance you may want to request that the salesperson log or report on what percentage of his/her time is spent on:

1. Actual time spent with current clients.
2. Actual time spent with prospective clients.
3. Time spent on waiting in reception areas or for the client/prospect.
4. On the telephone (whether it is a landline or a mobile phone).
5. Time spent on "chasing" or following up on orders or installations.
6. Actual time spent on administration and/or paperwork.
7. Time spent attending sales meetings (usually on a Friday).
8. Actual time spent in the office.

Once the entrepreneur sales manager has the results of the above then it will become clear as to how the salesperson's time is to be spent and adjustments can and must be made in order to ensure the most effective program for the salesperson and the company. The idea is to now carefully weigh up which activity will produce the best results and allocate this accordingly. Compare the allocation to the log results produced by the salesperson; make the necessary permanent adjustments and cement into the time planning schedule. The "log analysis" may reveal the need for more telemarketing, for a customer service representative, a sales administrator and what we call an "order closer" (a strong closer and a professional).

The route taken by the salesperson in each quadrant must now be contemplated and cemented. Planning effective travel routes (whether you fly, go by boat, hovercraft or train) will optimize the production time of any salesperson. The rule is clear: organize a salesperson's travel time and you minimize time wastage between sales calls and maximize time spent face to face with the client/prospect. Establish clear rules of route planning early on in the relationship in order to avoid failure. For instance, provide a clear visible map of the salesperson's territory clearly showing boundaries. Clearly identify and mark the locations of all current clients for easy reference purposes. Do the same for QUALITY prospects (QUALITY prospect is someone who has received a presentation and a proposal but due to the unprofessionalism of the previous salesperson managing the territory the prospect was not closed but shows both interest and great promise). A quality prospect to me is an interested party who stands at least 80% chance of turning into real business within the very near future. Also the salesperson must classify prospects and clients by visit frequency as has already been alluded to earlier in the chapter.

You must also understand that there are growth techniques, and while you may know this information, I shall not assume that you do, in that growth does not only come from opening new business prospects; however, business development also takes place when one effectively nurtures the existing client on the portfolio, and in many cases you will produce around eighty percent of your business from these good clients. The following is an example of a growth technique adopted by a service related business and has established this as a norm but also a minimum standard for all sales staff hired by the business. While you can change this to suit your own business needs I want to leave you with the following formula:

## Minimum Standard-10 sales calls per day

1. **5** Retention/penetration calls-existing clients.
2. **2** Service request calls on current accounts.
3. **3** Cold calls or follow-up calls on new prospects.

## Minimum Standard-Produce 1 New Business client per week

1. Closing Ratio = 15:1
2. See 15 QUALITY prospects per week

My recommendation here is that you consider your business within the context of your country and the target market as was identified by you. There needs to be a balance in that spending too much time on servicing existing clients at the expense of visiting prospects will negatively impact on sales growth. Existing clients can only be "milked" for so long before they reach saturation point. What happens then? The ideal situation is that you balance the two activities in order to maximize the desired result. Company growth is vital but so is taking care of the people who pay your bills right now. The question for you is rather: "What time allocation shall produce the best results for you and your business"?

As an entrepreneur salesperson YOU should be in control of your activities and your focus but you cannot be in more than one place at a time and so you may develop your business to the point where you hire one or multiple sales people. Beware;

do not get too busy with what is going on around you to the point where you neglect the activities and the planning of your sales staff. While I will be dealing with the key to time management planning for sales staff later in the book you have to understand that many unprofessional salespeople take chances and willfully misuse their time and you need to hold them accountable for every hour. This one thing that I recommend is that you and your sales staff MUST plan sales calls a week in advance. As discussed in this chapter these calls must be in writing either on their computer, tablet or paper Day-Timer (diary for some). It must be clear as to who they are seeing and what the goal of the meeting is. They must not call on UNQUALIFIED sales leads that have not been professionally:

1. Screened.
2. Analyzed.
3. Evaluated.
4. Updated.

Always ensure that you understand the use of the telephone as a sales tool and that you teach the same to your sales staff. The phone is used for setting up appointments; to answer client queries and to deal with service related matters, and finally, to write reorders and additions to contracts/agreements already in place. As a salesperson you must agree that you have certain hours to produce so understand what they are and the difference of being in the office and out on the road (or out in the field) and what time is allocated for these activities. Do not accept excuses for actions and poor performances – not from yourself nor from those around you. Salespeople have a habit of burying themselves in paperwork, and in doing so, they look "busy". Being too "busy" shuffling paper from one side of the desk to the other will be used as an excuse for not producing sales, and this, you must not and cannot tolerate at any stage. Salespeople are employed to sell! You must SELL in order to grow your business! No excuses from anyone when it comes to why they are prevented from selling. Do what I do, quickly remove any reason for why salespeople cannot produce sales and then they will hang themselves out to dry without fail. When the "paperwork excuse" is used you must analyze the paper load of the salesperson and immediately suggest reductions and ways of delegation if at all possible. Make sure that salespeople prioritize each day-tasks are to be listed in order of priority and ensure that "easy work does not become IMPORTANT work". Unprofessional salespeople also develop poor memories so you will have to spend a great deal of time in ensuring that some or all of the following tasks and principles are being met:

1. Set daily objectives and deadlines.
2. Focus on sales results at all times.
3. Develop alternatives to the day to day challenges.
4. Avoid procrastination at all costs.
5. Concentrate efforts-one task at a time ("multi-tasking" is for the unprofessional).
6. When overwhelmed use available company resources-delegate to existing staff.
7. Be reminded of scheduled commitments DAILY.
8. Plans are not etched in stone-be flexible.
9. ALWAYS maintain priorities.
10. Learn to say NO to:
    a. Clients/Customers.
    b. Fellow employees if you are an employed salesperson.
    c. Partners and staff if you are an entrepreneur.
    d. Suppliers and friends.
    e. FAMILY
    f. Anticipate hurdles and challenges.
    g. Develop and always have a contingency plan (a "Plan B").
    h. Manage daily interruptions professionally.
    i. Poor communication-a time waster.
    j. Lack of persistence-a time waster.

## *"Time Wasters and Time Traps"*

| 1. | | Private and long-winded telephone Calls |
|---|---|---|
| 2. | | Drop in "visitors", unplanned interruptions |
| 3. | | Unscheduled or scheduled meetings-a management weakness |
| 4. | | Crisis-firefighting ("putting out fires") |
| 5. | | Lack of objectives, deadlines, priorities-non-existent goal setting and time management |
| 6. | | Disorganization, cluttered desk and office-may be done on purpose to "look busy" to hide poor daily production |
| 7. | | Ineffective delegation to qualified assistants-control challenges ("I do everything myself that way I know that it will get done properly") |
| 8. | | Focusing on unexciting tasks-a way to put off the inevitable: SALES PRODUCTION! |
| 9. | | "Multi-tasking"-Doing too many things at the same time |
| 10. | | Unrealistic time goals-adds unwanted pressure |
| 11. | | Ineffective communication-poor listening skills |
| 12. | | Inadequate training-non-existent commitment to personal development |
| 13. | | Procrastination, indecision, day dreaming-a lack of self-discipline |
| 14. | | Inability to say "no"-poor leadership and self-management |
| 15. | | Unfinished/incomplete tasks-major result of "multi-tasking" |
| 16. | | Perfectionist tendencies-recognize this as a weakness |
| 17. | | Inadequate/poor performance by staff-poor motivation levels and unclear time management and goals |
| 18. | | Socializing, idle conversation-non-existent time management and accountability |
| 19. | | Lack of self-discipline-a poor personal characteristic but will lead to ultimate failure if not redirected |
| 20. | | Changing priorities-good only if planned for |
| 21. | | Non-listener-resulting in eventual failure |
| 22. | | Lack of feedback/information-poor communication skills |
| 23. | | Personnel problems/conflict-will effect production levels |
| 24. | | Worry, anxiety, fear-low self-esteem and low self-image |
| 25. | | Inadequate planning, failure to consider alternatives |
| 26. | | Waiting-this can be utilized effectively |
| 27. | | "Memo-itis"-focus on sales generation priority lost |
| 28. | | Poor memory-weak personal characteristic: changeable |
| 29. | | Confusing activity with results-being "busy" does not mean success |
| 30. | | Boredom, fatigue-a lack of achievement, no goal setting |
| 31. | | Blame shifting-lack of success and a need to remove focus from the guilty party |
| 32. | | Tension and stress-due to non or low production |
| 33. | | Inadequate equipment or facilities-a management issue |
| 34. | | Misunderstanding of company policy-read the documents |
| 35. | | Poor filing/computer system-lack of time management |
| 36. | | Excess paperwork-poor time management |
| 37. | | Travel, commuting-poor time management |
| 38. | | Pet projects/outside activities-must NEVER be allowed |
| 39. | | Haste, impatience-a poor personal characteristic but can be altered |
| 40. | | Failure to prioritize-a lack of time management and planning |

## Conclusion

Managing one's time professionally is imperative if we are to succeed in any area of life but more so in the area of sales. So much will rely on the ability of salespeople to produce sales; however, if time is being wasted on non-income producing activities then time is wasted and expected results are not met. When sales results are not met then this affects not only the salesperson and his/her family but it will severely affect business growth goals. Salespeople are notorious for wasting time on performing "tasks" which get them nowhere and this ensures their ultimate and continuous demise. The way they cope with this is to move from one company to another never achieving sales targets and always blaming everything else except their poor time management and laziness. I make no apology for why I believe unprofessional salespeople fail-LAZINESS! Companies must be aware of the "games" being played by many unprofessional salespeople. They are very good during the interview process to the point that many unsuspecting companies unwisely decide not to do credit and reference checks on these people to their own detriment. After a short while, despite time and money spent on initial training (the same training which they received from their previous employer), they show signs of their slackness by not achieving sales targets for the first few months. Sales managers and entrepreneurs will put this down to "settling in" and I cannot understand why a salesperson should "settle in". If he/she is a salesperson then they need to sell from the first day of employment. I do understand that the lack of product knowledge may be a challenge but this cannot continue on indefinitely.

When salespeople are interviewed it means that they made a conscious effort to seek employment with your company. They understand from the beginning the position entails sales and nothing else. Unless the position requires a person to be trained as a salesperson once the application has been made, once the trained salesperson as the applicant puts himself/herself forward for the position, it must be assumed that no further sales training is needed in order to close sales from day one. The unprofessional salesperson will soon produce the excuses which he/she hopes will gain him/her more time with the company before they are asked to clear out their desk. Do not employ these kinds of "salespeople" as they will waste your time and money. Make sure that you do the necessary background and psychological screening tests, if you have this available to you, BEFORE you hire any salesperson.

May I dare suggest that the very first question you ask is "May I see your time management plan"? If they cannot produce the time management plan which they used at their previous employer then you will have two choices (1) Do not employ such a person (2) You may decide to train them in time management principles immediately in order to enhance the chances of success. However, you will also now be aware that the salesperson's previous employer does not understand the concept of ensuring that salespeople have professional time management schedules to account for every minute of every day. If they don't have a time management plan then they will also not have a goal setting plan and together these omissions spell FAILURE and that is more likely the reason they were forced to leave their last employer! Therefore be aware of the following fact which will also help you to determine the level of professionalism of the person in front of you (being interviewed of course); ask them to produce a written goal setting plan which they have used to date and if they cannot produce this then move on as you are dealing with a time waster and the greatest disappointment will be when he/she wastes your time and your company's money.

Professional salespeople on the other hand have both a written plan for their business (as an entrepreneur) and life goals and use this as motivation for why they will produce the very best for you. The great achievers will also have a time management plan which will clearly outline the use of each minute of each day. The time management plan and the goal setting plan will thus be the driving force behind the professional salesperson (and entrepreneur of course) which will assure you that they are self-motivated and driven to achieve their personal goals. If they are driven to achieve their personal goals then the natural spin-off for you as an entrepreneur is that you will also achieve your sales quotas/targets ensuring the continued growth of your business. Time management is everything and when you add to this a written plan to achieve personal and business goals then you have a "perfect" recipe for success. Sales are vital for growth and this is why you will need to be careful when hiring salespeople. If you are the sole source of sales in your start-up business then consider the principles and admonitions contained in this chapter. Once you apply this to your business and your life you will wonder how you ever managed without them.

## My take on "MULTI-TASKING"

The word and concept called "MULTI-TASKING" has been misused by those who live their lives in a constant state of chaos in order to justify the disorganized state of their daily living in whatever form. Multi-tasking, in any form should be rejected and seen for what it truly is – CHAOS WITH A NAME! I can assure you, that while the concept of multi-tasking is touted by some as a positive attribute I want to assure you that in the life of the professional it has no place and is a most ineffective way to conduct your daily work life or any other part of life for that matter.

Multi-tasking is a term generally ascribed to the ability of computers to perform more than one task at a time for the effectual functioning of both the hardware and the software associated with this piece of equipment. Merriam-Webster.com states: "the concurrent performance of several jobs by a computer". Humans are NOT computers! Merriam-Webster.com goes on to define the term as: "the performance of multiple tasks at one time". It is a most overused and abused word and the original meaning has been taken out of context and used as a pretext to chaos justification. Can you imagine my consternation then when you and I look at the "jobs offered" column and we read: "The job requires someone who is 'good' at multi-tasking"? While I do not want to get into a gender "battle" here it must be pointed out that this weakness of multi-tasking has been attributed to the female gender as strength, and PROUDLY claimed as a female strength. Ladies, multi-tasking is not strength and if I were you, and someone attributed this to me as strength then I would reject this with contempt. Women, like men, are NOT computers!

I have often seen, when driving down the highway, women who "multi-task". They are capable of fixing their hair, applying their make-up and talking on a mobile, and all of this while speeding along the highway in a lethal weapon called an automobile/car. How many of them die doing this type of multi-tasking? Who knows? How many innocent people do they kill while performing this type of reckless multi-tasking? Who knows? While men are less apt to perform multiple tasks at the same time I have also seen my own gender going down the highway shaving their face, talking on the mobile and driving a vehicle all at the same time. What's my point? While this negative "attribute" has been ascribed to women men are just as guilty of trying their hand at multi-tasking. In the business world, pertaining to our subject matter at hand (time management in case you have been so busy multi-tasking that you have forgotten) effective time management will help you to focus on performing very specific tasks, as prioritized, and with a clear and concise goal at the end of the task.

As a professional I want you to forget about the notion and pathetic concept of multi-tasking and which gender is better at this weakness than the next. My desire for you is to organize your business and your personal lives for one reason only – IN ORDER TO ENSURE SUCCESS! Multi-tasking is a clever, but misused word for CHAOS and if you are to succeed in sales and in business the last thing you need is to foster CHAOS through "multi-tasking".

# Chapter 11

# Prospective Prospecting
## *The beginning and ending of the $ales cycle*

**Introduction**

While you and I have now had the benefit of being exposed to geographical farming a young salesperson by the name of Kirsten had not. While consulting for a client Kirsten came up to me and seemed pleasant enough but I could sense that something was amiss. "Trevor", she said, "may I talk with you for a moment?" I agreed and listened to her concerns as to her lack of production (sales) in her assigned territory. As I spent quite a while listening to her it became apparent that her challenge was not uncommon with salespeople in that she has not understood one of the most fundamental secrets of successful selling – PROSPECTING. She was good at what she did and apparently, according to her sales manager, she was a top performer. Kirsten was having difficulty achieving her personal life goals and business goals due to her inability to source enough new prospects. In other words, her situation may be likened to going into a food store but the shelves were empty. She had the ability to sell but found herself needing quality prospects to sell to.

As an entrepreneur I can assure you that this thing called prospecting can severely affect your ability to sell and to grow your business. Many salespeople fail in the sales environment simply because they have no one to sell to. Prospecting is vital and is so important to the selling cycle that it is the only step which is repeated. The selling cycle starts with prospecting and it ends with prospecting. Please allow me the opportunity to make it very clear to you once again – PROSPECTING IS THE ONLY STEP IN THE SELLING CYCLE THAT IS EVER REPEATED!

While we have discussed the pros and cons of geographical farming and working one quadrant at a time we now need to dig a little deeper and ensure that we understand what prospecting entails and how to apply it in a practical sense as without a prospect you and I cannot sell and if we cannot sell then we cannot close and if this happens then both the company for which we work or represent will not grow and we will not be able to earn a living and our personal life goals will not be achieved. For the sake of clarification then we all understand by now that there are two types of prospecting activities namely current clients and new business prospects. While we shall be touching on both aspects my focus in this chapter will deal largely with the big gap and need in the area of new business. The reason why I would like to do this is when you start a new business then the chances are that you will be starting with no or very little clients or customers at all unless you took these from a previous source or employer – not good! However, let's assume then that you have taken my advice and have performed the geographical farming exercise and that all time management planning has now been completed. The question then is: "Trevor, where to from here?" This is a logical question and one which we shall answer for you in this chapter.

The professional entrepreneur, sales manager and salesperson realizes that prospecting for new business is the life-blood to any business and continued sales success. As pointed out before, imagine walking into a store where its management has not taken the time to replenish the stock on the shelves. How long would such a store remain in business? Many may laugh at such a situation but the consequences would not be that funny at all. The same applies to an unprofessional entrepreneur salesperson! While you may be laughing at the above example and the consequences faced by this business you must understand that there are many salespeople out there who are neglecting to perform prospecting for "new or replenishment stock" for their own territories. The end result is catastrophic! However, the professional will ALWAYS consider prospecting as a way of keeping the "shelves" stocked. By prospecting for new business he/she realizes that this is the only way to ensure an adequate supply of leads ("stock"). May I suggest that you focus your attention now on one of the most critical subjects for sales success, and to learn quickly, and understand clearly, TO IGNORE PROSPECTING IS SIMPLY YOU COMMITTING BUSINESS AND CAREER SUICIDE!

The question then is why prospecting? The answer has to do with the future because if you fail to prospect then you will have no future. You will have no future clients meaning that there will be no growth and growth is a clear sign that the business doors will open again tomorrow. When you have a list of prospects you also have a thing called potential and the potential is that you may be able to convert the prospect into a client who will be spending much money with you. Thus, prospecting also means success because not prospecting means failure if we reverse the trend as depicted above. When you and I see a future and have potential then the outlook is great and we say that this is a great place to be. For instance, when a salesperson arrives at work on a Monday morning he should not be wondering what will become of him/her for the week as there are no prospects. If you have no prospects you will have a terrible Sunday evening as you will realize that you will get into the office in the morning not knowing what to do. However, the thing that is clear is that you have a monthly sales quota to fill and a sales meeting to attend in which you will be given all the opportunity in the world to explain why you are not meeting quota or sales targets. How pathetic is this may I ask? Prospecting, then, gives hope and I can tell you that you can take anything away from a man or a woman but if you remove hope then the person becomes well-nigh hopeless with no motivation to live or to go on. Ask someone sitting in jail for life with no hope of parole. Finally, prospecting opens up all kinds of possibilities in that goals will be achieved and in so doing self-esteem and self-image and motivation levels are high. If you have a positive mental attitude you will see all kinds of possibilities which all lead to success. Prospecting then is the hope that you will be able to sell tomorrow!

The idea of prospecting will be to ensure that proposal and quotation targets are met. For example, with a closing ratio of 10:1 (if this is in fact your personal closing ratio) you would need to ensure that you place ten proposals for every one sale. If you are to open one new business client per week that is four per month (with four weeks) and five for months with five weeks. However, even if you work on a four week month and assume the above closing ratio you would need to find forty prospects in order to submit forty proposals with a view to closing at least four of these in order to meet the quota each month. This is a lot of work so can you imagine what would happen to you if you did not have a steady stream of prospects? No prospects mean no proposals and no proposals out means no sales in. Simple! It is no wonder then that a lack of prospecting is the single greatest cause of failure amongst salespeople. The other consideration is that the salesperson will have to QUALIFY the prospects before making an approach. Prospecting is not simply a matter of numbers although we often refer to sales as "a numbers game" this does not apply to prospecting. When prospecting we must ensure that the company, or you as the entrepreneur, has a "prospect profile". This means that you have set parameters for which type of prospect it is that you would like to do business with and then go out and find these prospects and these people we refer to as QUALIFIED prospects. While salespeople are very concerned with filling the proposal quota they also realize that it would be futile to include prospects that have no potential of turning into real business – what is the point as no one will win? We have already established that the definition of a qualified prospect is that business entity that has at least eighty percent chance of turning into business before the first close has been attempted – "AAA" prospects.

In sales, prospecting is the process of keeping your name known among potential buyers. When I first started out as a salesperson many years ago I became fascinated with the concept of geographical farming (an old sales concept) and understood very quickly how this method could help me to become well known in the territory assigned to me. I broke down my territory into "bite-sized" chunks known as quadrants and then continued to break down the pieces until I found them manageable. It was during this time that I found out the tremendous benefit of prospecting. It was not so much the way that I dissected each quadrant but more about how I understood prospecting from that point on. I realized back then that people were friendly and receptive and they never had any preconceived notions and negative attitudes toward salespeople and so I used to park my vehicle outside of each QUALIFIED prospect and approach the lady (at that time the person at the front desk was usually a lady – very friendly people at that) at the front desk. I would introduce myself and the company which I represented and ask for a "compliment slip". For some of you that may not know a "compliment slip" is usually the top piece of a company's letter head but the words "With Compliments" have been added to the bottom left hand side. Many companies had these printed and included them when making check payments and any other appropriate correspondence-a form of advertising? The one thing about the compliment slip is that it usually contained all of the pertinent company information which I would need in order to turn the company into a prospect. However, in most cases I had to request the necessary information as this related to the correct contact person. I made sure that I got the name and last name spelt correctly, the direct landline number, the mobile number and the correct email address. I walked away with more than a compliment slip as I was friendly and professional and because of this I made friends – lots of friends! I handed out my business cards freely as I had printed all of our services and products at the back of the card so that prospects never became confused as to why they were calling me-a time waster. Due to my positive mental attitude (this is what I put it down to anyway) I was often asked to take a seat and to my amazement the prospect was ready to see me immediately – FANTASTIC! When I was not so fortunate I would need to call and schedule a professional meeting or appointment. By personally visiting every prospect in my territory I was able to "make friends and influence people" as was encouraged by Mr. Dale Carnegie in his book by the same title. Before long I became more known than the police in my territory and when there was a need for the services and/or products which I was selling guess who got the call? The competitors could not work it out at the time but I had found a secret and I pretty much kept it to myself for many years after that. I was not afraid to walk and I was not afraid to collect compliment slips and make friends. You see, I had goals, dreams and desires for my life and that of my family and I knew even as a young man back then that I would need to be different and being different meant that I was to put my laziness aside and develop clear plans for every part of my sales life. The best thing that I learned was most certainly that without a steady stream of QUALIFIED prospects I was not going to get very far at all.

Salespeople today are more fortunate in that companies generate "leads" which are then given to salespeople with a view to closing. However, many of these leads are random and unqualified, and as such, is a greater waste of the salesperson's time than anything else that I know. This is not only detrimental to the success of the salesperson but also to the company generating these poor quality leads. So I will say it again then and that is that prospecting is the beginning and the ending of the sales cycle as I know it.

1. Prospect.
2. Build rapport.
3. Qualify wants and needs.
4. Present and sell features and benefits.
5. Close (answer objections)
6. Prospect

The sad news though is that I have to report to you today that prospecting is avoided by most unprofessional and unproductive salespeople. How ridiculous! No wonder they fail and then blame everyone and everything else for their failure and move from one company to the next. Prospecting means that you actually have to meet people, and yes, it also means that you have to lift yourself off of the chair that you remain stuck to from morning until night. It also means that you have to do a bit of work and go meet and visit the prospects in your territory. So what! Why not think on the long-term benefits to you and your family not to mention your employer if you are a salesperson being paid such a wonderful salary – WORK FOR IT MY FRIEND WORK FOR IT!

Unprofessional and unsuccessful salespeople avoid prospecting and I want to tell you why. Three reasons:

7. The absolute fear of rejection.

Many unsuccessful salespeople are that way (poor performers) because they have an unmanageable fear of the word "NO!" While we have dealt with handling objections and the prospect's right to say "NO" you will still find salespeople and entrepreneurs who will never lose their fear of this word. You and I must understand that the word NO does not really mean what it says and I will once again refer you to the chapter dealing with the handling of objections. For those of us that do not fear rejection we may want to spare a thought for the unsuccessful in that their fear is real but most certainly not insurmountable. The thought of being rejected in any form has nothing to do with the sales environment although this is where they will pay the highest price for their behavior. These may be the same people who refuse to ask the girl next door out on a date or a long standing girlfriend for their hand in marriage. This is also the girl that is withdrawn and afraid to make an approach to be friends with some girl in high school or the girl that refuses to ask the boss for a raise despite the fact that he has not given her one in three years. Thus the fear of rejection is more often than not "home-grown" and has nothing to do with sales but is a major negative impact upon sales success if it cannot be overcome. This kind of person may find it easier to be run over by a steam roller that to do prospecting, and this, purely due to the fear of rejection.

8. They have developed low self-esteem over time and have brought it into the sales environment.

A low self-esteem makes it very difficult for such a salesperson to make and develop friends and unfortunately this happens to be what new business sales is all about. Doing prospecting will mean that this salesperson will have to meet and deal with people who they are not familiar with. Prospecting means cold calling and this word will incite fear into the heart of a low self-esteem sufferer. While dealing with people that they know, such as an existing client, contact is not a problem; however, they most certainly do not have the psychological ability to develop new relationships and so they would rather not place themselves in this situation called prospecting.

9. The salesperson has a bad perception of how he/she is viewed by the general public.

If I had to point a finger of blame as it relates to this perception then I would have to go to the door-to-door salesperson. While the life of door-to-door sales has dwindled down to the bare minimum in recent days there was a time when people were harassed from morning till night with high pressure tactics by unscrupulous and dishonest salespeople. This type of sales approach eventually affected us all.

However, we have to give credit to the general population as they have long ago understood the difference between door-to-door sales and professional sales. Professional sales is a salesperson setting up an appointment (meeting) which is for the purpose of a presentation and it is understood that professional salespeople do not barge into the work environment uninvited. The great thing is that most people find professional salespeople knowledgeable and friendly and are more than happy to deal with them. After all, when cold calling (prospecting) you and I are seeking information and not really selling a product or service until the meeting date has been set up.

**Professional tip:** Someone once said, "Do the thing you fear the most and the death of fear will be near".

There are certain basic prospecting fundamentals and philosophies which we will need to consider at this point. When prospecting with either an existing client or a prospective client you must understand an ancient life principle and that is to "give before you receive". The question is then what to give and what will you receive? The first thing that needs to happen is that you should give good service. Good service means that you make yourself available at the time appointed by the client and good service also means that you get into your car to view a challenge currently being faced by the prospect despite the fact the he/she is not as yet a formal client of yours. The idea is to give of yourself and your business in any area in order to gain a long-term business relationship. Recently, a corporate prospect had a problem with smelling drains in the kitchen area. They were not our client, and yet, I saw the opportunity and sent one of our service managers to the site for an inspection. The prospect was so impressed with the response and the proposed resolution that she is in the process of considering our proposal for a change of supplier. We did not have to go to the site which is about an hour away but we decided to "give before we receive" and it seems like it will pay off yet again.

Give before receiving will also mean that you will take the time to earn and to give trust. Many prospects are disgruntled over poor service and products. This will affect you as a new salesperson making an approach so the idea is to allow the prospect to vent before continuing on. By your willingness to listen to the frustration of the prospect it gives you the opportunity to earn trust and give trust. I once sat with a prospect and was forced to listen to his frustration for over a half an hour before I could get a word in at all. I sat and made notes while he was being abusive. After the prospect calmed down he asked me what I was doing. I stated that I was taking notes and he wanted to know why I was doing this. My answer was simple: "John, I am taking notes so that I never repeat these mistakes from my side and I also want to take this back to the office and share your current frustrations with them so that they too do not disappoint you should you be prepared to trust me to deliver on my promises not to frustrate you as you have been before my arrival. Furthermore, in order to put my 'money where my mouth is' I will make a note on the agreement, and sign it, that should you be disappointed in our service for any reason within the first ninety days then you will be allowed to terminate the agreement with no further questions asked". The prospect became my client and we have built a long-term business relationship for many years now.

Helping others cost nothing most times! I was sitting at home when I received a call from a concerned prospect. Her and her husband owned numerous franchised restaurants in the area and she was having a pest control challenge within certain of the restaurant. However, her challenge extended to the mall management's apathetic behavior to her challenge whom she also partly blamed for her situation. A customer had discovered a Cockroach in a plate of food and this caused frustration and embarrassment on the part of the restaurant owners. This discovery was not good for business and the good name of the restaurant. I had decided, without even thinking about it to go out and identify the cause of the problem. I found the problem, took photographs and developed a written report supporting her suspicions that the mall management was neglecting their responsibility regarding pest control. We now service all of her restaurants in the area. I can assure you that prospects will respond to someone who gives before he/she receives as they see a sincere heart and a willingness to serve and to resolve challenges before earning a dime. This shows that you have the prospect's interests at heart and that you are not only in it for the money.

As a salesperson wanting to develop a client base through effective prospecting you must be pro-active at all times and by being pro-active I mean that you must create the action rather than wait to be discovered – MAKE THINGS HAPPEN as they say! The idea is that you should be found guilty of being the best salesperson in your territory in that if you were arrested for being your company's or your business' representative they would have enough evidence to convict you. Whatever your product and/or service when a prospect in your territory has a need for the same then your name should be the first to come to mind. This takes a lot of work but can be achieved using the email and other approaches made to your list of prospects, due to your persistent personal visits into the area and to the prospect (building rapport and trust), because of the local advertising which you are doing and because of the consistent self-promotion program which you manage in the territory assigned to you. Never sit back and allow your competitor to gain ground on you as you must lead and you must be the most well-known salesperson in the territory.

My recommendation is that you develop a Personal Prospecting System ("PPS"). This is a prospecting system that you will develop from day one but "perfect" over a period of time. The system must work with you and for you and must be routine and procedure-based to produce the same response time after time. What do you want to achieve? The answer is simple! PROSPECTS, PROSPECTS AND MORE PROSPECTS! Remember your closing ratio and your goals and the great need, because of these critical factors, to generate a healthy stream of QUALIFIED prospects. The idea is that you want to ultimately develop a productive and profitable client base but most clients start out as prospects first – you need many of these for now! A "PPS" is the best way to produce a steady flow of prospects to keep your "shelves stocked" for future success. The great thing about developing the PPS is while you are developing the much needed prospect lists you are also developing a good referral base. The more people that get to know you and trust you the more they will refer you to their friends and family, and of course, other corporate entities. Referrals produce the highest closing ratio of any source-2:3. This means that for every three referrals you receive you should be able to convert at least two of them to business, and this, a far better option that 10:1 ratio when dealing with prospects having not being referred.

Referrals, in my opinion, benefit both the client and the salesperson. The question is how does it benefit the client? They get the opportunity to help you as compensation so to speak for the great assistance which you have rendered to them over the last while. Clients like to help you and me because they are truly interested in our success. They also help others when they refer you to them. It is hard nowadays to find a salesperson that genuinely cares and that does not disappoint other people. When clients find a professional like you they have no hesitation in recommending you as they know that you will not embarrass them as this is not in you. Your reputation has preceded you and so your clients' will feel safe in allowing you to deal with the people which they recommend – it is called TRUST! Therefore, they also feel that they will help others by putting your name forward as a referral. While they help others they also help themselves in that they take pride in being invited by their friends, family and colleagues to make recommendations of good reliable service providers and suppliers and to give opinions or recommendations on important matters. In many instances recommending someone turns out to be a disaster and one is inevitably embarrassed so it feels great to recommend a professional who will not let you down. When the feedback gets back to the client as to your great service then the joy is compounded. Great job! Clients also develop a sense of belonging. They feel that they belong to your network and a part of the network to which they refer you. Networking is great because people help one another and no one will want to help you more than someone whom you have helped in turn. Being a part of a network that actually works is important and when the client finds this then they feel that they belong and belong to something good and worthwhile. The client is also pleased as they tend to develop a broader knowledge. Depending on the services and/or products offered by your business, and by constant exposure to you, the client will most certainly develop his/her knowledge of whatever you have to offer. Many of the people which you and I deal with are purchasing agents and it is their function to meet with us but in meeting with us they learn all the time. They will learn about services, products and technologies which they, before meeting you, may never even have heard about.

The question then is, maybe more importantly depending on how one looks at the situation, how will the entrepreneur salesperson or salesperson benefit from all of the above? Developing a professional and productive referral base will produce the greatest benefit of all – IMPROVED INCOME! Surely, at the end of the day you have goals, dreams and desires and these must be achieved. The question is then do you want to achieve the hard way with the constant threat of failure or do you want to achieve and assure success by "working smarter and not harder"? Having a constant source of leads which are referrals means that these stand a great chance of turning into business without too much effort and the reason for this is that you and your services have in part been sold by the referring party. Wow! In sales, we simply cannot get better business and this is why I want to encourage you to develop numerous referral sources but you can only do this if you are truly well known in your territory to the point where you are a household name for your services and/or products. You will work hard to develop the territory and your name but once this is done then you will simply put "never look back"! In my previous book I deal with how you arrive at your personal value system and how to set achievable goals for you, the business and your family. In all honesty, I do not know of a better method for you to achieve the goals as you have set out according to the steps as I have shown you. Your own personal knowledge base will grow and be cemented as it stands to reason that the more qualified prospects you deal with the more you will present your product and/or services and the more proficient you will become in what you do. We are dealing with the old principle of "practice makes perfect". The other great thing about developing a professional referral base is that it is easy to talk to people, and to develop long-term business relationships, which have already been sold on doing business with you. You have taken the time to develop a professional reputation for prompt response and a solution based philosophy for the needs and wants of both your clients and the prospects presented to you through your referral base. I cannot tell you how many salespeople and businesses fail because they do not grasp this simple concept of developing productive referral based sources. As an entrepreneur you will need CASH to have a cash flow so your business can grow and this is how you assure yourself of success – DEVELOP REFERRAL BASES! As a salesperson or sales manager, you need to achieve sales targets or quotas so I want to assure you that you will have no problem achieving these if you would just seriously consider my advice and actually do something about it. Territories are not bad for you and they don't restrict you but they force you to work within a confined area for this very reason.

Over the years I worked a program which I have called "sourcing". If you are an entrepreneur salesperson or sales manager then you may want to pay close attention to this simple but effective way of generating quality leads.

It all started for me many years ago, before the information and computer age, when I made an approach to a major gold mining company. The business which I had started focused on providing workplace services to the corporate, industrial and mining industries. The idea was to take over services which were critical but unrelated to the mining house and the goal was to relieve the mine managers of managing unrelated services to their core business which was mining. For example, some of the service offered was a hygiene service, housekeeping service, healthcare service (installation and total management of all washroom products) and so on. We would thus manage all of the unrelated services to core business, which we refer to as "workplace services". When I did my market research on the prospect I had noticed that they were not happy with the current supplier base for these services. I also noticed that (and have seen this many times since) there was a senior manager on the mine who was considered the "god-father". A man whom everyone looked up to and a man used by one and all for any kind of mining related advice including personal, financial, administrative and technical. For the sake of the book I shall refer to him as Mr. McManus. Immediately, and instinctively, I decided to focus all of my attention onto Mr. McManus as my thought was that if I could close him then it would add the credibility I needed in order to secure additional business with the rest of the mine business units which were scattered over a large geographical area.

I can assure you that my goal was not easy to achieve. It took me around six months to get the man to take my call and the only way that I achieved this was to make the call at one-thirty in the morning when he came on shift. "Trevor, I will only have the opportunity to talk to you at this time so if you want to get your message to me then this will be the time or forget it!" I could not reach him via email as there was none and I could not text him as this did not exist at the time either. I only had three forms of communication open to me and it was facsimile ("fax"), the landline and a face to face sales call. I made the call and was on time for the meeting. Mr. McManus was impressed! I was given ten minutes to make my pitch and before I could close for the appointment I heard the news that I had been waiting for. "Trevor," he belted out, "I think that you had better come and see me!" We set the meeting date and time and I made sure that I was not late. The following week I introduced myself to the great man, presented my idea and services to Mr. McManus and the response was as follows: "Trevor, I want you to prove that your services work so how can you make this happen!?" I offered a no obligation (give before you receive) demonstration of a critical service which he had voiced the most concern over. The Hygiene Service is also known to many as a chemical deep clean service and my goal was to prove to my "friend" (he did not know it at that stage) that we were able to sanitize and decontaminate the washrooms and ablution facilities located all over the entire mine-the amount of potential business for this service was mind boggling to say the least. I arranged for one of our service teams to be on the mine and ensured that Mr. McManus was present for the demonstration. He was impressed! I was happy! The response which I received was the best news ever. "Trevor, formulate a proposal and have it on my desk by close of business this Friday!" FANTASTIC NEWS! However, I had not as yet closed the deal and would now have to make the service viable for both parties. When I presented the proposal to the man his response to me was: "When can you start!?" As the service had a monthly cycle we had decided to start at the beginning of the new month which was a week away.

Before I left I asked Mr. McManus if he could arrange with a few of his colleagues to be present for the first service. His answer did not surprise me but was most certainly typical of the man: "Trevor, you are here so that I have less work and can focus on my core business so don't ask me to do your job. Here is a list of all the mine managers so invite them yourself. Oh, by the way, tell them that I recommended you and that they should call me if they have any questions!" I knew then that he liked me and that we could build a long-term business relationship together for many years to come. I had my first contract "signed, sealed and delivered" and the way forward for more business was assured. My goal was to market and sell the service throughout the mine in order to generate the much needed cash-flow for the business to grow and to be financially secure. I invited around fifteen selected mine managers but only two showed up to view the service. This was the first time that I realized that my task was not going to be as easy as I thought. I still needed to promote the services and our business with a view to creating the kind of credibility needed in order to do business with the mine managers who were pretty set in their ways.

After the initial first service I was able to sign two additional contracts taking my total to three service contracts out of a possible fifty-eight. I had a great deal of work to do but saw the end result as a major motivating factor. I once again approached Mr. McManus with an idea which I was hoping that he would buy into. I wanted some time at the next mine managers' meeting in order to present our services and the idea of relieving the managers of spending time on non-essential services so that they can spend more time focusing on mining. I also asked his opinion on another idea which I had and that was promoting the services through a fax approach. I was astounded, he approved of both methods of spreading the "good news" and so started a chain of events which saw me eventually (over time) sign up all fifty-eight business units which took my business to an entirely new level. We finally had cash to manage!

The idea that I would like to leave you with is that when you open up a "source" then you will be able to work on a single source for a while and generate new business almost daily. It would stand to reason then that the more sources that you develop the busier you will become and that you will most certainly be in a strong position to fulfil your goals, dreams and desires. As a sales manager then you would be right to ask as to how this may be rolled out in light of the fact that certain sources may cross geographical boundaries? Obviously this would make things complicated but most certainly not unsolvable in practice. The idea for you would be to "cement" the geographical territory as "first prize". Then the option of developing sources within the territory must be discussed. For instance, if I have been allocated territory "A" and want to develop a source within the same then I would need to identify a Home Office/Head Office located in my territory. It just so happens that the Home Office for Wal-Mart is situated in my territory while the Head Office for McDonalds is located in the next territory ("B") over. As the Home Office is located in my territory I will have all the rights to develop the business for Wal-Mart in the entire geographical area covered by the company and my colleague retains the right to develop business with McDonalds. It is therefore critical in order for the salesperson to develop a productive business relationship to be seen as the sole contact for services and/or products for the company. The source can now be professionally cultivated. While you may choose to make any and all changes to the above in order to make this work for you, in your peculiar situation, but the idea of developing productive sources must not be negotiated and must be a part of developing your business at all cost.

A personal prospecting system will force the entrepreneur salesperson to develop more professional work habits and personal habits as he/she determines to provide a service on unsurpassed levels within the industry. The more well-known you become in the territory the more pressure you will be under to perform both for the company and personally and this is a good thing. As when you grow professionally so does the prospects trust factor of you. The more the prospect and client trusts you the easier it is to do business with anyone needing your services and/or products within the allocated territory. You will also notice as this growth takes place so shall the client base under your management. The goal with a prospecting system is just that as it must grow you, your business and the client base, and this, all in order of you achieving your personal and family goals. When you are assured of a continuous flow of sales leads, largely due to your personal prospecting system, you grow as a professional and in confidence which in turn has a serious positive affect on your self-esteem and self-image. When you become confident (not arrogant) you exude professionalism and success, and people, would rather do business with a successful person than do business with the unprofessional salesperson. I know of no other way, within the business and sales environment, to boost your self-confidence than when you are constantly referred by someone who trusts you as a person and your professional abilities.

## Sourcing for Sources

When considering developing a source, or sources, as you must do if you are to succeed in business and/or sales, you have to understand the concept of the term "source" as used in the sales environment. Source as referred to in our context must be taken to mean a cause of something with recurring and growing benefits-in this case qualified sales leads. In a sense also the originator of multiple business deals and the development of long-term productive business relationships or the starting point for the development of future business with a clear view to promoting a positive cash flow. This then will epitomize the term that "nothing happens without a sale" in that a sale cannot take place without a good lead and good leads cannot be generated from thin air but they come from a source who is interested in your success and their good reputation. In other words a source must be the beginning of something good or it will not work. The easy way to identify a successful source is to ask, if by entering into a business relationship with this person, will it lead to a once-off single sale or is there the opportunity of multiple sales within the business units attached to the relationship (prospect/client)? For instance, you may make a sale at an ABC company but they are a single entity with only one branch. However, developing business with Wall-Mart has massive long-term and multiple opportunities for repeat and expanded business. Which one would help you to achieve your personal and business goals quicker? ABC Company (single entity) then will not be considered a source but Wal-Mart (multiple entities) will most certainly be considered a source. My advice to you then in this regard would be to secure multiple sources as soon as is possible and spend your time working those.

While there is a multitude of ways within which to source prospects and sources I want to list just a few in order to get you thinking in the right direction:

1. Current client base.
2. Past buyers-no longer clients but are now viable prospects yet again.
3. Acquaintances-interested in your success.
4. Family members-interested in your success.
5. Company leads-quality leads generated by company advertising and promotion.
6. Third party influences – "someone who knows someone".
7. Associations – join industry related associations and network.
8. Corporate contacts – great for generating new sources.
9. Fellow salespeople – those not associated with your industry but come into contact with prospects looking for your services and/or products.
10. Business neighbors of your current client base.
11. Vendor lists – large companies have a preferred supplier list get a copy if you can.
12. Compliment slips – as discussed above (graduate from this to working sources as soon as you possibly can).

## Conclusion

Prospecting is the beginning and ending of the sales cycle. What I mean here is that you must never forget about asking for a referral once you have completed a successful close. My approach to ensuring a continuous stream of prospects is simple – I ASK FOR THEM! Once I have closed my priority is to ensure that all runs smooth with the installation, the service and/or the product delivery. Once I am satisfied that the client is happy I will ensure satisfaction by making yet another approach to the client. I will only do this if I am sure that the client is satisfied, and if not, then I will ensure complete satisfaction BEFORE making an approach. The goal will be to eventually say something like this: "John, I would just like to again say a big thank you to you for placing your trust in me as this relates to our business providing the workplace services to your company. May I ask are you happy with what we have been able to deliver to date?" The client will hopefully respond in the following way: "Trevor, yes, I was surprised as to how smooth and professional the entire process has been and I have been receiving positive feedback from several of our staff-thank you!" I usually see this as a sign to close for a referral.

"John, I appreciate the positive feedback and compliment from you, so may I ask you a question that would help me? I have no doubt that you are well connected and want to know whether you would be kind enough to refer me to a few of these good people so that I may be of service to them as well?"

I am yet to have a satisfied client say NO to me and have learned over the years that as long as I have fulfilled my promises the client is only too happy to help me as he feels that he/she can use the opportunity as a way to giving me something back for my good service. Your business and career is in your hands. If you are able and willing to understand the importance and the urgency of prospecting then you will be assured of success; however, if not, then you will join the millions who have gone before you in despair and failure as this relates to developing a successful business and a sales career. If you fail to prospect then you will fail and this is not conjecture this is a fact. With the concept of geographical farming you are assigned an exclusive territory belonging to you, and the instruction is that you manage the same professionally at all costs. The territory gives you the right and you have been given a mandate to grow the area for the good of the business and/or company which you represent. This chapter teaches you the concept and importance of prospecting so that you can achieve the above goal with ease.

The goal therefore is that you become a household name within the territory assigned to you and the only way to achieve this is for you to promote yourself and the services and/or products which you are selling. Remember, you need to do this so well that if there is a need in your territory for your services and/or products then the ONLY name that should come to mind is YOURS! Never allow a low self-esteem make you afraid to prospect as this will mean failure which will further lower your self-image and destroy any confidence which you may have. Always understand that effective prospecting and self-promotion is what will separate you from the mundane and unprofessional entrepreneurs and salespeople out there – the ones that ultimately fail. Your ability to place prospecting in the correct perspective as this relates to the sales cycle will ensure that you become a "lean mean money making machine".

# Chapter 12

## Competitor Advantages
### *$ell what makes your business stand out!*

**Introduction**

"Ignorance is [not] bliss" in this instance and to go about business believing that a competitor has no influence upon your business is tantamount to behaving like an ostrich – head in the sand. Some competitors are stronger than others while your biggest rival may not be the biggest supplier or service provider available to prospects in any given marketplace. It is imperative that no matter how many competitors your business faces you will need to know them all. As a salesperson managing a territory the same thing will apply as your competitive advantages may just be the thing that gets you ahead of the game. While you will need to know as much as you can about the competition you must also understand that there will be differences between the way you do business and the way the competitor does business – you must clearly identify these for the purposes of "neutralizing" these when called upon to do so.

Competitors, in a sense are considered rivals, and while you may come across your competitor and even have coffee with them there will always remain a sense that you are on opposing sides. Competitors consider themselves rivals and understand that they compete for business almost every day. A competitor may be responsible for you not achieving your sales quota or revenue budgets as an entrepreneur. The competitor may be seen as the greatest hurdle to your success so I admonish you to take these people seriously. A competitor will challenge you for the same business and will have no mercy on you or your business as he/she will not have your weakness in that they will most certainly view you as an adversary or an opponent. Let me assure you that despite appearances the competitor will consume you at any moment given half a chance to do so and this is why I say ALWAYS be careful and ALWAYS be aware of who your competitors are and how they operate.

The idea in knowing your competitor in every critical aspect is simply that you want to gain and ensure that you have a consistent advantage within the sales arena. The advantage though must be intelligent and not based upon an unintellectual approach and attitude toward discovering the competitor. When identifying the differences between you and the competitor you must find the benefits in doing so with a view to the discovery leading to tangible "assets" which can be used to gain the competitive advantage in the field. Anything which you find out about the competitor must assist you and help you (and aid you if you will) to deal with objections which are raised by the prospect as this has to do with what your competitor can do and what they cannot do and what they are in a position to offer and what they are not. The ultimate goal then of discovering the competitor's strengths and weaknesses has got to be your ability to use the knowledge in your favor when called upon to do so, and this new found knowledge must show clear gain at the close of each sale. The knowledge must be used to exploit weaknesses and to manipulate your strengths to your advantage for profit.

Many books have been written on competitive behavior in the market place; however, we do not need to become overcomplicated in our approach. As an entrepreneur salesperson or salesperson you will not be (for now) sitting in the boardroom with some high flying marketing managers discussing the technical side of the competition. The knowledge that you require is important but not overly complicated in any way. Our theme throughout this book is not to overcomplicate our lives and while this topic could very well become that we will do our best to avoid the same. The idea then, in order to sell effectively, and to build our respective businesses, we must become familiar with the advantages and disadvantages of competitor services and/or products. In fact, for the sake of our discussion we will focus our attention on the following competitive advantages:

1. Features.
2. Benefits.
3. Company image.
4. Services and/or products.

I have to mention again that it is so much easier today to discover what the competitor is up to than it has ever been as they place all the relevant information on a website for all to see. However, there is still some critical information that you will not be able to find out, and this, will have to be sourced elsewhere. For instance, most competitors will not reveal the company price structure on the website or a list of its key clients. I recommend that you consider developing spread sheets (which may be altered as the competitor details change from time to time) called Competitor Information Sheets (or whatever name you decide upon). You will use these sheets in order to compile all available intelligence as this relates to your key competitors. These CIS's are working documents and must be available and updated for use at a moment's notice. There is no point in developing the sheets and then you never look at them ever again. Your competitors will change product, service, price, marketing and distribution all the time and you need to be ready to adjust for these changes at a moment's notice so it stands to reason that you will not be able to respond if you have lost touch with changing developments.

While the following list is by no means exhaustive competitor information may be obtained from:

1. Websites.
2. Suppliers.
3. Friendly and loyal clients.
4. Other experienced and industry unrelated salespeople.
5. Newspapers and trade magazines.
6. Credit reports.

I always make it a point to encourage my clients to help me and I can assure you, barring the exception to the rule, I receive the kind of help I need. For instance some of my clients have no problem, based upon the loyalty between us, in handing me entire proposals of my competitors and this includes the current pricing structures, brochures and the like. I also have a policy with prospects in that should they receive a better competitor pricing offer then I will match the price but do one better by offering a further ten percent discount on the competitor proposal. In order to qualify for this deal I insist on a copy of the competitor proposal. This way I keep in touch with competitor pricing and any other pertinent information which appears on the proposal or in the enclosed package of information.

Suppliers are also a good source of competitor information as many times they supply the same competitors with product which we also use. An "innocent" question to the delivery guys from time to time will not hurt but may guide you as to whether the competitor is purchasing more product than you or whether they are having payment trouble or even developing a bad reputation in the marketplace-something to take advantage of.

Salespeople who have worked for the company before and salespeople in general can be a wealth of information as this relates to what they know about competitors. A friend or an acquaintance may be working for a competitor and is not happy. I have had a situation where a competitor treated its staff so bad that they were sending me information even though I did not request the same from them. Once your organization grows you will teach your experienced sales staff to always be on the lookout for information that will keep you abreast of what competitors are up to. This information must be brought back to the office for the very reason of updating the CIS. Salespeople are a wealth of information but they must be taught to understand the importance of securing competitor information and then getting this back to the office.

Newspapers and trade magazines contain company advertorials and/or editorials, and these, more often than not reveal new products and new strategies which are announced by the competitor. While they may not divulge the pricing structure (or they might) for the proposed new service or product they will reveal all the necessary features and benefits enabling you to consider and counter these. They may also reveal sensitive information regarding their shareholders and the future direction of the business and how this may affect you and your business.

Websites contain just about everything which you will need to know about a company, including at times, their annual audited financial statements which is public record if they are a listed company. You will pick up as to the local, national or international footprint so that you can have a clear understanding of how their footprint compares to your target market. You may be able to pick up the amount of salespeople which you are up against and how this will affect your sales and marketing efforts. Credit reports are usually available to everyone but not in all cases. However, should you be able to do a credit check on a competitor then you must understand that this information is confidential but can be used to help you understand how the competitor company is managed financially. One of the goals of gathering all of the information as has been discussed above is to understand the strengths and weaknesses of the size of your business as opposed to that of the competitor.

For instance, being a medium-sized business within any particular industry competing against major competitors may have the following benefits:

1. More flexible than smaller competitors.
2. More flexible and more personal than larger competitors.
3. More lenient on passing credits than many larger companies – too much "red tape".
4. The owner/s may handle complaints personally.
5. Service complaints are handled in-house and not through a foreign call center.

In a competitive environment everybody seems to know everybody and it may be that prospects know your competitors better than you do. You should never let this happen to you! Be awake, be knowledgeable and be ready always to give a reasonable explanation when the competitor is brought up as an objection. Prospects enjoy watching salespeople squirm when they mention the competition but the professional takes things in stride and has confidence due to pre-existing knowledge and understanding of virtually every aspect of his/her competition. You are not called professional for nothing and your research and intimate knowledge of each competitor is why you are placed in this category. It may very well be that the prospect may prefer doing business with a corporate entity and you will need to overcome this objection or you will not close the sale. While I will help you to overcome this objection in the following paragraph I need you to know that there are numerous other objections that may be raised as this relates to your business versus any one of your competitors who are competing for the same business. As an example then let's deal with the objection that is raised with regards to the size of your business as opposed to that of your corporate competitor.

The first thing that you will need to convince the prospect of is that as a medium-sized business you tend to be situated between the small business and the large corporates. It is your feeling that you are better positioned for two very good reasons (1) Your business is at the least more reliable than the smaller competitor (2) Your business is most certainly more personal and flexible than that of the larger competitor. For instance, and I must add that I don't mind going up against a large corporate, as currently, one of my biggest competitors is a large national corporate. We take more business away from this large conglomerate than from anyone else. The reason that this happens, if you would ask the prospect (now client) is two-fold: (1) overpriced (2) poor service delivery. Larger corporates become "top heavy" and develop complex systems which make satisfying the client's needs cumbersome and time consuming. In a medium-sized business (or a smaller business for that matter) reaction times to a service complaint are so much quicker, and in fact, control over the quality of service provided far supersedes that of the larger competitor – this is a distinct competitive advantage so never forget this and use it to deal with any objections that are raised. The other clear advantage is price! The larger competitor has major overheads which need to be met on a monthly basis and this pressures the company to force its price upward. Some of your prospects may want to go for the "big name" of an organization without thinking things through. High price for poor service, and this, all for the sake of a BIG name! This is not good business at all! In order to have the big name corporate to respond to a service call may take days depend upon the "red tape" in place. However, same day service will apply to a small to medium-sized organization where they still care about the client's satisfaction and where they are still motivated to retain the business at all costs.

Have you ever tried to get a credit note out of a large business for anything at all? The system is so complex that it could take "forever" to accomplish. Generally a decision to grant a credit in a medium sized company is done in an instant and the task is performed the very same day if not the very same hour. There are no complex systems in place and if there are systems in place they remain client/customer friendly to the point where the transaction can take place soonest. The other great thing about dealing with a medium to small sized company is that it is not difficult to deal with the owner and in many instances it is the owner who will deal with the client's complaints and it is the owner who will resolve any issues to the satisfaction of the client. The owner is usually highly motivated to ensure that the client is kept happy at all times as he/she understands that the client is the most important person in the organization. The owner also understands that when growing a business it is difficult to gain new business and when this has been accomplished the owner becomes highly motivated to hold onto each new client and will ensure that the client is kept happy. The entire motivation and client management philosophy is more client satisfaction based as opposed to the client getting lost in a quagmire of systems and red tape. The customer service department, in most instances, is operated as an in-house department, and thus, complaints are managed on a more personal basis. A larger competitor nowadays is all about cost saving due to their large appetite for consuming money for massive overheads and many have now opted to have their procurement, payments and services department "offshore" compounding the ability to satisfy the needs of clients. This is vital information so you will need to discover the process followed by your biggest business rivals and exploit the weaknesses as and when needed.

Some other areas to consider when dealing with competitor objections is the impersonal voice messaging systems being employed by some of the larger competitors. For instance a client makes a call and the phone is answered by a voice recording. The voice recording asks the client to choose a number in order to go through to the correct department and once the choice is made goes through to the correct department only to find out that they will have to leave a voice mail as "all of the operators are currently busy". How frustrating! Does this approach make anyone feel that they are important? No! To me personally I feel that this is a distinct competitive advantage should your business be able to take its calls using a human voice on the receiving end of the client's call, and in my case, I use this a great deal when confronted with a competitor objection. This is why it is important to know what your competitors are doing, and in particular, in critical areas such as have been mentioned here. How long does it take for a larger company to prepare proposals? In many instances prospects have to wait for days in order to receive proposals for product or services offered. In a smaller organization everyone is so focused on the growth of the business that there is a high motivation to get proposals into the hands of the prospect as soon as is possible but generally within twenty-four hours and in many instances (as in my business) the same day for certain products or services. The point here is that the smaller business understands that the prospect cannot make a decision if he/she does not have a proposal containing the figures. Figures are important as this is the only way for the prospect to "compare apples with apples". On the other hand the large corporates don't seem to worry when the prospect receives the proposal as they are too busy with the day to day challenges of running an oversized conglomerate. Who would you rather do business with? When a client needs to make a change to his/her order or service contract it could take weeks in some cases to affect such changes when you are dealing with a larger supplier. Once again, I must point out the complexities and red tape of some organizations which in essence is strangling their businesses and frustrating their clients to no end. As a smaller business this does not usually happen and queries, complaints, change in order quantities and contract changes are usually dealt with speedily and without delay all leading to a pleasant working relationship between client, customer and the supplier or service provider. Finally, you will need to point out a common fact in most cases and that is in a small or medium-sized business, the client receives more personal attention and is treated more as "family" and as the most important person in the business almost all of the time.

While there are many areas which you may need to focus on when gathering competitive information, and while I shall give you a list of suggestions to follow, my feeling is to reduce your requirements down to about ten critical points. For more complex deals and products you may have to dig just a little deeper. Some suggestions are:

1. Pricing.
2. Payment terms.
3. Contract/Agreement terms and conditions.
4. Hidden costs such as call-out fees.
5. Installation/delivery turn-around time.
6. Response times to service and delivery complaints.
7. Variances in installation and delivery charges.
8. Quality guarantees.
9. Product warrantees.
10. Services/products offered in comparison.
11. Type of service support.
12. Policy on collections-invoices and statements.
13. Major client base.
14. Reputation as to image and ethics.
15. General strengths and weaknesses.
16. Years in business.
17. Overall staff numbers.
18. Number of salespeople.
19. Method/s of selling and techniques.
20. Current advertising program – "where, what and how much".
21. Financial stability.

## Conclusion

We have dealt with handling objections in depth in this book; however, always be ready to give an answer to the prospect that is determined to compare you with another competitor. Not understanding the competitor who operates within your target market is not very smart, and this, in particular, if the prospect knows more about the competitors than you do. I want to encourage you to understand that nothing must be left to chance in the selling cycle and that as a professional you must anticipate the most unusual of objections. Knowing the weaknesses and the strengths of your competitors is vital and these need to be compared against those of your own company's. Identifying the weaknesses and strengths in other businesses will help you to make changes to your own and the idea then would be to make you stronger and more appealing to the prospect.

Knowing what someone else is doing is not a new phenomenon in the world but rather the activity has been going on for years. While we are not dealing with industrial espionage in the least we are talking about you knowing your competitor's business so that you can grow and protect yours. Countries spy on one another all the time and again I am not advocating that you "spy" on your competitor but you simply must understand the basic differences between you and them. Many of the differences are public knowledge so nothing illegal should or must take place in order for you to gather the same.

We want to be able to give the differences between our businesses and that of any competitor which we face so we must know the features of products and/or services offered by the competitor. What are the products and/or services-features? What are the benefits-what features may do? Understand your competitor's company image. The largest of businesses in the world may have a bad reputation for providing poor quality products and service and this is not good for their image. You could exploit this if you know how to do so without offending the prospect. It is also critical to understand all products and services offered by the competitor who includes a variety of services, whether sub-contractors are used and whether multiple services are provided under one umbrella.

"Mind other people's business so that you are able to mind yours"

# Chapter 13

# Client Knowledge
## *Understanding who you are $elling to*

**Introduction**

The moment of truth has arrived. You are now ready to present your product or your service to a prospective customer/client. The question here is, are you really ready to make an approach to the prospect? What do you know about the person we all call the decision maker? In fact, is the person that you are about to communicate with the actual decision maker? Not sure!? The idea is then that you make sure that whomsoever you are about to approach with a view to sales is in fact the person who can make your day with the kind of decision which will enhance your business. What you don't need is to spend a great deal of time introducing the person in front of you to your business and products and/or services only to find out that you are dealing with nothing more than a personal assistant who has to refer your discussion to a more senior manager-the decision maker.

In many businesses the inability of the entrepreneur salesperson to professionally target a prospect makes the difference between sales success and failure. When I refer to the word TARGET what am I actually referring to? This is also something which you and every other entrepreneur salesperson ought to consider and understand. It goes without saying though that the end result must justify the means. By this I mean that if you and I expect to reap sales rewards then we must be prepared to do all in our power to ensure that we have a successful close at the appropriate time. The more you put in up front by way of research of the prospective company and the decision maker the easier it will be to ensure additional business time after time. There are some businesses whose product/service may not need a significant amount of professionalism and research but we are not talking about the local hot dog stand we are talking about your business, and if, your business is in fact the local hot dog stand then all you have to do is to make enough hot dogs and be in the right place with the right amount of feet passing you by and you are all set for success. Most businesses do not operate at this level of simplicity though and the sooner you understand this the sooner you can get the research complete and the sooner you are then in a position to make a professional approach. The difference here that I would like to point out to you is that there is an "approach" and then there is a "professional approach". The professional approach is calculated and researched with one goal in mind and that is to secure a CLEAN AND SUCCESSFUL CLOSE!

I would like to draw your attention to two keys words which most certainly apply in context with this chapter: (1) FOCUS; (2) RESEARCH.

**Focus as a definition**

Please note, do not lose sight of the "focus" of our discussion in this chapter and that is doing all to understand the prospective client which you are about to make a professional sales call on.

In understanding the prospect then we must be guilty so to speak of focusing on what is important to our successful conclusion of the sales attempt. We need to discover very specific things about the person and the company making up our prospect BEFORE we make the initial approach. James Bond 007 is usually handed a file containing all the relevant information about his next assignment. He never seems to go in "blind" and why should he – he is a professional after all? Before you and I take on our next "assignment" we need to focus on what matters and thus we must concentrate on all aspects that could ensure a smoother and a sure close. We need to pay direct attention to all aspects of what will impress the prospect and make the prospect want to do business with you no matter what it is. The term focus thus means that you and I need to fix our business attention or home in on all relevant aspects of what will make the prospect change suppliers and/or make a decision to do business with you. To focus means to "spotlight"! To focus also means to "aim at", to think about, to "center on" and to MAINLY "look at" within the sales environment.

## Research as a definition

When we research our prospective client we focus on the relevant information only. However, in the focusing process we need to ask very pertinent questions with regards to the prospective company and decision maker and the answers to these questions are generally answered through an activity called RESEARCH. Research will thus mean for the sake of our discussion, and common sense, the act or actions of investigation into, an enquiry into and a searching for relevant information on a very specific (focus) subject or subject matter. Research will also then mean to "study" someone or something within our context. We want to "probe" and to even go as far as to say "explore" all the possibilities which would ensure professionalism and success during the closing phases of each sale. The result of the focus and the research actions must surely be to obtain the necessary information about the prospect in order for you and me to analyze all information at hand with a view to determining our chances of success and/or whether we want to do business with the prospect or not as they may not fit into the target market parameters set as a viable prospect for the business model. We also use the information gathered then to qualify the prospect as an "A" prospect or a prospect that you will not waste your time on. For instance, during your focus and research stages of prospecting you discover that the prospect has a poor reputation when it comes to paying bills on time. Do you feel that this will qualify them as a potential client? Is this the kind of business that you want to build in always "running after" your clients/customers for payment? No! Of course not, so focus and research may both qualify or disqualify a prospect. When you disqualify then it means that your focus and research has led you to believe that the prospect will not make a good fit and that this has now saved you time; however, on the other hand your information may have led you to believe that the prospect will be perfect for your business and this will give you much needed confidence as you make the sales approach and then ultimately the close-SUCCESS THROUGH FOCUS AND RESEARCH!!!

Now, the question is "what to research and what to focus on?"

The answer to this question will be determined by your product and/or service offering surely? For instance, let's assume that we have two service related entrepreneurs. The one has a service offering the cleaning of kitchen extractors and canopies while the other provides services providing washroom rental products. When cleaning a kitchen extractor we generally assume that these only exist in restaurants but in effect this is not true. Kitchen extractors are also prevalent in the mining industry and industrial and commercial kitchens and research will reveal this fact to you and me. It may be that our research will reveal that restaurant owners may not be good payers whereas management of the mining, industrial and commercial kitchens tend to pay as per the terms and conditions agreed upon. In fact, our research may also reveal (not to say that this is the case as we are just using this as an example), that franchise related kitchens have owners who are more responsible in abiding by payment terms than those that is privately owned. We have to then research the culture of paying bills on time and as per the agreed upon terms of payment. This is a big thing in a small business as when you cannot get your money in on time you will face cash flow difficulties.

When researching for a business that predominantly provides washroom rental products to the commercial and industrial industries the idea would be to ensure that they actually have sufficient washrooms in order to make the service viable. Do they have a culture of cleanliness and/or of promoting a healthy and hygienic washroom environment amongst employees or don't they care either way. You and I want to do business, in this instance, with companies that have a caring culture as to approach a business who has management that don't care at all will not help us in a successful close. Research has thus saved us time and frustration and will allow us to focus on our target market.

While the merits of following a "focus and research" strategy may be debated for a long time my goal here is to get you to understand a simple fact, and that is, that you should know as much about the prospective company and company representative (decision maker) as is humanly possible BEFORE making the initial approach for a meeting. While there are many, many parameters for research and focus, and these will be determined by industry, product and service (to mention just a few) I do want to give the following direction and examples in order to assist you in arriving at a set of parameters that may apply to your business and sales environment.

Before we discuss the area's most likely to be covered during the focus and research stages of the pre-selling cycle I want to ask you a question which answer will undoubtedly help us to keep focus on why so much work is necessary prior to the initial approach. The question is this: "Who do most entrepreneur salespeople believe is the most important person in their organization? I have had many answers given to me when I have asked this very fundamental of business questions. Some entrepreneurs have suggested that they are the most important person in their business and some have suggested their spouses and families are. I have had some say that the bank and/or the business accountant is the most important person in their business while others have suggested lawyers, sales staff, services staff and even administration staff. I have even had some well-meaning entrepreneurs impress upon me how important their suppliers are to their business. However, not one of the abovementioned answers is correct as the only correct answer within our context is as follows.

## THE MOST IMPORTANT PERSON IN ANY ORGANIZATION IS THE CLIENT/CUSTOMER!

Your understanding of this will be revealed by the way you treat them and the way that you focus on them and research them from day one. I truly believe that the research and focus phase adds a new dimension to customer/client relationship even before a single call or meeting takes place. When you know your prospect better than they know you they will sense this during your first meeting. You will be seen as someone who is genuine, who cares and who has a clear understanding of which it is that you are dealing with. This understanding and caring must not only come from your research into new business prospects but also of the current/existing client base doing business with your company on a day to day basis.

Thus, the entrepreneur salesperson must review and discuss with additional sales staff that may be added to the business, and all other relevant staff, the research and focus results of all current clients which form a part of the current client/customer base. In fact, I would go as far as to say that all staff, at all times, should be well aware of who it is that they are dealing with whether in person, on the telephone or by any other electronic means. Should you be fortunate to see your business grow to the point where you appoint a sales manager then this should be impressed upon him/her as a basic fundamental part of the job description. As an entrepreneur you may say "nobody does this" and "nobody cares this much" and I will say to you that if you hope to grow your business and compete against the BIG BOYS at some stage then it would behoove you to instill some long-lasting good CRM in your business from the foundation days. The idea is to separate yourself from the mundane in sales and to stand out as a company that truly understands that the most important person in your organization, EVER, has got to be the CUSTOMER/CLIENT.

When territories are established and new salespeople are taken on to manage these then it will be the first duty of the entrepreneur salesperson or the sales manager to go through each and every current client outlining and impressing a fundamental business fact: "We know our clients/customers and we know them well".

Each client should be reviewed when it comes to sales potential, by service and/or product by size and Dollar amount. In each territory the question of local and national trends should be determined through research-the trend up or down and why? The following question must ALWAYS be asked when considering each customer: "Is it possible for sales to these customers or clients to be increased by simply leveraging the current relationship to date?" Are there other branches locally or nationally? What if we added new services? What if we expanded on current services? What services and/or products is the client looking to add? Do we provide these additional services? Why? Why not? Do we want to take on these new offerings or not, if not, then why not?

The entrepreneur salesperson or the sales manager must analyze each client and/or prospective customer once the focus and research activities have been completed. The goal here should always be to enhance new business through the current client base while seeking to grow the new business base with quality new customers who pay on time. During the analyzing phase some of the following pertinent questions need to be asked and then discussed.

1. Who does the buying in the organization? The idea here is to understand who you are dealing with so you want to understand her reputation for doing open and honest business. What are her expectations of a supplier or service provider? Discover all of the demands which such a person would place on you and your ability to accommodate her needs as a person and personality.

2. What is the best time to reach the decision maker? Remember, these people consider themselves "important" and will more than likely employ the use of a gatekeeper. Generally a decision maker is a high achiever and in saying this they tend to work abnormal (to some of us) hours which means that they are more at the office than at home. When working hours start, believe it or not, calls usually go through to a gatekeeper of sorts but BEFORE and AFTER working hours (don't forget lunchtimes) you may have the opportunity to make personal contact without any problem at all if your contact is by mobile or landline.

3. You may want to make contact with the gatekeeper and ask pertinent questions about the decision maker's likes and dislikes regarding the way she/he conducts business. For instance, meetings with salespeople are strictly reserved for Friday and Wednesday mornings BEFORE 12h00. She will not tolerate you walking in unannounced or without a set meeting time as was pre-arranged. If you arrive late she will show you the gate!

4. If possible, discover his/her personality. What I am talking about here is the character and nature of the person. The temperament, the disposition and individual identity of the decision maker. You may receive this information directly from the decision maker (if you are professional enough when asking the questions) or it may be better for you to allow the gatekeeper to talk to you. Most gatekeepers are great people

and will do almost anything for you except not put you through to the decision maker most times when calling for a meeting date. But talk they will and help you they may more often than not.

5. If you have developed a decent relationship with the decision maker then discuss pertinent and related "hot-buttons" if any. It may be a subject/topic that will arouse a strong reaction from the person such as "poor service" or "false promises by salespeople". You will want to discover what the hot-buttons are and then do your best to stay away from these at all costs.

6. Discover company buying policies and procedures. For instance, do they go out on tender or do they require three estimates/quotations at all times? What is the turnaround time for decisions?

7. You will want to know as to who the lowest and highest ranking individual is that is involved in the decision making process. Some companies have spending authority limits so if your estimate is above the threshold of your decision maker then in this case he/she cannot be determined to be the actual decision maker and you will need to change strategy.

8. Inquire as to the prospects current credit challenges and corporate culture. Do they require unreasonable credit (i.e., sixty days from date on statement)? Does their corporate culture show fiscal responsibility and do they settle suppliers as per the agreed upon terms and conditions?

9. Has there been or is there a negative or positive attitude or perception toward your business? Your research must lead you to both aspects if at all possible and a means of correction if the result has been negative.

10. If there has been a past relationship or an association, and the prospect or client has been disappointed, then you will want to know how and why. Until you discover this you will not be able to move forward and understanding this will also give you the opportunity to investigate the claim and to come back with an acceptable solution.

11. Does the client or prospect have any special challenges, problems or needs that you could use to successfully close? A

current service provider not measuring up? Products being delivered late and sometimes not at all? These may be the very reason/s you conclude business – NEED SATISFACTION SELLING (as a reminder).

12. What competitive services and/or products are currently being used or provided? If you are to expand your business with a current client or customer then you will need to know what services you can add. As you may be making an approach to a new business client then it would also be good to know what services they currently use and how this will fit into your current service offering. Both sides will also provide a dollar value which will assist you to determine the client/customer hierarchy ("A", "B", "C" etc.). The goal will obviously be to gain the business currently being provided by the competitor in the long term. If at all possible try to get the competitor pricing structures for the various services currently being paid for by the client – ask for an invoice/statement and/or a service contract/agreement.

13. Is there an existing agreement or contract in place? This is important as in order to do business with the prospect or existing client (if you want to add a new service or product) they will have to be free of contractual obligations first. I have seen salespeople do the full sales pitch only to be told by the prospect "sorry but we are locked into a three year agreement with your competitor". The idea is to get this information BEFORE you make the approach hence the dire need for a focus and a research strategy with all prospects and the existing client base. You cannot do business with a business if they are locked into a contract/agreement unless the client makes an approach to the competitor for a "contract buy-out" and this will not happen very often at all.

14. Is the client or prospect's business growing? Adding GROWING businesses to your portfolio of clients' means that you will be adding quality customers to your portfolio of clients. Management who grow their businesses usually knows what they are doing and what you want to do is to get your business to grow in tandem with your successful clients/customers. In a sense you "link" or "attach" your

business growth to that of your successful clients as when they grow it stands to reason that they will require additional product and/or services – YOU BENEFIT!

15. Who or what is the driving force behind the success of the business? This is the kind of person that you may want to have a cup of coffee with or invite out for a meal and your focus should be to show an honest and an open interest in both the person and the methods employed for success. Who knows? It may very well be that you learn something and apply the principle/s into your own business as if it works for one who says that it may not work for all? The greatest benefit though, for you and your business, is the confidence which you will come away with knowing that you will develop a business relationship with a client who has clear vision for continued growth and stability – HE WILL PAY THE BILLS!

16. Do the prospective company PAY THE BILLS ON TIME? You may say "wow, how many more times are you going to harp on clients/customers paying the bills on time?" When you "have more month at the end of your money" then you will thank me for pushing you to ALWAYS consider the clients who are able to pay. You can have a great relationship with your customers and get in great orders but if they don't pay you on time then the pressure will become unbearable and this type of poor payment habit may cost you your business. You MUST do business with businesses that PAY THEIR BILLS ON TIME! Do NOT do business with businesses that are late, poor or non-payers no matter who they are and no matter how great their orders are.

I want to also suggest to you as the entrepreneur salesperson (or your sales manager if you have already appointed such a person) should develop a clear list of prospective clients/customers which match your target market within any given territory. The idea then of developing such a list is that your focus and research becomes more organized and that one quadrant will be researched and worked at a time until the territory has been covered. NEVER lose such lists that have been developed so save them on the server or on the cloud or on the moon for all I care but SAVE THEM. Once you have developed these lists by whatever means then you MUST ensure that these lists are maintained, and by maintained, I mean that these need to be updated and upgraded on a continued and consistent basis in order to ensure their "current" status. Do not keep outdated client lists as these become an exercise in both futility and frustration for any salesperson managing a territory.

Lists such as described above must include the following key factors:

1. Decision maker/s name/s and titles and position within the company.
2. Company and decision maker/s contact information such as: (1) Landline number (2) Mobile number (3) Email address (4) Physical Street addresses of Home/Head Office and associated branches and/or businesses (5) Any other pertinent information regarding the ability to contact the prospect/client/customer.

Again, you may say "don't you give up?" No! This is why I will ONCE AGAIN take the opportunity to impress upon you, only for your own good I assure you my friend, you simply MUST believe me when I tell you and encourage you to discover the decision maker's name and details. The act of identifying the true decision maker must be done as soon as is possible during the process of setting up the abovementioned lists and a constant effort will be required in order to keep these names and positions current at all times. I have seen so many times the frustration of entrepreneur salespeople, sales managers and salespeople in that they do a full presentation of their services and products only to be told that a decision cannot be made as the entire decision making process is in the hands of some other person. What a complete waste of time and money! This type of poor (or non-existent) research mentality will result in a great deal of frustration, and will, if allowed to persist will result in the total demotivation of the sales person, and even more so, the entrepreneur.

While I understand that we have all come out of the dark ages, and that many forms of recording information is present today, I do want to encourage you to consider placing each prospect and client on cards or even files containing the pertinent and important information only. One color card for existing clients/customers and another color card for prospective clients/customers. However, you may think that this is just a little archaic so you will find a way to accomplish the above in a more modern manner and this is alright as long as it is done. The idea is that the lists are available at a moment's notice and that they are ACCURATE. As you grow as an entrepreneur and as your sales force grows with you ensure that all client lists are protected at all times and include in any employment agreement/contract the fact that ownership of client lists will rest with the employer and must be returned IN FULL (without these being copied in any form) prior to departure from your business.

## Conclusion

Now that you have read this chapter and understand the importance of focused research on those companies and decision makers whom you will choose to do business with (target market) may I ask you one more time: "Who is the most important person in YOUR organization!?" Your answer simply MUST BE the CLIENT OR CUSTOMER!

The one thing that I am sure that you will understand as I do and that is that research parameters will change from time to time as the territory evolves and grows. The parameters will also change when your target market undergoes a "shift" and when it expands to suite the growing needs and changes of your prospects and or customers. YOU need to understand the parameter changes in the needed and ongoing research and adapt to these. Above all, ensure that the parameter changes are instituted immediately and without fail and that all company owned client lists are up to date and protected at all times. It is clearly understood that prospect lists are freely available all over the world; however, in many instances these are inaccurate and do not apply either to your target market, your services or your focus. Researching and updating prospect and client information on a regular basis using the sales force and managed by the entrepreneur sales person or sales manager is likened, in my opinion, to "business gold". Researching the details and abilities of your target market will reveal the potential revenue available to you in each territory and will keep you focused on what works for you and what does not. The idea is to focus on each territory as we have stated before so never lose sight of this fact as combined research will reveal the "harvest" for you to reap. Focused research will assist in avoiding the frustration of reaching and dealing with non-decision makers who waste your time, money and cause untold frustration. As an entrepreneur you and I can ill afford to waste time and money on non-productive sales calls as when we call we must get to the person that can ultimately shake our hand when clinching the business deal time after time after time. They say that "time is money" in the business world and for an entrepreneur with limited resources the way you manage your time will obviously determine the amount of money you and I make. Know who you are dealing with and ensure a fit between the client's and the prospect's needs and wants and your product and/or service and your business will grow beyond all expectations. The opposite may become true for you should you ignore the good advice in this chapter!

# Chapter 14

# Your Friend: The Telephone
## *Understanding the use of this great $ales tool!*

**Introduction**

Here is a categorical statement and principle which you simply MUST adopt before we go any further and for always in sales objectives of your business: "The number one objective, when using the telephone, during the sales process, is to GET AN APPOINTMENT/MEETING with the prospect or client (DECISION MAKER). The foundation is, as you will see throughout this chapter, face to face meetings with the prospect are most conducive to closing the sale than any other means. I would like to qualify this statement by making it clear that we are referring directly to the action of securing NEW BUSINESS sales for your business. There are many other reasons why your staff will make use of the telephone but we are talking only of the sales environment at this juncture. However, I am sure that you have already accepted this being the professional that you are.

Many entrepreneurs fail when it comes to producing sales and I can assure you, through experience in my own business, if a sales person fails you may be forgiven for assuming that it started at the inability of the sales force to use the telephone to their advantage and in a professional manner. What I would like to achieve in this chapter with you is to ensure that by the time you conclude the absorbing process you will understand very clearly that the telephone can be your best friend if used wisely and professionally or your worst enemy if you don't. Like I said, if you, or your sales staff are struggling to achieve sales then you will understand that there is no need to look further as they are more than likely not able to set up meetings if they have no clue as to how to professionally use this most amazing of tools. This is technically the very first step in the introduction process and must be managed and achieved on a professional level.

As a professional, and an entrepreneur who understands the importance of generating sales on a consistent basis you will not need me to convince you that the telephone is a salesperson's most valuable tool. It will behoove you and me then to do all in our power to understand how this tool is to be used and how it should not be used. We will also understand the constant need to improve this skill as to do so will directly affect the "bottom line" as sales are generated more consistently and on a professional basis. Calls come in and calls are made but the difference between success and failure lies more often than not in the way that the instrument is used or misused. Many entrepreneurs will attest to fearing the telephone (when used in our context) as will many sales people around the world but my questions remains: "WHY?" The only reason, which I have found for this "fear" is that very few sales people, let alone entrepreneurs, are ever professionally trained in the professional use of the telephone. We want to change that in this book and in this chapter. Knowledge, they say, is "power" so a lack of knowledge in the use of the telephone must therefore represent FAILURE. The other objective in this chapter is to get you the entrepreneur and/or the reader to learn to respect the telephone as a means to an end. One should neither fear nor disrespect this tool at any time. Our ultimate goal here then is to learn how to use the telephone both EFFICIENTLY and EFFECTIVELY.

## The significance and importance of the telephone in the salesperson's business life

When securing much needed sales for your business you and I must understand that the telephone will generally be used to expand two areas of the business: (1) Contact with NEW BUSINESS prospects (2) Contact with the CURRENT CLIENT base. When we consider the new business development within any organization we refer to both incoming calls, for instance, a response to a commercial (advertisement for some) and calls made in order to solicit new business. You, the entrepreneur, has decided to promote your services and/or product in the industry associated magazine and so it is expected, if the advert achieves the desired results, that your business will receive calls in response to the same. Another way new business development is achieved is by means of a third party referral, and at this time an outgoing call has to be made, the goal will be to: SET UP THE APPOINTMENT/MEETING! Yet another way to develop new business for your company is to consider the "cold call". The term "cold calling" is not accepted well by unprofessional salespeople but you must understand that making an approach to new prospects is the very nature of developing new business. The only time that cold calls should become negative to the salesperson or entrepreneur is when no research has been performed on the decision maker and the associated business. Cold calling becomes more like calling a friend if one knows more about the person whom one is calling. Researching the decision maker and the company which you are about to approach turns the "cold call" into a call to "someone you know" and there is a very big difference psychologically in how the call and the contact is perceived.

When using the telephone to make a call to an existing client the tension levels drop drastically as does the pressure and apprehension brought about by the familiarity with the client/customer. Once again, I say that it is my view that the more research that is done on the prospect (cold call) the more familiar you will become with the decision maker BEFORE the call is made. The tone, inflection and the entire attitude will be different (positive) when the cold call is made and the receiver will feel more comfortable as it will sound as though the salesperson is known to them for a very long time-friend. Thus, when calling an existing client/customer the call is courteous, friendly and focused on the needs of the customer. Usually there are no hurdles to overcome and business (of any kind) can be conducted in harmony with very little conflict unless it is a service complaint.

**The telephone and professional courtesy**

To be "courteous" on the telephone (keeping to our context that is) means to be professional as a start and, in particular, we will understand this act of professionalism to mean polite, helpful, considerate, respectful, civilized and very important, to be well-mannered. While I am sure that you are able to add to this list I feel that we have enough to understand what I mean by telephone courtesy.

In order to summarize the above I would like to propose a PLATINUM rule as a BASIC rule for telephone courtesy and professionalism: "TREAT PEOPLE ON THE TELEPHONE AS YOU WOULD LIKE TO BE TREATED!" May I dare to say that this includes our clients? My experience to date has led me to believe that the basic principle of respect has left most unprofessional entrepreneurs and salespeople and we need to get back to basic good manners once again. Please consider the following other good practices principles and rules when wanting to come across as a professional while on the telephone.

1. Always speak into the mouthpiece. The poor habit of the unprofessional salesperson is to allow the mouthpiece of the phone to "hang" off the shoulder and for some reason this bad habit is thought to be cool. I can assure you that a prospect can quickly conclude that the salesperson is not talking directly into the mouthpiece and in particular when they are not able to hear the caller clearly. The message this sends is that the caller must be doing something else in the background like messing with their mobile phone, distracted by someone else in the office or typing on the computer keyboard. What a start to building rapport with a new client? I can tell you that it will not happen! Talk directly into the mouthpiece at all times, focus on the prospect and do not become distracted by anyone or anything else while making new business calls.

2. I am sure, like me, you have been placed on hold when calling as the switchboard may be busy or because the person whom we are calling to speak to is busy and cannot take a call at present so we are placed on hold. There are many such instances where we are rudely and abruptly placed on hold without consultation. The professional entrepreneur salesperson will always understand the negative impact that such rude behavior will have on the sales target and will seriously consider applying good manners in this instance. My rule for the professional then is to *ALWAYS ask the caller or the receiver's permission to place the call on hold.* The process is fairly simple so there is no excuse for poor manners: "Joan, I would like to check the agreement for you may I place you on hold for a few seconds [no longer]?" It is this easy so there is no excuse (clearly stated once again) for behaving in an unprofessional manner.

3. Always thank the caller/receiver for holding! No more said as this is self-explanatory, and again, 'good old mama taught' good manners.

4. Make the caller/receiver feel important at all times. The best way to stroke the ego of the caller/receiver is to mention

their name as often as possible throughout the call without coming across ridiculous. The professional entrepreneur will recognize the psychological benefit in that stroking an ego generally breaks down unnecessary barriers and skepticism. The more the name is used the more familiar one becomes with the prospect and the quicker and easier rapport can be built so use the caller's name EARLY and FREQUENTLY throughout the conversation. Making the receiver feel important is a secret used by the professional salespeople only so I shall pass this on to you at this time.

5. Do NOT cover the mouthpiece while talking to the caller or receiver. Most people are not that ignorant that they cannot work out that if you are covering the mouthpiece with one hand then the chances are good that you are having a second conversation with someone else in your office. Do you think that this will make the prospect feel important? No! Of course not as it will solicit the exact opposite reaction and is deemed rude in almost any culture that uses the telephone for communication purposes-whether mobile or landline! The rule then: NEVER TALK TO OTHERS IN THE AREA BY COVERING THE MOUTHPIECE WITH YOUR HAND!

6. Here is an action dealt with in much detail in ENTREPRENUERSHIP (*minus*) 101. In fact, the subject is so important I dedicated an entire chapter to the art of listening. My advice, LISTEN to what the caller/receiver is saying at all times. This means you have to actually LISTEN in order to HEAR. Focus all of your attention on to the caller/receiver and if you don't feel that you are able to at any given moment in time then DON'T MAKE THE CALL UNTIL YOU ARE! Clear your office of people, clear your mind of useless thoughts and focus on the caller/receiver if you want to succeed.

7. Thank the caller or your prospect for listening to you or for giving you some of their valuable time. This is a sign that you respect them and their time. My mom always used to say,

"Trevor, saying thank you never killed anyone but using it frequently will get you far in life my son!" She was right!

8. The following recommendation may astound you as it did me when I first realized the ramifications should I not adopt this policy. ALWAYS place the telephone receiver down AFTER the prospect or client. The one thing that you do not want the prospect or your client to believe is that you were in a hurry to get off the line or that you were, simply put, rude and ended the call by hanging up. A good way to do this is to replace the receiver back on the cradle in slow motion and not abruptly as is the practice of the unprofessional.

## Using your imagination-Imagery

A foundation must be laid at this point if you and I are to clearly understand both the development and use of imagery and the vital reason for the concept's implementation when using the telephone. While entire books have been written on the psychology of the human imagination I don't feel for the sake of our context that we need to expand beyond what we need to in order to understand our use of imagination when using the telephone within the sales environment. However, it does become critical to understand why it is important to use the God-given gift to our best advantage as professional entrepreneur salespeople. So what do the terms IMAGERY and imagination mean for the purpose of application?

## Imagination

"... the act or power of forming a mental image of something not present to the senses or never before wholly perceived in reality ...

- Webster's Ninth New Collegiate Dictionary

"The faculty or action of producing mental images of what is not present or in one's experience"

- Collins Dictionary

By the above, and our personal life experiences with regards to imagination we understand then that the ability to imagine is a creative gift, and yet, we are all capable of using this gift for our own betterment, and in particular, when using the telephone within a sales environment. We thus have the ability to create mental pictures by simply using a voice coming through over the telephone. Being able to create a mental picture of the person behind the voice is critical if you are to break down barriers or "break the ice" as we say and to build critical rapport. When you and I are able to speak to someone for the first time and make them believe that they know us for a long, long time then this demonstrates yours and my ability to use our gift of imagination and create a picture of the person we are talking to, and this, to the point where we become a friend and not a cold caller. It is so much easier to set up an appointment, which may lead to a long-term fruitful business relationship, with a "friend". In order then to use your imagination throughout the telephone conversation you will understand that your mind will be going through a process by creating an image of the person to whom you are talking, you will be original in your creation, inventive and you will be inspired to say the least. What you will also use of your gifts will be vision, insight and most certainly sensitivity to the caller and in creating a mental picture of who you are talking to. You will be thoughtful and sensitive to the voice as a voice has the most amazing ability to make you think and to stir up your curious senses as to the physical make-up of the person on the "other side of the line". The more you practice the use of your imagination over the phone the better you will become at setting the caller or receiver at ease and the quicker you can do this the easier it will be for the caller or receiver to listen to your message rather than trying to get rid of you as a possible time waster in their lives.

## Imagery

"… the art of making images … mental images; *esp.:* the products of imagination"

-Webster's Ninth New Collegiate Dictionary

"… mental images …"

- Collins Dictionary

The goal then when you are on the telephone, if success is your objective in setting up the meeting or appointment, is to talk to the person as though he/she were sitting directly opposite you in a room. While you have the ability to create a physical picture of the person many professionals will tell you (particularly if you are dealing with the opposite sex) that they have even developed the ability to imagine the scent or fragrance and the kind of office décor which may be associated with the caller or receiver. Now this is what I call a gift! While using your imagination and ability to create an image, you will also need to learn to recognize the tone of your voice (if you are the caller) and the words you select in the message which you convey. The question then is WHY is this so important? From a psychological point of view the answer is quite obvious:

DURING THE COMMUNICATION PROCESS, 55% OF ALL OUR ABILITY TO COMMUNICATE INVOLVES **NON-VERBAL** COMMUNICATION KNOWN TO US ALL AS **BODY LANGUAGE**.

Actions such as gestures, facial expressions, and body positioning and all related physical actions cannot be seen on the telephone. All of these body parts are a language which you and I read constantly as a part of the verbal process and between the two functions we are able to arrive at certain critical conclusions within the sales environment. Without the ability to see someone our job becomes at least 55% more difficult with more than half of our communication ability gone. However, having the ability to use imagery, and our imaginations, we are able to reduce this weakness for both parties with a positive outcome in most instances.

## Understanding the psychology of the incoming call

As professionals you and I will understand that the old saying still applies today: "You have around 10 to 15 seconds to make an impression". The problem with this is that as an entrepreneur salesperson you have it in you to create two kinds of impressions and this being either a NEGATIVE impression or a POSITIVE one. As you are smart you have already worked out that the latter is the kind of impression which I am doing my best to get you to create within the first few seconds when calling for a meeting (appointment) time and date. The "old school pro's" have also left us with another piece of good advice, and again, I do believe that it still applies in modern times: "You never get a SECOND CHANCE to make a good FIRST impression". The goal then would be to ensure that we are prepared before making calls.

It matters not the task, however, I can assure you that if you have prepared for any task at hand then the chances of you succeeding will be greatly enhanced. Do not allow, over confidence and arrogance to lull you into a false sense of security. As an entrepreneur salesperson you will deal with some truly smart people who are highly trained, well-educated and have all the life skills needed to put you in your place should they have a need to do so. The goal then will be to plan and be ready for any and all eventualities which may arise during your session calling to set up meetings. Remember, the client/customer will buy from people and not organizations so it is imperative that you get to meet the very person that will put bread on your table at the end of the month.

Did you know, according to my own personal experiences within my company's sales environment (service industry), it costs me around $210.00 (per lead) to get a salesperson in front of a serious prospect? This is why I have impressed upon our salespeople to ensure that they are prepared and by being prepared I specifically refer to them knowing their product and/or service offering. Companies spend so much money on developing all kinds of selling tools, a website and hard copy brochures (and many other new technology sales aids) for the prospective client/customer but they never seem to focus on ensuring that all of this knowledge is placed into the heads of those selling. The result of this lack of focus is that the salesperson will flounder around when being questioned on a product and/or service by a well-trained and experienced prospect. I consider this lack of product knowledge a major reason why some salespeople exhume a total lack of confidence in their abilities on a daily basis. They have no idea as to what it is that they are selling and it shows clearly. Once you are confident that you and your sales staff know and understand better than anyone else what it is that you are selling then there is yet another key psychological aspect that will need to be considered.

It will take time when you first start on the road to professional sales but a key factor to your success is that you understand the caller and/or the receiver's state of mind at the time of you making or receiving the call. However, before I get into the callers/receiver's state of mind you simply must understand and come to terms with the following critical piece of information. Somewhere along the line some "fool" has made you believe that the general public out there do not like salespeople and that they would prefer never to be contacted by a salesperson in their lifetime. Let me assure you that this useless piece of information, given to you and implanted somehow into your brain, is not true! I will however agree that some unprofessional and unscrupulous "salespeople" have most certainly done damage to the noble profession of sales; however, I can assure you that it has been my experience that the majority of prospects out there, in any sales environment, will be more than happy to deal with a professional salesperson who has the correct product knowledge training and that "knows his/her stuff". What about the caller/receiver's state of mind then?

Most of the people you talk to WANT to deal with you and WANT the information which you have at your disposal. These same people know what you and I already know: "NOTHING HAPPENS WITHOUT A SALE!" However, many of these good people will also know what I know and that is that SALES DO NOT HAPPEN WITHOUT A GOOD SALESPERSON! Salespeople have the wrong impression that prospects do not want to talk to them so as an entrepreneur salesperson never fall into this trap as the consequences for you will be dire. If you believe that people don't want to see you then you cannot believe that "nothing happens without a sale" and if you don't believe this then your business is literally doomed my dear friend. The answer to the success of your business, may I remind you yet another time, is SALES, SALES and SALES! However, in saying all of the above you must understand that in general people do experience a certain amount of anxiety even at the thought of dealing with or talking to a salesperson and this is largely brought about by the public misconception of salespeople, which misperception has been brought about my unprofessional salespeople who are unscrupulous in their dealings with the public. Furthermore, people do not like to be sold to and pressured into making decisions which they will regret – The answer then? Don't sell to prospects but be guilty of satisfying their needs and if there is a match between what they want and what your product or service can provide then you have a sale without any undue pressure at all. In other words, sell to the prospect but don't let them know that you are selling to them. Have a conversation with them and supply their needs and a win-win situation will exist for one and all.

Callers/receivers, it must be conceived, have had bad experiences. It may well be that you or your business had nothing to do with the experience recorded by the prospect and client but they do exist. The reason I share this with you is that when you get what I call a hostile prospect then don't be

316

surprised. People become disappointed because expectations were never met and because unprofessional salespeople, for the sake of the sale, have once again over promised and under delivered. In other words they have misrepresented their product, their service and their company and the prospect or client has had to pay the price for deception and lies – they NEVER forget the experience and every salesperson they come across in their life (whether related to any particular industry or not) will feel the wrath of such an one. Would you not react this way had you been lied to and deceived? Of course you and I would so you can expect a negative reaction from time to time. The professional will quickly recognize what is going on and the state of the caller's and the receiver's mind and will make very quick adjustments psychologically.

The professional entrepreneur salesperson will encourage the receiver to discuss the experience. The more the prospect talks the more they "vent" the more they vent the more they will understand that you care and that YOU are not the source of their frustration. The more they talk the more time you have in order to get your brilliant mind to think of the next step in the entire process. You are professional so behave like any other professional out there. Your next step then must be to reassure the prospect that you are a professional, and while this does not make you perfect by any stretch of the imagination, you will do all in your power not to repeat the same mistakes as your predecessor but that you will avoid these same mistakes at all costs. However, this will not be the only state of the prospects mind at the time of your call that you will need to be concerned about.

You must understand that many callers or receivers are professional at managing their time. The attitude which you may come across more often than not is the one where you may be deemed to be a waste of time and that you ought to be scratched off the list for not being able to come up with a solution to the prospect's challenge. In other words, the prospect's state of mind at the time may reflect the following: "The quicker I can eliminate this salesperson from my list of calls, the quicker I can find a lasting solution to my challenge." Your wise reaction to this state of mind should be as follows:

1. Do not give out too much information during the telephone conversation – you want the face to face appointment/meeting remember?

2. Always give just enough information to arouse curiosity and interest in you and your product and/or service.

3. Always reinforce the caller's decision which made them call you in the first place.

Another consideration during the calling process is that both the prospect and the salesperson may, more than likely, have conflicting goals and ideas. Remember, the objective of the prospect together with the conflicting values systems of both parties will make for some interesting psychology as the two go head to head in achieving different goals. You will have conflict if there are differences but you will have absolute failure if these differences are so far apart that they cannot be reconciled. Always narrow the gap between what the prospect sees as a conflict and what you see as a victory. If the client wins then you win and not the other way around! For instance, at the risk of repeating myself, the caller may want to eliminate your business from a particular list of potential suppliers thereby you, the entrepreneur salesperson, will be eliminated. Your goal, in the role and objective as the salesperson, will be to satisfy the prospect's needs thereby ensuring a successful close. The conflict of objectives thus becomes apparent. Because you are a professional the prospect does not want to call it quits with you but holds on for something more. Once again, you are the professional so you will understand that your objective on the telephone is to arrange a meeting/appointment and that is all, so you do not give away too much information but enough for the prospect to say "yes" to your close for a meeting. This is true sales professionalism! What I am trying to get you to see is that when the prospect says no to you in this instance (on the telephone and specifically to the appointment) then it is almost all of the time seen as a "time saver" by the prospect. The conflict between you and the prospect is now apparent! The basics and the principles are now stated so what do you do when the phone rings and it is a prospect calling to enquire regarding your product and/or service offering?

The goal now surely, and using simple logic, is to create interest in the mind of the caller. You will have a maximum of between fifteen to thirty seconds within which to achieve this most crucial of goals. You cannot fail now and that is why I tell salespeople everywhere to ALWAYS be ready to take a call as the cost to being unprofessional will not only affect you but your business, and more importantly, your family. You need a "hook" meaning that you need to say something that will IMMEDIATELY arrest the attention of the caller/receiver to the point where they would want to carry on and successfully conclude the conversation. For instance, but most certainly not limited to: "Suzanne, thank you for calling our company today! Did you know that as a prestigious workplace services provider [your company name] services some of our country's top 100 national corporates?"

When the calls come in here is some good advice for you- STOP WHATEVER YOU ARE DOING AND FOCUS! Do not be distracted by anyone or anything in your office (shut the door if you have to) and concentrate on the call as not to do so may cost you in the long run. Relax! Take a deep breath if you are feeling uneasy or apprehensive (it gets better with practice I can assure you). A caller, believe it or not, is just as adept at using imagery and their imagination as you are and they will quickly decipher your emotional state at the time of making the call. Instead of coming across uncomfortable rather portray a confident and friendly demeanor. In order to avoid the above mentioned uncomfortable situation may I suggest that you SMILE when taking a new call from a caller/prospect/receiver/client/customer? While you are doing this take time right away to try and visualize the face of the person which you are now talking to. In other words, put into practice the principles taught in this chapter. Understand this as well, you should expect to feel a little pressure at least (as said before this does get better with practice) as much is at stake. The caller represents the opportunity to develop a lasting business relationship which will have positive financial repercussions for you, your family and your business. We have also concluded already that ALL pressure is not bad for you! We have also understood that certain pressure is good for you as you will surprise yourself as to what you are truly capable of. The salesperson must expect to remain in control of the conversation if you are to conclude for a meeting. The best way to lead a conversation to a successful conclusion and show leadership at the same time is to ask questions which lead you from point A to point B successfully. Devise a set of questions which work for you (not etched in stone as you may need to be flexible from time to time) which start at creating interest but then leading to the closing question for an appointment/meeting. Be in charge, feel confident and be prepared at all times. The phone rings but first things first.

You will need to obtain the caller's name – My advice in this regard then? Make sure that you obtain the caller's name early on in the conversation and then use it throughout the conversation. Nothing makes a person feel more important than someone else mentioning your name a few times. Many professional salespeople will agree with me that usually using the prospect's name frequently during the phone call or sales call frequently leads more often than not to a successful sale close. Obviously, the more you and I use a person's name the more likely we are to remember the prospect's name. We have come a far way now in understanding principals, conflicting objectives, how to respond to the caller and how to use imagery so the question is WHY consider and implement all of these? Does all of this information lead us to our number one telephone objective, and if so what is the NUMBER ONE OBJECTIVE when talking to a prospect on the telephone at this stage of the selling cycle?

# TO GET THE FACE TO FACE MEETING!

This means then that your focus is clear so you must understand that the more you "give away" while talking to the prospect over the phone the more chance you stand of "losing the prospect". I don't care how good you are as a salesperson and while it may be possible in our time to sell over the phone you cannot build rapport over the phone that will lead to a long-lasting and successful business relationship. The best way to sell, and I don't care who tells you any different, despite modern technology, is meeting someone face to face. The face and other body language say it all and you lose at least 55% of this while you are on the phone. Furthermore, the more information you give out over the phone the more chance you stand of being "taken out" and scratched off the list as a potential time waster. I can assure you that one of the most common mistakes made by unprofessional salespeople is that they try to do too much while on the phone when securing a meeting date and time. I want to make my position clear to you today in the hope that you will NEVER forget this fact and that is that face to face meetings are more conducive to long lasting and repeat business than trying to sell your product or service over the phone. There is a place for this type of selling once the relationship has been firmly cemented! I also want to add that my feeling is that the strongest attribute which you have going for you in sales has got to be your personality so use it to create long lasting and successful business relationships. Presenting yourself to the prospect as a complete person is impossible to do over the phone.

I know that what I am about to do may seem out of place to you but I would like to go back to my admonition to you to develop a list of questions which will help you to remain in control of the call and lead you to a successful conclusion when seeking the meeting date and time. However, I felt it better to "ground" you in the other previously mentioned facts as a first step before finalizing the questions and leadership role. That now said and done I am sure that you will be happy that I came back to this for you as you will soon see the benefit to you on a personal level.

We have discussed controlling the conversation when the phone rings and I have recommended that you remain in control of the conversation by using pre-designed questions to help you do so. My goal now is to give you some EXAMPLES of what I am talking about with a full explanation to follow.

The phone rings:

*Good morning [smiling of course], thank you for calling [the name of your business], my name is Trevor and your name is?*

*John, I'm glad you called, what can I do to help you today?*

Please note: the delivery of your statement and question as stated above is vital in that you need to come across friendly, welcoming, inviting and willing to help. Smile! Smile! Smile! In order to be emphatic and sincere I would suggest that you finish the opening statement/questions on a high note as this will also help you to project enthusiasm to your prospect. If the caller states that they are calling in response to an advertisement, promotional activity or commercial of some sort (you should know about this and be ready to answer calls when these have been placed or aired – don't flounder and don't ask the client "what advertisement?") you should consider responding by saying:

*John, the advert was correct; we do have the perfect solution to your hygiene challenge!*

This is perfect as it does not give away any more information than was originally given to the caller in the commercial or advert but you know he/she wants more information so you want to enhance the curiosity and interest without giving away too much more information. You may want to continue and state the following:

*John, I can assure you that we have not as yet met a hygiene challenge which we could not solve!*

The less you reveal the more you are saying here as at this stage the prospect is going through so many emotions. However, whatever doubt John had before making the call this is now starting to dissipate and any apprehension which he had before making the call is turning into the following sentiment: "at last, a solution". The idea is to get the meeting remember! Why waste time?

*John, the good news is that I have samples and a short presentation on the proposed solution to your challenges and will need to see you soon.*

You have just closed for the meeting; however, BEFORE the prospect responds you may want to consider cementing the close by stating the following:

*However, John, may I check my calendar for my soonest available meeting date? May I place you on hold for a few moments, John?*

What you have achieved so far is that you have shown and retained leadership hereby controlling the conversation. Should you ever lose control of the conversation then you will not win but the prospect must not feel like you are "controlling matters" as the process must come across friendly and painless but he/she must also know that they will only get more information when meeting with you.

By referring to your calendar you have created apprehension about you being able to meet soon (hang the carrot out there and make the caller reach for it) so the urgency of meeting you now shifts from you to the prospect. Always check your calendar for the appointment as suggested to the prospect and do not lie or deceive callers. Do NOT place any caller on hold for more than TWENTY SECONDS. Again, the goal here is by placing the caller on hold at this juncture the action may increase the caller's interest and urgency.

*Thank you for holding John, according to my calendar my first available opening for a meeting is[state the date and the time].I will confirm the meeting then for [restate the date and time]and send you a meeting request from my calendar as a reminder to you.*

You may also want to add the following question in at the start of your conversation or you can save it for when you meet the prospect:

*John, may I ask what appealed to you most about the commercial?*

The answer to the above question is vital as this could very well be the key to you closing the sale successfully. You must remember this NEED/WANT when you are ready to present your final proposal for the close.


## Dealing with a difficult telephone prospect


You and I have experienced persistent and difficult prospects, and in general people, in all walks of life. However, this prospect is different in that he/she represents a business relationship with potentially a great deal of financial reward as you and your company services their needs over the years. Be patient! Be careful! Remain calm! But also remain in charge and be ready to lead the conversation no matter how difficult the prospect. In fact, it may very well be that the discussion between you and the prospect may lead to you and the possible client/customer wanting to discover more about each other which in itself is not a bad thing, and this, ONLY if it will help you in the closing process later in the sales cycle. The key here though is to retain control and leadership as to lose this battle will mean that you are scratched off the list as a time waster. The goal at this stage then is to guide you to a successful close for the meeting/appointment. Furthermore, if you (or the prospect) feel it absolutely necessary to continue with the qualifying process (remember the prospect's goal is to extract as much information from you while on the phone in order to determine whether you are a time waster or whether you are actually capable of solving his/her challenge) then design some well thought out questions to keep you on track for a successful close for the meeting date. NEVER forget your goal and that is to CLOSE FOR THE MEETING! Some examples of how to question and why are as follows:

1. Determine the prospects motivation for wanting to change the current service provider and/or supplier. For instance,
- "Suzanne, why are you considering a change?" or
- "Suzanne, why are you considering [name of your company]?"
- "Suzanne, I understand that your current supplier has not been able to resolve your challenge but what have they done so far to resolve the issue?"
- "Suzanne, are you familiar with our focus and level of service? How?"

2. Determine the prospects physical needs–do not get too involved remember you will discuss this in detail when you meet.

3. Determine if there are any special requirements that you ought to know of currently not being met by the existing supplier or service provider.

4. Determine their financial ability and terms of payment – be careful at this point as you may upset the prospect but you will need to understand this at some point. Try this question or ignore the point if you already know the financial credibility of the prospective company:
- "Suzanne, what is the budget set aside for this project so that I may formulate my solution accordingly?"

The idea would be to close for the meeting at this point. However, let's assume, for the sake of the discussion at hand that the prospect is located across the country and it may not be as easy as to get into your automobile and "pop down the road" for a meeting, what do you do then? The answer is obvious in that you will have to qualify the prospect even further, but notice, you will still retain a leadership role, and as you may still have to meet with the prospect you must not lose track of closing for a suitable meeting date. One reason prospects want to make a change of service providers and suppliers is because there are clear areas of discontent. These areas of discontent vary from prospect to prospect so when you are discussing this on the phone then you may need to focus in the following areas:

5. Is the prospect frustrated and tired of the complaints which their company receives due to poor service and inferior products?

6. Many decision makers become disillusioned, tired and frustrated at not being able to find an effective solution. Find out if this is the case with the caller.

7. Many good procurement departments have been taken to task for wasting financial resources on solutions which hold great promise but which don't work. Discover if this is the case with this decision maker.

8. This prospect may be calling you because many salespeople and companies which he/she has called before you show no interest in their challenge and move on without proposing any type of a solution at all. Find out if this situation exists and assure otherwise.

Should the above qualification process be fruitful and you and the prospect agree then CLOSE FOR THE APPOINTMENT/MEETING. However, should the "distance" between the two of you remain a challenge for the time being then I will guide you to one last phase and batch of questions which may assist you with LONG-DISTANCE prospects only. You will understand that you must never get this far with a locally based prospect. Under normal circumstances you should have closed for the appointment a long time ago. Should you or the prospect need additional information for an effective solution then you may want to focus more on the benefits which your product, service and company has to offer. While there are many benefits associated with many different products and services around the world you may want to consider the following as a guideline:

9. Installation crews are reliable and will install on the pre-determined date.

10. Your solution is quick and easy to implement and is a long lasting solution.

11. Your products and services are a hassle free solution.

12. You will ensure that the prospect's current frustration comes to an abrupt end.

13. The proposed service is a full and comprehensive service and covers all the prospect's needs.

14. When you meet for the presentation of your services and subsequent proposals these are based upon no obligation on the part of the prospect and at no cost.

15. The pricing structure you present in your proposal is an all-inclusive rate so the prospect should expect no additional or "surprise" charges.

16. You must be able to assure the prospect that the products offered to him/her will be amongst the latest technology and expected standard.

17. You will assure the prospect that the services on offer are fully supported and you will be on site personally in order to ensure a smooth installation so the prospect need not be concerned and can continue with normal daily activities during the process.

18. Should the prospect be happy with your proposal, and move ahead within seven business days you may be in a position to waive the installation charges as well as come in under budget.

## Close for the meeting

The idea before the close is for you and me to offer our service, but more important than that, we need to make it easy for the prospect to do business with us. In closing for the meeting/appointment then consider the following final questions:

1. "James, I would like to work with you in finding a lasting solution that would fit both your needs and your budget!"

2. "Mary, my schedule is more flexible at this time than yours, so I would be happy to meet with you on Thursday at 10h00!"

Once the question has been asked: CLOSE FOR THE APPOINTMENT/MEETING!

I know that I must sound like the proverbial "stuck record" but ALWAYS remember when a prospect calls in; the number one objective for you is to get a meeting date with the prospect and the sooner after the initial call the better. While I am sure that you have great talents and abilities do not try to sell your services and/or your product over the telephone. As a last resort, and I want to repeat this, as a last resort, if the prospect is adamant that he/she does not want to meet then offer to at least send some additional company information regarding the product and/or service. Promise to make a follow-up call after their receiving the information, and try one more time for the meeting close.

May I offer another word of advice at this point and spare you the embarrassment of being labelled "unprofessional"? Make sure that you never DOUBLE BOOK meetings! I can assure you that prospects are looking to deal with professionals and not rank amateurs. Think about this with me will you? You have just used all or some of the above questions, you have maintained the leadership role, you have promised all the solutions in the world to your prospect and you have finally closed for the meeting. The prospect agrees to a meeting with you, and then, a day or two later you realize that you have double-booked the meeting. You "the true professional" will now have to start the business relationship off apologizing for your unprofessional conduct. Do you still believe that the prospect will have enough confidence in you and trust you to resolve all of her/his challenges? Try it then and see how it all lands up for you! The one thing that you never do then is to double-book meetings and the second action which will most certainly reflect poorly on you is when you cancel a meeting which you have set with a prospect. This action is not only poor and unprofessional but is unforgivable unless you have died or have had some kind of family emergency such as death.

When closing, I have found it more effective to use what I call (or what most salespeople have come to call this type of close) the "alternative choice" close.

"Paul, according to my calendar I am able to meet with you next Friday at 09h00 or would 10h00 be more convenient for you?"

Once you have asked this question then BE QUIET! Don't say another word but wait for the answer! Let me say this again! Once you have asked the closing question you MUST wait for the answer from the prospect and the prospect knows this so DO NOT say anything until the caller does! Once the response has come back in the affirmative then you may want to confirm some of the following:

1. Promise to send the caller a meeting request from your calendar and ask them to confirm the meeting time by return email.
2. Invite the caller to call you at any time (provide your mobile number) between now and the time you meet should they have any emergencies.
3. Confirm the prospect's company name (ensure that you have the correct spelling of all names), contact details and street address.
4. Lastly, THANK the prospect for calling (state the name of your business) and let them know that you have certainly enjoyed talking with them.

## What to say when cold calling on the telephone

Your business, products and services will dictate the make-up of your script but I would recommend that you develop a script that works for you. Design a script then that takes on the culture of your business and your personality and a script which allows the prospect to sense the professionalism in you. As a guideline, I would like to present the following script that I have used in my sales career successfully for many years. My suggestion is that you develop your own but if mine works for you then please feel free to try it out. When using a script it must not sound as though it is being read, it must come across in conversation format and be interesting to listen to with all the hooks attached and formulated to get the sought after YES answer to your request to meet. The script must also be "short and sweet" and to the point. Please see as follows:

*Hi Fred, my name is [add in your name] and I am calling you from a company called [add in your company name].*

*[Your company name] is a health and hygiene services company [add in what YOU do] providing workplace services such: washroom rental products, washroom hygiene services, pest elimination services and housekeeping services [add in you services/products].*

*Fred, I am the Healthcare Salesperson [or add in whatever title suits you] in your area and I am calling you for two reasons:*

*1. I would like to set up a meeting with you in order to introduce myself to you personally, while at the same time,*
*2. Presenting our services [and/or products] by way of a short but effective presentation.*

*Fred, I can assure you that I don't intend wasting your time in any way at all.*

*Fred, I am in your area next week Wednesday and can see you at 09h00 or would 10h00 suit you better?*

## Conclusion

The telephone is a communication device without adding a body or a face. YOU have to add the body and the face using your vivid imagination which will produce an image of the caller or receiver. Never fear the use of the telephone, rather fear your inability to use imagery when trying to connect with the caller on an emotional level. Building rapport does not start at the meeting but on the telephone and during the very first call. You do not have long to make a positive first impression and this first impression may be perceived and received as either negative or positive. You had better consider ensuring that all first impressions are positive or start counting the financial losses as new sales begin to dwindle. Maintain control of every call and lead the caller/receiver to one goal and one goal only – GET A MEETING DATE AND TIME!

Understanding that the telephone is a tool to be used in order to achieve success is not only pivotal but fundamental to sales success and to your business growth and personal goals. I can assure you that if your sales are down then chances are that you or your sales team is not using this tool professionally or effectively. Remember, being effective on the phone, leading through asking the right questions and gaining valuable and much needed information during this process will go a long way in ensuring success during the services and/or products presentation stage. Prospects or callers/receivers do not only develop perceptions of who you are when you sit in front of them; perceptions are more often than not already formed (albeit superficial at the early stages of the sales process) during the first few seconds on the telephone. Once this first impression is made I want to warn you that it generally lasts throughout the sales process, and that is, if you are even allowed to get that far.

# Chapter 15

# The Gatekeeper: Getting Past
## *Overcoming this impediment will bring ultimate $ales success!*

**Introduction**

Many well-meaning salespeople absolutely detest making cold calls for fear of hearing one single word – "NO!" You and I will agree that to the untrained and to the unprofessional setting time aside to make calls needed to set up crucial sales meetings in order to achieve sales targets is a most dreaded task, and this, many times, caused by the inability of the salesperson to overcome the constant negative responses handed out by the "gatekeeper".

The first thing that we need to accomplish before we proceed is to de-mystify the term gatekeeper. The only way for me to accomplish this for you is to help you to see that the gatekeeper is a person who is made up of all the physical and psychological attributes that you and I have. In other words the gatekeeper is a person, and yes, a human being. They have feelings, they have blood running through their veins (just like you and me), and they have hair, eyes and even ears. They run and walk like you and I do! They brush their teeth and comb their hair on a daily basis (some even more than once per day) and they even dress, and some, the same way as you and I do! Again, they are human beings! Many have spouses and families which mean that they have goals and aspirations as a family unit. A job or career is one way for both spouses to earn a living and to achieve their dreams of buying a home, a second car and going on an overseas vacation or holiday. Children need to be educated and a career or job provides for the education of the young ones as well. Being human is a serious business and with it comes responsibility, and more importantly financial responsibility and stability which only a secure career and job is able to provide. Most people out there are not entrepreneurs and would prefer NOT to work for themselves. However, I want to assure you that the working class (as opposed to the "owner class" or the "sales class" for the sake of our subject matter) is no less committed to what they do as a career than your commitment to being an entrepreneur. Some "gatekeepers" are as passionate about what they do as the rest of us, and in many cases, are more loyal and more committed to their job descriptions than most unprofessional entrepreneur salespeople and salespeople in general. You will now begin to understand why the friendly neighbor across the road can be so bubbly and outgoing on a weekend but become an absolute solid "block of ice" when she sits behind her desk defending the decision maker's time. That is exactly what she is doing and instead of labeling such a person a gatekeeper you will also be wise for referring to her as a "defender". The decision maker is usually a senior purchaser/buyer/executive within most organizations and EVERYONE wants to book time to see them. Many people call and simply waste the time of the decision maker, and so, enter the defender (gatekeeper).

The question then is what is the defender defending? In my opinion two things: (1) Time (2) Access. During the interview process the defender is specifically asked about her screening skills. What does the screening process entail and involve then? In order for the defender/gatekeeper to perform his/her function effectively (to the point where they don't lose their job) they will have to understand and perform three tasks (1) SCRUTINIZE (2) EXAMINE (3) INVESTIGATE. In other words considering the abovementioned three actions you, your product, your service, your company and your very call will be VETTED or questioned. The definition of vet simply means that everything about you will be scrutinized, examined and investigated; however, will also be inspected, assessed, appraised, and in modern day terms, you will be "checked out" and thoroughly so. Why do I tell you all of this? For one simple reason, and that is, so that you will understand that the defender/gatekeeper has a job to do and that he/she does NOT hate you but is fulfilling the very serious role for which they have been hired! Should the defender/gatekeeper fail to defend the time and access to the decision maker then the negative consequences for such a person may lead to dismissal (being fired!)

Communicating with the decision maker is crucial in any sales situation. With the above now said and done, the professional entrepreneur salesperson usually has good intentions of reaching the decision maker, with a view to setting up a meeting date, he/she is sometimes prevented for achieving this goal by the defender/gatekeeper. The defender, within the sales environment, may take many forms and hold a variety of positions within an organization. You and I must therefore understand that the secretary, personal assistant, administration assistant and receptionist are well trained, and experienced, in the art of screening any and all incoming calls to the decision makers. Please, also remember, that many of these people have the added advantage of years of experience and ongoing professional training throughout their tenure. They are PROFESSIONALS! As a professional entrepreneur salesperson it will behoove you then to understand that the gatekeeper is well equipped and very able to prevent you from reaching your target audience-the decision maker.

**Please remember, the DEFENDER/GATEKEEPER is the one person who is able to stand between success and failure in the selling process.**

Some defenders have the attitude that their job function is to say "NO!" and they feel to say "YES!" to you and me would be defeating the entire purpose of their position. They understand, and take the role very seriously indeed, that it is their job function to act as both a BUFFER and a FILTER when it comes to screening calls to the decision maker and this is why many times salespeople truly feel like they are "hitting their heads against a brick wall" when on the telephone.

You must understand that the entire purpose of the gatekeeper is to screen calls as described in this chapter so far but NOT to turn away ALL calls! Believe it or not there are certain calls that do go through to the decision maker and your goal and mine will be to ensure that our calls go through to more decision makers than anyone else. I can assure you success when making calls for meetings and appointments but you will need to apply the contents of this chapter and to understand the psychology and dynamic of this particular phase of the selling process as this phase is critical if you are to continue on in the process. The idea, as stated MANY times before in the last chapter, is NOT to give away too much information when requesting your call to be put through to the decision maker. We have now reached the point where we need to understand then as to how to deal with a stubborn defender, or for that matter, any defender/gatekeeper at all. I would like to take this opportunity to consider three techniques which I have used throughout my sales career. While I most certainly have not achieved a 100% success rate I am able to assure you that I have come close to achieving this milestone throughout my years as a professional entrepreneur salesperson. Please consider and apply the following sales techniques.

1. Hit then head-on!
2. Evasive action!
3. Ignore them!
4. Catch a "wake-up!"

**Hit them head on!**

To me, personally, there is nothing like taking the direct approach when wanting to set up a meeting with the decision maker. Don't misunderstand me please! What I am not referring to is an approach where you and I seem like high pressure salespeople. We are professionals who are seeking the most EFFECTIVE way to get to the decision maker and more often than not the most direct way is the most effective way which in turn leads to the most successful way to achieve the goal. Hitting the defender "head on" must be done with finesse and utter professionalism in order for you to achieve success time after time. The reason for success here has more to do with our ability to use "verbal blockers" to distract the gatekeeper but also to keep the salesperson on track for the appointment. I will give you an actual scripted example of this shortly. Distracting the defender from her/his goal will many times allow you to achieve yours. This move may be likened to an offensive line that assists the receiver of the ball to get across the line. While the defensive team is confused by a myriad of activity the ball carrier slips across the line. What we are trying to do here is to conceal the ball through much "off the ball" activity so that the "opposition" loses sight of the ball or their game plan.

The key to understanding the use of this technique has now been mentioned many, many times in this book to date (and may be mentioned even more-who knows?) and is:

1. NEVER sell a service and/or product to the defender/gatekeeper. This person is not your target as the decision maker is. This person is only interested in determining whether to put you through or not and if you spend your time wasting his/her time then you will most

certainly not be put through. Decision makers buy products and services but defenders/gatekeepers do not.

2. You must rather spend your time and energy on getting the gatekeeper to put you through to the decision maker and the sooner the better. This is what gatekeepers/defenders guard and this is what they defend so never get the roles confused and let me say it one more time. Do NOT sell your products and/or services to the gatekeeper as in all honesty THEY ARE NOT INTERESTED! However, DO sell the defender on putting you through as this is in her/his control but buying from you on behalf of the company is not!

You will notice one "attribute" ascribed to the gatekeeper by many tried and tested salespeople worldwide: "Gatekeepers ask many, many questions!" May I ask you to consider WHY? The main goal should be obvious but just in case it is not let me point out that he/she does this in order to extract as much information from the salesperson as is possible. The goal through the "interrogation" process should be just as clear but let me state the obvious anyway. The idea is to get as much information as is possible to decide whether or not to put you through to the decision maker or not. The more information the unprofessional salesperson feeds through to the defender the LESS chance they will have of being put though so that the sales process may continue on to the next phase.

You will remember that I have admonished you to ALWAYS remain in charge of the sales process and that includes the telephone approach. The one who should be asking the questions is who? Exactly! Well done! Yes, the professional entrepreneur salesperson has by now come to understand that the one asking the most questions in the sales process becomes the leader so if the prospect, the defender or the gatekeeper is asking most of the questions then they, by default, become the leader in the situation and this is why many unprofessional salespeople never achieve their goals when on the telephone (or any other part of the sales process for that matter if I may add this). As the leader then you and I must ask very specific questions all of which should lead us a step closer to being put through to the decision maker. The following are the reasons why specific questions are asked and why unrelated questions are totally discarded:

1. As discussed, to maintain control of the conversation.
2. The professional salesperson does NOT want information from the gatekeeper.
3. The professional entrepreneur salesperson desires a very specific action from the defender.
4. The goal, action and desire for you are to be put through to the decision maker without any further delay.

When a request to be put through to the decision maker has reached the ears of the gatekeeper then the professional salesperson will perform the following three tasks with the utmost respect:

1. Respond in brief to the question posed by the gatekeeper.
2. IMMEDIATELY follow up with a "command statement".
3. Use a question which will confirm that the gatekeeper understands the received command.

Chapter eight dealt with the use of empathy so I will once again refer you now to your new found knowledge in this regard. As you and I will use empathy throughout the selling cycle it is also very important that you use this psychological technique at this time. When doing so then you will understand that the gatekeeper has clear knowledge of the fact that it is their job function to screen calls. Think about this from his/her side and understand the tension and pressure to do the right thing and the consequences should the wrong decision be made in letting you through. They also have the understanding that to reject the right types of calls could have the very same negative result so they are in a very difficult situation most of the time. Consider this! Understand this! The only way to screen calls is to do what? Right! To ask questions and this is why most of the time you and I get the "third degree" before the decision is made to put us through or not. When using empathy then you will also understand that there is a certain dynamic as this relates to the gatekeeper's relationship with the decision maker and he/she is highly influenced by the express wishes of the decision maker. Think about it, how would YOU react if your boss says to you that he/she would be happy if you screen all calls carefully? Also then think about the disappointment in both parties if this instruction is not carried out and the subsequent frustration which will ensue. Finally, when using empathy you will then come to a clear understanding as to why it is that the gatekeeper will feel like a total failure if there is a lack of questioning during the screening phase. This is why I would exhort you to understand that you should not volunteer any more information other than what is absolutely necessary in order to satisfy the gatekeeper's question.

Using the above as a foundation then how does the professional entrepreneur salesperson react to the filter's questions in such a way as to ensure success? The first thing that needs to happen is that you must make the defender feel as though they are fulfilling their role and performing their task professionally. Allow questions but control the quantity and the quality. The second key is to ensure that you do not give away too much information, and so much information, that it will cause the gatekeeper to make the incorrect decision about whether to put you through or not. "Verbal diarrhea" is neither a friend nor an attribute of the professional! The third consideration and step to success is to ensure that the first two are achieved and in doing so you will be assured of greater success as you move forward.

They say that, "honesty is the best policy" and this rings true (so true) during the meeting setting phase of the selling process. If you lie, and get caught out doing so then you will lose ALL credibility with the gatekeeper and the decision maker. For instance, you cannot tell the gatekeeper that you need to talk to the decision maker because his/her house is burning down if his/her house is not in fact burning down- THIS IS CALLED A LIE! Do not use "tall stories" to get through to the decision maker at any time! The goal is to get through to the decision maker providing the minimum of information but a one sentence blatant lie does not qualify in the least. Let me state this again, the less the amount of information given to the gatekeeper the better your chances of going through to the decision maker so that you are able to set up the desired meeting.

We have discussed much previously so please allow me now to set the stage in the hope that the following scenario will help you to put into practice the mentioned principles so far in this chapter. The scenario is in the form of a script (previously promised in this chapter) and deals specifically with a salesperson asking to be put through to the decision maker.

Gatekeeper: *Mr. Smith's office!*

Entrepreneur: *Did you say that this is Mr. Smith's office? [1st question – remain in charge]*

Gatekeeper: *Yes, I did!*

Entrepreneur: *Thank you! Who am I speaking to? [2nd question]*

Gatekeeper: *This is Stacey. How may I help you? [1st question – makes Stacey feel like she is doing her job]*

Entrepreneur: *Hi Stacey, my name is [add your name] calling for Mr. Smith. Could you put me through please? [Remaining in charge and going the direct route]*

Gatekeeper: *What company are you with? [2nd question – feels like she is doing her job]*

Entrepreneur: *Stacey, I'm with a company called [add in your company name]. Please tell Mr. Smith I'm holding for him [a command – or "I'm calling from New York" if long distance as it adds pressure and urgency]*

Gatekeeper: *Is he expecting your call? [Doing her job asking questions so the salesperson allows this]*

Entrepreneur: *Stacey, I don't believe we have set up a specific time, [no lies, tell it like it is] but please let him know that I am on the line [a command action].*

Gatekeeper: *And may I say what it is in connection with? [Fishing for reasons why to say no – just doing her job]*

Entrepreneur: *Stacey, you may let Mr. Smith know that I have been instructed by the President of our company to personally schedule a meeting to go over our company services with him in more detail. [No information has really passed to the gatekeeper but she has been allowed to do her job and she is still in the dark as to the services and/or products] He is supposed to be in today would you please put me through right away? [A command action]*

Gatekeeper: *Does he know you at all? [Fishing for more information as she is now feeling the pressure but must continue to question as this is what she has been told and taught to do]*

Entrepreneur: *Stacey, we haven't met personally, but I do have the much needed information for him so please let him know that I'm on the line. [The answer is short and to the point and again does not give anything away that should not be revealed and that should give her a reason NOT to put the salesperson through]*

Gatekeeper: *Please hold while I transfer your call. [There was nothing else left to do]*

## Summary

Let's summarize the call as stated above. You will notice that the entrepreneur salesperson identified the name of the gatekeeper early on in the conversation – this is a critical action. You then stroke the ego by using the name throughout the conversation. The name should also be used frequently and in our example this is exactly what happened. Understand that people like to hear their own name so never forget this throughout the sales process. When you use the prospect's name frequently this will help in breaking down resistance and assist in building vital rapport. It was clear that the entrepreneur salesperson gave away very little information and the script was well planned. He also allowed the gatekeeper to do her job which is fair and vital in getting put through to the decision maker. The outstanding thing in our example was that the gatekeeper was allowed to ask questions but the salesperson retained control of the conversation at all times using commands to achieve this. Pressure, but not undue pressure was placed upon the gatekeeper and she/he felt that she/he had sufficiently been allowed to screen as was her/his instruction and as is her/his job description. She/he was allowed to ask questions but did not seem to get anywhere and the logical conclusion for her/him was to put the call through to the decision maker.

*The key aspect of the above script example was the fact that the entrepreneur salesperson never placed the conversation in jeopardy by giving the gatekeeper enough information to make a decision not to let him/her through to the decision maker.*

**Evasive action!**

Should we consider the defender/gatekeeper as a defensive line (which he/she technically becomes in their role) then it may be more prudent at times (and smart) NOT to make a direct approach and NOT to "hit them head on". In fact, it may very well be that you decided to use the previous technique as stated above and you failed, meaning, that despite your best efforts to go through the gatekeeper he/she refused to put your call through. The script (or your own personal script) simply did not work and no matter how hard you tried you could not breach the "defense" of the gatekeeper. On the day she/he was too good for you! This is not the time to give up so don't even go there; however, this is the time to change tactics and to use that great brain which was given to you by your Maker. Understand that if one way does not work there are ALWAYS other ways of achieving your objective. If reaching the decision maker means that much to you then it is time to be creative and find another solution (technique) to the challenge which lies before you. It just so happens that we do have a "few more tricks up our sleeves" so to speak. The **EVASIVE ACTION** technique is also used to go around the gatekeeper and is used to get us into the decision maker. The idea then is for you and me to simply run around the defensive line-that simple!

Just as wide receivers (football), and left and right wings (soccer etc.) are used to breach a defensive line in sport we will use this tactical move to get through to the decision maker without the help of the gatekeeper. Thus we are saying that there are two ways to get around a stubborn defensive line.

1. Most decision makers have direct lines.
2. Try calling a different department.

There are many ways to get the decision maker's direct line number but the receptionist (if he/she is not also the gatekeeper) is one of the ways in which you can achieve this. You can also ask to be put through to the HR department and ask for the number and the company website may also list the number. Once you have access to the number you will then have direct access to the decision maker without involving the gatekeeper at all. A logical move if you ask me! If none of this works for you then you may have to go and see the receptionist and ask for a business card belonging to the decision maker. She could also get the number off the email template used by the decision maker when sending out emails. Some companies have a corporate directory with all relevant extension numbers, and once you obtain an extension number it is far easier and more successful to simply ask to be put through to a particular extension number without using a name at all: "Please put my call through to extension 2156 [the decision maker's extension number] please!" The point is that there is always a way to get the direct line number so get thinking!

However, should you not be able to get the direct line number through conventional means, and the gatekeeper stubbornly refused to put your call through to the decision maker then you have yet another option which I like to call a "sneak attack". "All is fair in love and war" they say and as long as you are ethical and have high moral standards then you will always find a way to get what you need in order to achieve what you need. The technique here is for you to call the same company but ask to be put through to a different department. For instance, when calling back ask to be put through to the HR department or sales department or even production if you have to. Once the call has been put through to the unrelated department you should ask to speak to the decision maker by name of course. The receiver will obviously inform you that you have come through to the incorrect department, and if they don't offer to do so then apologize for coming through to the incorrect department but also ask the receiver to put your call through to the decision maker-again, by name.

**Ignore them!**

A stubborn gatekeeper is usually no match for a well disciplined and determined entrepreneur salesperson, and in particular, when the decision maker holds the key to a lucrative long-term business relationship. Use this motivation to think your way around challenges which prevent you from achieving your goals, dreams and desires. Once again, if you cannot get through to the decision maker by conventional means then consider yet another technique namely: "IGNORE THEM! How do you ignore the gatekeeper? CALL THE OFFICE OF SOMEONE MORE SENIOR IN THE COMPANY! This is a very similar technique to when you have gone through to a different department but this may work out even better for you. Why? Well the more senior person will realize that you have come through to the wrong extension and usually offer to transfer your call through to your decision maker. Generally, the transfer of your call may go something like this: "John, hi it's Kirsten, this call is for you". Now let me assure you that a call being put through from a more senior person will work in your favor as the call will immediately receive a level of importance and the attention which it deserves. I can assure you that you will have all the attention from the decision maker at the time of the call. The rest is up to you!

## Catch a "wake-up"!

Decision makers, such as the person which you are seeking a meeting with have old habits which, seem to "die hard". They get to work early and they leave the office late. In fact, it is quite possible and consistent with their personalities, due to their commitment to their positions, the company and their responsibilities, that they will arrive at the office or workplace ahead of everyone else and leave long after the regular staff. Think about this one with me! They arrive early meaning that when their phone rings they understand that they have to answer it as the personal assistant is obviously not at her desk that time of the morning. You will bypass the line of defense and do so without having to "wrestle" with the gatekeeper and reach the decision maker.

You may also want to know when the gatekeeper goes on lunch as most senior people (decision makers) don't usually go out for lunch (unless it is a business luncheon). This will be another of those times when the decision maker understands that the gatekeeper is on lunch and he/she will have no option but to take the call. What about making a call after working hours? The habits of "workaholics" are well known on a company by company basis so find out what the "working habits" are of your prospect and consider calling after hours if the technique has not worked when calling early morning or lunch times. This is the kind of call, as is the case with the early morning call, which you can place from home so there is no need to be at your office when doing so. If all else fails what do you do? Another technique which professional salespeople do is they would even consider calling the prospect over a weekend. I want to caution you here though and ask you to think very carefully before attempting such a call at such a time. However, if this is the only way to achieve your objectives then I have no doubt that most decision makers will be impressed enough with your levels of motivation to offer you a few minutes to get your point across. "Good morning, Mr. Sharp. My name is Trevor Whittaker. Please accept my apology for calling you on a Saturday morning. In all honesty I have found it impossible to reach you during normal business hours as I know that you are extremely busy. Do you have a few minutes for me, sir?" What you say after this will either impress the prospect or you will not achieve your goals. You will sell the meeting date only (not the product or service as stated numerous times now) after stating the name of the company which you represent.

## Conclusion

As an entrepreneur salesperson you should have one goal and one goal only and that is to generate sales. However, a stubborn gatekeeper has the power (through training, experience and through instruction from his/her boss) to keep you from achieving your goal. You must never allow such a person to stand in your way and you must NEVER give up on your mission to get through to the decision maker in order for you to set up the vital meeting needed so that you may introduce yourself, your company and your services and/or products. The techniques presented to you in this chapter are but a few successful ones used by me and many other sales professionals over the years, here is the secret though and it is that these techniques actually work but they will only work effectively if you use them as instructed and with professional experience gained over the years. I am hoping that the foundation laid in this chapter will give you enough insight so that you are able to assess each "gatekeeper challenge" on merit and come up with a way out. You are smart (because you made a decision to buy this book in the first place, and secondly, because you have shown a desire to learn from the best) so think the challenge through as I can assure you that there is ALWAYS a way past the gatekeeper. Ingenuity and determination are critical ingredients in overcoming in this part of the selling cycle. The professional entrepreneur salesperson is always on the lookout for ways in which to achieve his/her goals. Being able to overcome the challenge of the gatekeeper's questions and defense is sometimes both time consuming and frustrating; however, in overcoming, the rewards are surely satisfying and sweet.

# Chapter 16

# The Presentation
## *The Entrepreneur's SHOW-WINDOW!*

**Introduction**

The critical moment has arrived! You finally managed to get put through to the decision maker who has been more than happy to meet with you. The one thing that you will need to understand (and NEVER forget) from this moment on is that what the decision maker has given you is his/her valuable TIME. The time belongs to the decision maker so don't waste it and never squander an opportunity to now develop a long-term business relationship. You have worked hard to get to this point, and understand as every other corporate does out there, it cost money to get you to this point so don't waste this opportunity. Many unprofessional businesses out there never spend time in training their sales staff in the basic fundamentals of selling so it is quite possible that once they actually set the meeting/appointment with the prospect that they arrive for the meeting really not knowing what to say and what to do. How sad is this!? Others have so much to say, and say it in the most boring of ways that they lose the prospect after a single minute. What a waste! The Boy/Girl Scouts have a motto: "Be prepared!" While you and I are not scouts (well some may still be) when we are presenting to a prospect we must BE PREPARED! It is imperative that we show organization which in turn leads to a professional image and professional prospects prefer to deal with professional entrepreneur salespeople.

The question is then: "What are we showing?" the answer is that you are showing (1) Yourself (2) Your business in general (3) The products and/or services on offer. You start by showing yourself because if the prospect has not "bought" who YOU are then the rest will not matter. Remember, buyers buy from people they like and not companies. What is the goal in the initial presentation? TO DISCOVER THE PROSPECT'S NEEDS! I refer here again to the philosophy of need satisfaction selling and you cannot satisfy the prospect's needs with your products or your services if you have no clue as to what the needs are. I am sure that you agree but the unprofessional reading this concept may have difficulty coming to terms with this. However, read on, my friend, as you and I will work together and you and I will win. You will have TWO opportunities during the selling cycle to do a presentation. The first one we have discussed above and this one happens before the close of the sale. The second presentation has to do with closing the sale after presenting the final proposals for approval.

The first presentation is more commonly referred to as a "show and tell". This is your show-window and we thus refer to this as a multi-media presentation. This presentation is usually made up of PowerPoint slides, but should include interesting items such as short video clips of some of the services in action if at all possible and animations and humor when used in good taste can lighten up the mood and show that you have a sense of humor. Humor in good taste in the presentation is one of the most underrated positive attributes of a presentation and the entrepreneur salesperson that I know of. Many salespeople tend to shy away from the use of humor and I can never understand why as some of the most successful sales pitches I have ever done were all filled with good clean humor. People love to laugh so make them laugh and you will not be forgotten for doing so. I will soon be giving you a seven step format for the presentation process but before we get into this vital part of the chapter I would like you to fully understand the concept of a presentation and why it is necessary to present in an organized and professional manner.

We have already discussed aspects of the use of the five senses in this book so I will not repeat the entire idea here but your understanding of the use of the five senses during the presentation phase is critical if you want to leave the prospect with a lasting impression. Thus the use of samples is important so use these in your presentation as well. For instance, if your business provides soap dispensers then allow the prospect to feel the unit, touch the soap for texture and smell the soap. Also allow the prospect to wash their hands so that they can feel the difference between your soap quality and those of your competitors'. Explain and show the ease with which the soap cartridges are replaced and even encourage the prospect to make the change with your guidance.

To show then will require that you produce (as in production) an interesting multi-media presentation with a view to entertaining your prospect as though he/she was sitting in an audience and you were the main actor. Your presentation then must be a "spectacle" and able to keep the viewer (prospect) interested (as opposed to boring him/her to death) and in a sense come across as a wonderful display of interesting content (including photographs) and be an exhibition of all that you have to show and tell the prospect. Most of all the entire presentation must leave the prospect with an indelible impression of you, your company and your services and/or products. Let me reveal a secret to you. If you prepare and present a great presentation then this will allow you to set forth the GREAT VALUE of the prospect doing business with you and VALUE is what all buyers are more concerned about, and at times, even more so than the price of your product and/or service. Use your presentation to create GREAT VALUE and you will soon see how pricing objections disappear during the closing phase of the selling cycle. The greater the value the higher the pricing expectation and once you have raised expectations on the coming pricing structure during the proposal presentation then the greater the reduction of the "pricing shock" at the end. More often than not your price will seem so much lower when you present this to the prospect because the GREAT VALUE increases pricing expectations so never forget this key aspect of sales known to only a few professionals like you and me my friend.

**Presentation Format**

Structure is a key word when developing a professional presentation. If I had to use another key word then it surely would be "brevity". You and I have often heard the term "K.I.S.S.", ("Keep it simple Simon!") and this philosophy might be no more appropriate than when developing a professional presentation. When preparing a presentation you must use empathy-look at the presentation from the prospect's perspective. If you use empathy and conclude that your presentation is boring-then guess what? It is probably boring so make changes! Having huge amounts of data on each slide (mainly because you may not know your product and/or service) is not the way to go either and I will condemn this in the strongest possible terms. The LESS placed on each slide the better. All you are looking for is a guideline, or as I often refer to such things, a "skeleton", so that YOU can add the "meat" so to speak. This obviously means then, and goes without saying, that you need to know what you are talking about and understand yourself, the company which represent and the services and/or products which you are selling. You will also need to time your overall presentation, including the use of samples but excluding a question and answer session after the presentation is done. Most times, should you be able to present completely and professionally I can assure you that prospect questions will be limited or even eradicated as all questions are usually answered by the prospect actively listening to your interesting and lively presentation in its entirety. The maximum amount of time to spend on the presentation process, depending on the complexity of your business, should be forty minutes. Seven principles to follow are:

1. Building rapport (Old school: "Breaking the ice").
2. Building credibility.
3. The needs foundation phase.
4. Doing the presentation-action time!
5. Performing a COMPLETE survey of the prospect's overall needs.
6. Preparing the proposal/s.
7. Close for the business.

However, during the very first presentation you would want to professionally complete steps one to five only. Depending on your business you, more than likely, may need two meetings with the prospect before closing happens. The first meeting in the service industry (as an example) is considered more information gathering so that it will lead to the preparation of the proposals. A second meeting will then take place, the prospect is told of the second meeting upfront, and at this meeting the entrepreneur salesperson will present the proposal/s and CLOSE. Obviously, if you are in a position to, then complete all of the steps at the same meeting. For instance, I have everything set up on my laptop (Notebook for some) and am able to do a phase one and two using the same meeting meaning that after completing the information gathering I am able to input all of the information and get a confirmed proposal by simply printing it out for presentation to the prospect. I ask permission to use an unused office or boardroom. If I don't have access to a printer I will simply email the completed proposal to the receptionist and ask that she/he print this out for me.

## Building rapport (Old school: "Breaking the ice")

Don't forget the obvious PLEASE! Introduce yourself in a professional manner. Men, when shaking a woman's hand I suggest that you take it easy, but do not shake her hand as though she is a fish or porcelain. The handshake must be somewhat firm but not overbearing. LOOK THE PROSPECT IN THE EYES WHEN GREETING THEM! Ladies, when shaking a man prospect's hand you do not have to prove anything at all. He will see your gender and will not break your hand when he shakes the same in greeting you. However, from your side make sure that your handshake is not overpowering but firm enough to suite your gender. The idea here is professionalism and you must understand that building rapport or breaking the ice has already started and your time to leave a positive first impression has also started at the eye contact and the handshake, and guess what, you have not even sat down yet. This will be a good time to hand the prospect your business card and to get his/hers at the same time. In order to "break the ice" may I suggest that you have something UNRELATED to your visit to talk about and make the short conversation more about the prospect than about you? For instance, at times I would look for photographs of the prospect's family and simply focus on building a short discussion around this, and on other occasions, I may see trophies and create a conversation and show interest around this. Some prospects are proud of their studies and have degrees up on the wall or they collect model planes, boats or cars. The idea is to be alert and discover the source of you breaking the ice the moment you enter the room. Again, please understand, this is not a moment for you to talk about you! The focus must be on getting the prospect to talk as the more he/she talks the more comfortable they become with you and the more you stroke their ego through this "talking" process the more important they feel and the more important they feel the more cemented your relationship. I say again, buyers buy from people they like and not from companies. Your job, in a nutshell then, is to get the prospect to LIKE YOU and the sooner you can do this the better – trust me on this. If you are not able to build rapport (break the ice) then you may be wasting your time with the prospect – you MUST get the relationship to GEL if you know what I mean.

**Building credibility**

The rapport building stage as stated above deals with YOU building credibility (becoming likeable?) as a professional entrepreneur salesperson. However, what I am referring to now is that you will also have to build credibility as to the capability of the business which you are representing. If you are approaching a large corporate or multi-national then you must forgive the prospect for wondering if your company is able to manage the kind of workload which they will require of any supplier and/or service provider. You will only have a short time at the beginning of the presentation process within which to accomplish this goal. The other consideration is that you approach a client who considers your business as an "unknown quantity". In other words they have never heard of you or your business before. On the other hand, while they may have heard of your business they still have no clue as to what the business is capable of and its current reputation. Please refer to chapter 6 of this book for "Responding to $ales Resistance". The main goal during this phase is to create TRUST! As we have seen before, without TRUST you and I have nothing and this includes those people that know us very well. You can then only imagine how difficult it will be (using empathy of course) for a prospect who does not know you as a person or anything about your business. You have simply GOT TO change this so use the advice that I have given you above. During your presentation then, give an interesting short version (3 to 4 minutes maximum) of your business, what products/services it provides/performs and who you are currently doing business with (not a long list but sufficient enough to impress with you using as many compatible names as is possible). This helps to add much needed CREDIBILITY and thus means that you develop the much needed TRUST scenario for business and the development of a long-term business relationship.

## The needs foundation phase

There are two opportunities in my presentation format within which to do what the legal profession commonly calls "discovery". I have often shared how important it is that you discover the needs and the wants of the prospect and then you NEVER forget these as the prospect's needs and wants will be used to ultimately close the sale at the end of the selling cycle. I now give you two opportunities to put this secret into practice. At the outset the conversation is casual and you really want to use the time in order to find out what made the prospect agree to the meeting/appointment with you. The scenario may lead to something like this: "Bob, thank you so much for meeting with me today. I am curious and want to ask you a question that may seem odd at this time but your answer may help me to help you going forward. Would you mind very much if I asked you my odd question?" "Yes, Trevor, please go ahead!" "Bob, I can only assume that you have current suppliers for our products so with this in mind I am curious as to what made you decide to see me today?" I again want to admonish you to get your pen ready and write as fast as you can as somewhere in what the prospect will tell you after you asking this question lies the need and/or want that will help you close the business. This is not the time to get into long conversations as to the answer to your question as this will come along soon enough in the presentation. Your goal here and at this stage is fairly simple. Allow the prospect to answer your question, take notes, and BRIEFLY discuss your understanding of what the prospect is telling you by way of feedback: "Bob, so what you are telling me is …" Also be task oriented during this part of the presentation and help the prospect to understand, in brief, how your product and/or service may satisfy the needs as were presented by him/her. It would also be good to enquire as to the prospect's current challenges with regards to the products and/or services under discussion. Lastly, you may want to consider, clarifying possible new activities that will elicit further information or needs revelation by the prospect. WRITE DOWN ALL OF WHAT YOU DISCOVER!

**Warning:** *Don't move ahead with the presentation until you are convinced that you have at least uncovered the reason WHY you were granted the meeting in the first place!*

### Doing the presentation – action time!

You have a professionally prepared, tried and tested presentation so present IN FULL – no shortcuts. You have three goals at this time:

1. Present the "usual" PROBLEM/S clearly.
2. Present a clear SOLUTION to the problem/challenges encountered by past and present clients.
3. Present TESTIMONIALS that will support your proposed solutions.

The PROBLEM/CHALLENGE may have been given to you by the prospect but your product and/or service has already overcome these for other clients before your presentation on the day. The prospect, like me, will want you to have a clear understanding of any challenge BEFORE you can understand what solution is applicable so demonstrate this understanding in emphatic terms through your product/s and/or service/s. Problems which underscore a need for your product/service must already exist otherwise why offer your product and/or service? If there is no need for your product/service then you have no target market and you are simply wasting your time in business and sales. Focus on three things in this section as a priority: (1) Current available service/service levels in the marketplace (2) Staff morale and motivation levels (3) External audits which are and may be faced by the prospect (if applicable)

Present a clear solution to the problem/challenges encountered by past and present clients/customers. Besides the obvious the introduction of your products and/or services may have a positive effect on staff morale and motivation which in turn will lead to more effective production in the long term. For instance, let's assume that one of the services offered by your company is what is commonly called a hygiene service. Staff morale is down as the washroom areas have a malodor which will in all likelihood represent the strong possibility that the area is fast becoming disease filled. You recognize the problem and present the solution which will reduce the disease build-up in the washroom area meaning that you will also successfully reduce the risk of cross-infection amongst the staff and in turn you will create a positive effect on production which will ultimately benefit the prospect's company. The HHS (Health Department) may also perform unannounced inspections and demand to see proof or evidence of what is being done to contain the situation. Your service is done professionally and thus certificates are issued after each service thereby protecting your prospect or clients in the event of audits. The focus in this section of your presentation format should also be threefold: (1) Present your business focus (2) How your company manages staff (3) Guiding the prospect to the way forward (or the next step if you will).

Present TESTIMONIALS that will support your proposed solutions. Present testimonials clearly and do not go overboard with presenting too many in this forum. I would propose a maximum of five testimonials from clients who have been happy with your services and/or products. Choose only the best testimonials and ensure that they are unsolicited as the prospect may request copies and decide to call and verify personal references on you and your business or the company which you are representing. If the prospect wants more testimonials then provide those at a later stage. What types of testimonials are we looking to include in your presentation? Create a selection of three of the following: (1) Corporate Clients/customers – BIG NAMES (2) Government (3) Industry-related mining, commercial and industrial. The idea is to align the testimonials, as far as possible, with the industry to which you are presenting.

## Performing a COMPLETE survey of the prospect's overall needs

In step three you made an attempt to seek and discover the SERVICE/PRODUCT areas of the prospect's discontent. However, as a professional entrepreneur salesperson you are still not satisfied, and as a professional, you know that there just has to be more than what you have already discovered to want to make the prospect make such a drastic change from a service provider/supplier with whom they have been doing business with for so many years. The question is WHAT must still be discovered and how SERIOUS are the areas of DISCONTENT? The question then is should you probe even more in order to discover the SOURCE of the discontent? My answer to you then! Of course you should continue probing! Please remember (I am going to make this stick in your head no matter what), the only way to close the sale is if you base your entire philosophy on need satisfaction selling. If you have not as yet discovered ALL of the areas of discontent then do so NOW; however, the other critical discovery is for you to find out what the SOURCE is of the current discontent. Is it poor service levels, high pricing, lack of communication, poor CRM or repeated concerns in all the areas already mentioned? The result of all of this is frustration for the prospect so you will have to find out what the cause (the source) of this frustration is and the sooner the better as you will be reminding the prospect of this when you are in the close.

You will also want to discover what the prospect's expectations are as this relates to both your products and services and how this should be implemented to the prospects complete satisfaction. Issues such as delivery, and installation dates, and the subsequent service dates and expectations will need to be discussed. It is important to understand what services are important to the prospect and what services/products have priority at all times or just some of the time.

## TAKE COPIOUS NOTES WHILE THE PROSPECT IS TALKING

If you are in the workplace services industry then this will be the time to request permission to complete the presentation stage so that you are able to perform a site survey of the prospect's premises with a view to using the information in order to formulate the proposal/quotation. Once you have completed the survey then you have two options as discussed before (1) make yourself comfortable in a spare office or boardroom and complete the proposal for presentation on the same day or (2) remove yourself from the site with a view to preparing the proposal at your office and then arranging a second meeting for closing purposes.

### Preparing the proposal/s

Business practices regarding legally binding agreements around the globe vary from one country to the other. However, in most modern businesses today we no longer work off the "good old boy" handshake where a man's word is his bond – this is sad but a sign of the times I'm afraid. Should your business make use of legally binding agreements then prepare these for presentation. Check, re-check and double-check the agreement/proposal in order to ensure that all the client details and financials are one hundred percent correct. Legal documents require the full legal name and legal format of the business so ensure that this is placed on to the proposal or agreement. Again, ensure that your figures, both order quantity and dollar calculations are correct as once the prospect authorizes the document you and the prospect are bound by the same. You are now ready for final presentation and close!

## Close for the business

The moment of truth has arrived and all that you now have to do is to present the final proposal and move into a professional close as has been presented in this book way back in chapter 3 and 4. Three steps apply:

1. Summarize the NEEDS.
2. Summarize the BENEFITS.
3. ASK for the order.

## Conclusion

The definition of presentation:

*... the act of presenting ... something set forth for the attention of the mind ... a descriptive or persuasive account (as by a salesman of his product) ... an immediate object of perception, cognition, or memory ...*

- Webster's Dictionary

*The act of presenting or being presented 2 the manner of presenting 3 a talk or lecture; the manner of presenting ...*

- Collins Dictionary

Think about a "show window" for just a moment. Show windows exist all over the world and are used almost exclusively by national and international department stores.

You and I walk past show windows all of the time when we visit the shopping mall. The one thing about a show window is that it is purposefully designed for one thing only and that is to attract your attention. No matter where you are in the world the show window is attractive and its design is ever luring to the passer by. Color and perfection are the order of the day in a show window but only the very best of products are displayed in the show window. Many show windows are filled with multi-media presentations such as video, big bold lettering and photographs. Mannequins are the order of the day in a clothing department store but these too are designed almost to perfection, and once clothes are placed onto them one would be forgiven for thinking that some of them may be real and will walk out of the show window at any moment. The clothing, the service or any other products are carefully chosen and many are unique (one of a kind), and this attracts attention as well.

The goal though, and the purpose of the show window is what? Yes, it is there to represent the company, and yes, it is there to attract attention, and yes, it is even there for you and I to admire. However, the main function of the show window is to do all of the above but it MUST get you to come into the store. It must therefore generate enough curiosity in you and me to want to take another look and to go into the store to use some or all of the five senses (touch, feel, smell, etc.) with a view to actually PURCHASING the items/s. Show window is in a sense advertising and the essence of advertising is to lure people into the purchase. Thus there is no difference between the show window and your presentation if you consider it in the above terms. Your presentation then must be organized, professional but also STRIKING. It must be striking and luring enough for the prospect to want to know more (go into the store to use the senses) and attractive enough to cover all the needs and wants which you discover from the prospect. If your presentation is like the show window then it will be interesting and to the point.

No one should know more about your show window than you. Do not have a cumbersome presentation of your services and/or products; however, keep it short and to the point but the key word is interesting and covering the entire basis as was set forth in this chapter. Your prospect must be in awe of your presentation, but YOU remain in charge and YOU are the key to their challenges and YOU are more than capable of closing successfully for the sale. So, what are you waiting for?

# Chapter 17

# Post Call Introspection
*Self-correcting for $ales $uccess!*

**Introduction**

One of the most PRONOUNCED differences between an unprofessional and utterly professional entrepreneur salesperson is his/her ability to recognize that there is ALWAYS "room for improvement". The old adage of "one is never too old to learn" is a motto lived by when it comes to professional salespeople. Recognizing that mistakes exist and can be made is another difference between the professional and the unsuccessful. Making mistakes is a part of learning and once you have learned then DO NOT make the same mistakes again. Repeating mistakes will become costly for both you and your business but before you can determine not to repeat mistakes it is thus logical that you have to be able to identify the errors made after each sales call. The idea is to identify the error, affect a solution and develop a personal plan which will ensure that the same is NOT repeated EVER again. You have met people, like I have I am sure, who on a consistent basis, are saying sorry for repeating mistakes, but my view is that it can no longer be considered a "mistake" or an "accident" if the same negative action is repeated time after time once recognition has taken place. Should this in fact happen then it simply means that the perpetrator has developed a bad habit and does not have the will power and discipline to overcome the challenge. It is this type of personality that will cost a company dearly.

Thus, the professional salesperson will quickly learn and come to terms with the fact that being teachable is profitable. Again, understanding that mistakes can be made and are made during the sales call will help in taking corrective action prior to the next sales call, and not to do so, will cost. ALWAYS be open to analyzing your physical, mental and verbal actions after each sales call, and better yet, realize right up front that you are not perfect and that continuous error in judgment and in your presentation can and will cost you and your business a great deal of profit. Failure in this regard will also mean that a great chance has been lost to add a new client/customer to your current portfolio. What a waste!

How is post call introspection accomplished?

You have just completed a sales call, and it matters not, the activity. For instance, you may have messed up on a phone call the goal of which was to set up a meeting. This did not go well or it may have in fact ended well for you. By the way, things don't only have to go WRONG for you to do post call introspection as it is just as important to know what you are doing RIGHT so that you can keep on doing the right things that bring you success. So I want to encourage you to analyze every aspect of the sales process and perform this act as often as you can until you think you "have arrived" and even beyond.

Let's understand then what it is that you should evaluate. The first question you should ask yourself throughout the sales cycle is "did you achieve your objective/s?" Did you close? Why not? Did you get the meeting date? Why not? Did the presentation go well? Why not? Did you discover the needs? Why not? Another question is, "what went right and what went wrong?" The idea is to discover about yourself what you did well and what you did poorly, and in fact, what you did not do at all that you know to do, but "forgot" to do. You also want to ask yourself: "I have identified my weakness so what follow-up action is required?"

Asking the right questions about your actions, or lack thereof, will ensure a better performance the next time around so learn to ask many meaningful questions. Never forget to ask questions about what you omitted to do. Did you enquire about the complaints the prospect was experiencing in his/her dealings with the competitor or even with your own company if there has been a history of working together? Did you use sales aids such as samples? Using samples, as has already been discussed, adds a different and interesting dimension to your presentation but sometimes salespeople becomes lazy and in a hurry so they decide (in their "wisdom") to omit the use of samples and thereby do not create the "five senses experience" with the prospect. The logic here is that it is always better for a buyer to actually see and touch what they are buying-the impression is real and long lasting. Did the salesperson present a key benefit or were the very best testimonials presented or were they ever presented at all? Why and why not?

The most important question of all is DID YOU GET THE ORDER? Why not or why if you did? Did you obtain all the correct information or were you nervous about asking for this and did you do a great rapport building (breaking the ice) or was this either poor or non-existent when you met with the prospect? Was your meeting with the decision maker? If not why did you allow this as you are now disappointed at the result, and if you did, have you now decided to ensure that you ONLY meet with decision makers in the future as I have encouraged you to do? Did you find out about the frustrations and challenges faced by the prospect? Did you get surprised by a demand which you could not answer or an objection which you could not answer?

When you do self-correcting introspection WRITE IT ALL DOWN!

It will be necessary, of course, to visit the CURRENT CLIENT PORTFOLIO from time to time as has been decided upon during the geographical farming stage for territory management. Have you documented all the relevant parts of the discussion, and in particular, the client's/ customer's request for additional services? Have you documented any of the client's pricing concerns and quality control questions? Have you answered these correctly? Did you have the necessary information to effectively deal with the customer's query? Were you organized, prepared and informed enough about your products/services and the company itself?

WRITE YOUR FINDINGS DOWN FOR FUTURE REFERENCE!

When visiting existing clients do you have a "Current Account Call Sheet" to record all relevant information and the discussion? See a primitive example below but it is the idea that you can develop for your industry and current client/customer base.

Self-correcting introspection should be very specific. You need to ensure that the following three questions are achieved at all times for all sales calls. :

1. What happened?
2. What was learned?
3. What is the OBJECTIVE and STRATEGY for the next sales call?

**Conclusion**

As an entrepreneur salesperson and a professional you will understand the absolute importance of realizing very quickly that we all learn and improve our skills by consistent self-correcting introspection. Once again, an old adage: "Learn by your mistakes" will apply and if this is good enough for our old school ancestors then it should be good enough for you and me. The idea at this point in the selling cycle is to focus and build upon our clear strengths after each sales call. We should ponder and contemplate each strength and how it was used and the result which it produced. The key here then is to repeat performing the strong parts of our expertise and personality over and over again when dealing with a prospect that can add to business turnover and profit. On the other hand many salespeople also have weaknesses but we can even learn buy these. Weaknesses are simply an opportunity to improve. Identifying a weakness is always a good thing but it is what you and I do with these weaknesses that matter. Weaknesses simply MUST be turned into strengths or discarded or replaced entirely. The end product then must be to turn negative errors into positive results. Never neglect to take a long hard look at yourself after each sales call, and never, be lazy to contemplate your actions (whether negative or positive) as it is in this action that you may yet reap the best rewards, and these results, will be long-lasting and produce more positive fruit than you can ever imagine.

# Chapter 18

# W.A.R. ("WAR")
# Weekly Activity Report

## Introduction

It is important at this point that you, the reader, understand that I absolutely admire the salesperson in any industry. I have been a salesperson for almost all of my life so when I discuss matters in this chapter, and I will get deep down and very personal, you must understand that it comes from the heart and in no way am I meaning to be derogatory toward my fellow salespeople. However, there are certain home truths which need to be discussed in this chapter, and my friend, if YOU are offended by some of my statements then one of two things may be wrong: (1) you are guilty (2) you are guilty but understand the need for change. Once again, due to the nature of the topic of this chapter it is imperative that we lay a firm foundation as many unprofessional salespeople out there will argue AGAINST the need for a rigid reporting system. If YOU are a salesperson and if YOU are one of these unprofessional people who argue against the need for a clear and concise reporting structure relating to your weekly activities then I would ask that you bear with me, keep an open mind and consider the chapter as a whole before you reject the contents at the outset.

I will state one more time that I have been a salesperson for many decades; I have sold all types of commodities and/or services and have done so in many various economies, cultures and countries. The reason that I make this clear is to instill in you an intrinsic understanding that I know salespeople probably better than most. I know all of the short-cuts, the floundering, the LAZINESS, the lack of commitment, the lack of direction and the lack of loyalty to the company which employs you. I also understand that you will blame everyone and everything else for your lack of production and achievement but the finger of blame will never go your way – according to you anyway. You will blame the "lack of support" which you perceive coming from your sales manager or entrepreneur sales manager. You will blame the lack of training (this may be legit at times but you can self-train) for why you are not achieving quota/targets. You will blame the lack of sales aids, lack of printed material and the lack of a company strategy. You will blame your wife and family for your failure, your friends and even the traffic congestion. In fact, you will find a reason, other than yourself, to blame for your laziness, lack of direction and lack of production on almost anything else except YOU. In my opinion then, and excuse the following forthright comment: Taking the above into account I have a different point of view: YOU ARE TO BLAME FOR YOUR OWN FAILURE!"

Sitting in coffee shops will not help you! Spending time visiting friends and family during the day when you should be selling won't help you! Going to the local shopping mall and doing "window shopping" will not help you to sell and achieve quota! Going to a movie while you should be selling is pathetic but this action will not help you and your loved ones achieve your personal and family goals in the least. What you do and how you deceive others and yourself will ultimately destroy your own goals but it will also disappoint the company you work for, and in particular, when they see that you are not producing a sale which was the very reason for spending so much money on you to begin with. The other issue I have with unprofessional salespeople is that they seem more than willing to take any job offer (as a "stepping stone" in most cases) with a view to immediately start looking around for something "better". There is no commitment, no loyalty and no trust from such a one. This is the worst kind of fool in the sales world as they simply waste time, and while I am never concerned with their own time they waste as this is largely self-inflicted, I remain concerned about the utter wastage which such a person generates for a well-meaning business and entrepreneur. If you are the kind or person described above (hopefully you are not) then I want to attribute one other characteristic to you and that is that your main daily activity will probably be to lie about your production activities no matter who you work with and for. You lie about where you are at any given point of the day; you lie about your activity and lie about "potential" business which never happens. You lie on your sales reports and you lie to your entrepreneur sales manager/sales manager but worst of all, and truly worst of all you lie to those closest to you – your family. I am sorry that I have to be this blunt but a lazy salesperson is also generally a very good liar. These two negative characteristics seem to go hand in hand.

The fundamental difference then between the professional salesperson and the unprofessional is simply this: THEY CANNOT BE TRUSTED!

This is the very reason why it is absolutely vital that you, as an entrepreneur learn from day one in business that you cannot trust yourself to stay on track and focus on bringing in new business through sales; however, more importantly you CANNOT trust any new salesperson which you hire to achieve quota simply by giving him/her the job. Salespeople's actions and sales related activities MUST, to me, be monitored at all times.

We have spent some time on discussing some rather serious problems relating to the unprofessional time-wasting salesperson. You may have felt that YOU are not happy with yourself right now so how do you change this? How do you go from someone that cannot be trusted to a professional salesperson who is serious about producing sales not only for his/her company or employer but also for your family? The very first item of business has got to be your willingness to recognize a few things and understand them clearly, the most important being, that you are well described above, and that you are in trouble and that you actually WANT to change. In order to assist this desire for change you will need to understand that there are certain key areas which I will now present which will help you in your new commitment. We will discuss:

1. Laziness.
2. Lies.
3. Deceit.
4. Direction

**Laziness**

The opposite of the term "lazy" within the working context must be taken to mean then "industrious". To be industrious I mean that a professional salesperson is action-driven with no excuses for why he/she is not achieving. They are noted by their ability to work long and hard hours if need be but they also have an unbelievable ability to focus on the task (whatever this is) at hand. While we don't often hear this word much nowadays the focus may also be likened to one being conscientious. A professional salesperson is also enterprising as generally there is no challenge that cannot be overcome and all problems must have a solution. They are, at times; painstakingly patient as it is their self-confidence that pushes them toward the ultimate actions which produce results no matter the hurdle/s. The professional salesperson is energetic, productive, keen to produce results and always active in "making things happen". In a nutshell then, these professionals display zeal in what they do each moment of the day and come across as absolutely tireless in their day to day goals which lead to sales and personal success.

The willful and deliberate act of laziness however depicts someone who is idle – doing as little as possible or just enough so as not to draw attention to one. This person is also considered to be shy of actual work and work-related activity in any form. Inactive is a good word for someone who is lazy and they are also both lethargic (even if they had energy they probably won't expend any at all) and most certainly slack. You and I have many of these kinds of people in our lives but salespeople have no excuse. This person does not perform well under any kind of pressure at all (no, not even a little bit) and is in their element if they can spend much of their time "relaxing". In other words, all in all, you are dealing with a salesperson with no motivation at all to achieve anything at all. The question which you may be asking together with me then is "why would one become a salesperson at all then as this characteristic is in opposition to the job description"? My response to this question: EXACTLY!

**Lies**

The problem with the above is that in the sales environment this characteristic develops the need to lie. How else do you "cover-up" all the obvious lack of production and missed sales quotas/targets? This is why I want you, as a business person, an entrepreneur and a sales manager to understand that when you conduct an interview for a sales position, in most instances you would be correct should the candidate give you the impression that he or she may be lazy and that the element of lying will also feature prominently as a cover up for why there is no sales success forthcoming. Do NOT be fooled into employing these people no matter how good the tongue as it is more about what is on the inside that you don't hear than being deceived by a smooth tongue on the outside.

To lie in our current context simply means that the salesperson is doing whatever they can to deceive you. There is no guilty conscience and deceit will come naturally to a liar. The goal of the salesperson here, to quote an old school phrase, will be to "pull the wool over your eyes"! Lies in our context again then will also mean that the entrepreneur sales manager will be fed a barrage of "half-truths", stories that have been invented a while ago and used with relative success over the years or a half-truth that is conjured up within a split second – such is the expertise of a "salesperson liar". Other words that best describe a liar may be false or falsehood, fabrication, falsification, deception and fiction. To once again quote an old school saying then, to such a one "truth is stranger than fiction". They lie so often that the line between truth and lies becomes blurred to the point where such a salesperson starts to believe their own lies totally oblivious to the ability of the entrepreneur or sales manager to see through their deceit and lies.

**Deceit**

While closely aligned to the term and action called lying there are some serious differences taking our context and discussion into account. Deceit is considered more "trickery", pretense, cheating, and a good legal word: MISREPRESENTATION! Deceit lends itself to the ugly side of a human being in that you can expect cheating in all forms from a salesperson who knows how to deceive management and clients/customers. A most untrustworthy and unsavory character I can assure you. Please remember the following should you be interviewing a potential deceiver: they are capable, and many do, of committing fraud and will not even think anything of both their actions and the results of their actions-they will also not care who gets hurt at the time.

## Direction

The absolute worst thing that can happen to any salesperson, (whether professional or not) is that he/she has a lack of direction on how to achieve sales quotas/targets. This is, if you will forgive me, the most unpardonable sales omission, and yet, the lack of this characteristic is still responsible for the downfall of many a salesperson, and in fact, companies all over the world.

Most unprofessional sales people are characterized as not having direction. Meaning then that these salespeople are directionless, no compass, no bearing and more than likely at a total loss of how to get from point A to point B so that sales quotas may be achieved. They don't know the route to success or the way to achieve goals and personal life dreams and desires. There is no course to their day and week and no line to follow. In other words there is a total lack of orientation and that is why when they wake up they already hate the day and what will NOT happen on the day. This is totally demotivating. There is nothing worse, in my opinion, than for a salesperson to be sitting on his/her couch on a Sunday evening not knowing what they will be doing to generate sales for the coming week. Sales managers and entrepreneur sales managers ought to take responsibility in this area as a lack of sales affects one and all. When a company's salespeople come into the office on a Monday morning it is not difficult to see those who have clear direction for generating sales for the coming week. They are happy and exhume confidence in all areas, are jovial and focused. They also have a burning desire to "get going" and are impatient at lengthy sales meetings. They are the "go, go, go" of your sales team.

What these people (the unprofessional that is) need are GUIDELINES! We have discussed the challenge or problem faced by the unprofessional salesperson in depth so we now understand the negatives and what we need to be aware of when employing new sales staff; however, we simply must find a solution or the only thing we have discovered is how bad certain salespeople are. The salespeople need a set of INSTRUCTIONS! They need a PLAN FOR SUCCESS and they need to be handed a set of orders (as in a military term) from the sales manager or entrepreneur sales manager (the "General" in command so to speak).

SALESPEOPLE MUST NOT BE LEFT TO THEIR OWN DEVICES BUT NEED TO BE MANAGED ALL DAY AND EVERYDAY AND EVERY WEEK OF THE YEAR!

As a sales manager it is not always possible to be with a team of salespeople every hour of every day but a carefully planned "WAR" (Weekly Activity Report) can achieve this goal and allow you to manage salespeople at the same time. I have developed a Weekly Activity Report and have fondly referred to it as the "WAR". While this in no way reflects a true war between nations it most certainly will allow the salesperson to think twice about "laziness", "lies", "deceit" and "no sense of direction". The salesperson will "WAR within them" as when you design a WAR then you must understand that it must cover the basis as stated above. The WAR must be designed to make it very difficult, if not impossible, not to achieve sales quotas/targets on a weekly basis. The course and direction must be clear and broken down into clear steps of achievement. The key though, once you have developed the WAR is that it MUST be strictly managed and the salesperson must not be allowed to get away with not performing even in a single allotted task. Each task MUST be monitored at least on a weekly basis if you are to achieve monthly and quarterly sales quotas/targets. The sales manager must accept NO EXCUSES for non-achievement on any of the KPA's as these are structured for success. If you are able to do this you will limit your damage as far as useless salespeople are concerned and you will have the ability to get rid of non-producers sooner rather than later, and guess what? You will also have written proof of why you have decided to terminate their services as not achieving the KPA's will be clear evidence of laziness, lies, deceit and not wanting to follow clear DIRECTION for success.

I have included a copy of a WAR which I developed many years ago and have used successfully ever since. However, before I start to dissect this for you, I want you to know that this is MY WAR (not yours); however, you are more than welcome to use it in your business and amongst your sales people. I must warn you that the WAR will apply to most service industries but it may not apply to you if you are in any other industry as a business. You can, of course, make changes or even develop your very own WAR. I will deal with mine because it is our example but you will quickly see that you will be able to modify the current WAR as presented to suit your own business activity and needs.

The WAR has been divided up into 4 sections. The one thing that you will notice is that it is a single page document but I can assure you that it is packed with DIRECTION in order to achieve success.

1. Proposals Report.

Item 1 deals with the physical amount of proposals which were presented to the prospect or existing client/customers for the week. You and the salesperson will need to consider the personal ratio between "sales in" and "proposals out" for each particular salesperson. While this will largely depend on each individual salesperson's level of expertise it will also have a lot to do with territory capacity, desired company sales returns and the salesperson's personal goals and value system. Goal setting and understanding ones value system can be found in chapters that are presented in my first book namely **ENTREPRENEUR** (*minus*) **101** (Publisher: Austin Macauley-ISBN 978 1 78455 148 3 Paperback; ISBN: 978 1 78455 150 6 Hardback www.austinmacauley.com).

Should the company decide that each salesperson is to see at least 2 new prospects a day then this, according to the "Proposals Out" section should be reflected as 10 new proposals for the week. Proposals Value is simply the total financial value when combining all of the proposals for the week. For instance, should the salesperson have achieved the week's quota at 10 proposals handed out then we must now understand the combined dollar value. Therefore, add up the dollar value on each proposal and place this figure into the "Proposals Value" section of the WAR. Proposal Value is what was ACTUALLY achieved for the week; however, this achievement must be compared to the desired company quota budget. There may be weeks when the quota budget is achieved, exceeded or equaled. Whatever the scenario the proposals Dollar value as combined, must now be compared to what was actually achieved. If there is a shortfall then enter this figure in under the section for "Proposals Surplus/Shortfall".

Example: From Monday to Friday 10 proposals were presented to new business prospects and each, with varying values naturally, when calculated together to produce a dollar figure, amounted to a total dollar value of proposals out for the week as $5000. However, as we secure our services by means of annual (automatically renewable on an annual basis until terminated by the client) agreements/contracts we want to know the annual value for each contract/agreement. In this case then the ANNUAL value will amount to $60000. In order then to determine the difference between the quota TARGETS/GOALS one would need to set these with the salesperson and in line with your expectations and budget projections. However, for the sake of our example let us assume that the quota target is set at $60000 per week then this would mean that this salesperson would have achieved quota for the week as far as his/her "Quota Value" is concerned and thus deserves a "pat on the back". However, if there is a shortfall then the "Quota Value" is subtracted from the "Quota Budget", and this total, either way is placed into the "QUOTA SURPLUS/SHORTFALL section. Quota shortfall figures are represented in the negative so place these in parenthesis at all times to be able to instantly view negative figures for either motivational or discipline reasons. Whatever you do as a salesperson NEVER take negative reflected figures lightly as these add up over a quarter and before you know it your quotas are behind and you are called in for some severe discipline of the worst kind. My feeling is that if you can't make it then you must go. If you are the entrepreneur sales manager or sales manager in your company then I want to warn you that you simply CANNOT allow salespeople NOT to achieve targets/goals of any kind. It should be your goal to deal with poor and non-performers each and every week. Dealing with poor or non-performing salespeople on a weekly basis gives you the opportunity to identify weaknesses and shortfalls and make corrections to attitude, activities and training. A word of advice if I may? NEVER be afraid to get rid of non-performing or poor producing salespeople. If you come to the point (it may be sooner rather than later) where you realize that you have done all in your power to train and support the salesperson and yet there seems to be no positive change by way of sales achievement then make a change NOW. The only positive change which you want to measure is QUOTAS OUT AND SALES IN.

2. Sales Report.

The "Sales Report" section of the WAR works in pretty much the same way as the "Quota Out" section as the calculations and parameters work in the same way. However, as a fair warning to you salespeople who are not closing sales professionally tend to focus YOUR attention more on the "QUOTA REPORT" section for obvious reasons. If they feel that they have handed out enough proposals then you will be "happy" with this as this surely represents POTENTIAL NEW BUSINESS!? Not true! ONLY signed (authorized) agreements/contracts are a true reflection of a sale and NOTHING ELSE! I have already warned you of deceitful salespeople so here is where you will be deceived I promise you. ONLY signed contracts (duly authorized in some circles) must be considered as sales and QUOTAS OUT are just that, they are proposals which have been handed to a prospect but in essence were not even closed professionally or you would have every proposal represented as a sale and placed into the SALES VALUE section of the report. NEVER confuse the two although they do tend to work hand in hand as you simply cannot have sales if the salesperson is not face to face with the decision maker presenting proposals. However, if the salesperson is handing out his quota of proposals and this is not coming through in the sales section then it is time for you to ask some serious questions relating to the salesperson's ability to close the sale. This weakness will need IMMEDIATE and URGENT attention as you may be wasting your time on someone who is good at the initial aspects on the sales process but weak on the most critical part of selling-CLOSING. If a salesperson cannot close professionally, or at all, then you will be wasting your time with such an one as the way your business will grow is not through the amount of proposals which are placed into the field but the amount of SALES CLOSED! Never forget this and if you do then you can expect to develop cash-flow challenges sooner rather than later which may even lead to you losing your business.

3. General Report.

The "GENERAL REPORT" has 7 sections as you can see. This section deals with the salesperson ACTIVITY for the week. Once again, if you are going to be deceived then this section will assist you to eliminate this threat. You will notice that there is no place to report visits to the mall, the coffee shop, the movie house or any other non-selling related activity. The focus is on activities only which will promote the selling process. These activities will assist when it comes to giving both you and the salesperson DIRECTION. We have not included room for non-sales related activities as this is what they ought to be focusing on every minute of the day if you are to succeed. Let's consider the individual reporting KPA's shall we?

4. "Number of cold calls this week":
Unprofessional salespeople hate cold calling! While you may not need to include this in your personalized reporting

structure you must also understand that when you develop NEW BUSINESS then in most cases the very nature of this activity is to FIND new business. Cold calling is a time-tested and proven way to generate sales leads for new business introductions and new business SALES. No entrepreneur salesperson/sales manager or sales manager will ignore the importance of this activity and I would encourage you to seriously consider this activity as the life blood of your business. Set a quota AND STICK TO IT! For each cold call done during the week you should demand proof of the same, and such proof, may come in the form of a business card, company "compliment slips" (usually from the receptionist of any business) or if any other method fails then the salesperson should be required to hand in a company letterhead containing all the relevant details. I want to warn you that you WILL be lied to and deceived in this KPA as well in that more often than not you will receive "repeat" business cards and the like when this is handed to you on a weekly basis. For instance, three weeks ago you may have received a business card (or whatever is handed in as proof of the call) and the unprofessional deceiving salesperson will assume that you have by now forgotten the name of the company and simply include another of the same business card in order to make up reporting numbers. The other area of deceit and lies comes in when a business card was handed in about three weeks ago; assuming that you had forgotten the name of the cold call, but a company letterhead may now be handed in as cold calling evidence. DON'T be fooled! ALWAYS BE ON THE ALERT! Remember, the turnover, profit and cash-flow of your business is at stake so be aware of deceivers and liars at all times. I agree with you, it is sad, but one has to resort to knowledge in order to be aware of salespeople who are out to take you and me for a ride. I want to emphasize that NOT all salespeople are alike but I will warn you against the exception rather than the rule as this relates in particular to the unprofessional. The physical evidence of the cold call must contain the name and ALL contact details of the decision maker.

5. "Number of meetings this week":

If 10 meetings a week were set as a quota for new business presentations (proposals) and closings then this is the figure that is inserted. However, a copy of the salesperson's calendar/diary/Day-Timer must be included in the package to be handed in each Friday. You will then cross reference these with the meetings as presented in the last week's WAR – the figures for last week stating the meetings for the coming week must match as this was the "meetings for next week" commitment. If the meetings do not match then you need to ask why.

6. "Number of meetings for next week":

The idea is to keep the salesperson setting up new business meetings as this way he/she ALWAYS has direction for each week. Under no circumstances are you to entertain directionless/headless salespeople. Pre-set meetings give direction and these meetings allow the salesperson to have a good rest over a weekend in knowing that they have direction for the following week and the weeks thereafter. This is highly motivational and does wonders for self-image and self-esteem levels. As a reminder then, the commitment of how many proposal closings the salesperson has set up for next week will be reflected in and checked by using the calendar/diary/Day-Timer copy of the following week.

7. "Number of AAA accounts visited this week" (see example of CURRENT ACCOUNT/CALL REPORT):

As discussed in the previous chapters on territory management, it may be that the territory allotted to any particular salesperson has pre-existing business relationships with current clients/customers. As the entrepreneur sales manager you have added the servicing of these existing clients/customers as a duty. With this in mind you and the salesperson will need to have a clear understanding of how many service calls will need to be made on a weekly basis. This figure needs to be placed into this section. ALWAYS ensure that a CURRENT ACCOUNT REPORT is included each week which coincides with the number of calls made. ALWAYS check these sheets and ensure accuracy as it is just as important for you to look after your current client/customer base as it is to generate new business. What is the point of bringing in new business on the one side and you have to deal with cancellations/terminations on the other hand. The business MUST grow and can only do so if you are ADDING new business.

8. "Number of AA accounts visited this week":
Same procedure and practice as above.

9. "Number of A accounts visited this week":
Same procedure and practice as point 4 above.

10. "Number of sales leads received this week":
Most companies support their sales staff by ensuring that they have a stream of QUALIFIED sales leads for the purpose of turning these into sales. It costs money to generate a sales lead so whatever you do keep TRACK OF SALES LEADS AT ALL TIMES! You will want to track the sales lead from the time it comes into the company until the result comes back from the salesperson. All sales leads need to be monitored every step of the way but particularly once it has been handed to a salesperson. Should the salesperson NOT be able to convert sales leads into business then you need to know why and determine first of all if the lead is as QUALIFIED as you have been led to believe. ALWAYS do your best to "pre-qualify" sales leads, or hire someone to do this for you, BEFORE you hand these to your sales staff. The last thing that you want is to demotivate your salespeople and having a heap of time wasting "leads" is frustrating considering the amount of time that the salesperson must spend on trying to convert these into a "live" sale. The long and the short of a sales lead though, ONCE THEY ARE QUALIFIED, you must track these after they are handed to the salesperson. The amount handed to the salesperson each week must be reflected in this section and all activity in working these must be submitted each week (supporting documentation to be handed in).

## REMARKS SECTION

The remarks section may be used for just about anything EXCEPT excuses for the lack of sales and/or any other production failures.

If a salesperson is out in the field a great deal and is running out of sales and promotional material then this section may be used as a request to replenish stock. If the salesperson is having difficulty with a current account and needs the assistance of the sales manager then this request may be placed in this section. If additional training is needed or there is a request for the entrepreneur sales manager to attend a critical closing with the salesperson the following week, or sometime into the future, then this request is placed in this section. However, under no circumstances are you to allow a salesperson to place ANY EXCUSE (I suppose death would have to be an exception) for why sales and/or proposal quotas were not met. There is no point in the salesperson having a bad week and then feeling that this section alleviates the need to meet with a superior with a view to explaining sales failure.

4. Supporting Documentation.

The goal is to keep salespeople on track so that you can grow your business. A reporting structure such as the WAR (or any other structure as designed by you and for your business) must be comprehensive, yet practical but MUST keep the salesperson focused and on course for sales success. Direction is vital and this can only be achieved if there is no confusion as to what is expected by the salesperson each week. The WAR will achieve this goal. In order to ensure that there is no confusion as to reporting expectations a summary of all the needed "SUPPORTING DOCUMENTATION" is included as a final reminder as to what must be submitted, when this is to be submitted and to whom it is submitted to.

You will notice that I have our sales staff hand their reports in to the sales manager BEFORE 15h00 on a Friday, and this is generally after the sales meeting each Friday. I also ensure that each salesperson is aware that the ENTIRE DOCUMENT (WAR) must be completed in full each and every week. In fact, the sales manager will make sure that no WAR is accepted without being scrutinized for completeness. Furthermore, we ensure that no confusion exists around what must be included in the WAR in order to make it COMPLETE:

1. "Photocopies of all proposals as given to prospective clients": It matters not if the salesperson works through the server to generate proposals or whether he/she uses pre-approved templates, the point is that EVERY proposal that is handed out for the week must be copied and handed in together with the WAR. The proposal copies are then validated like any other document in line with the claims on the WAR.

2. "Photocopies of all signed (authorized) sales agreements/contracts": If the salesperson has made a claim to closing whatever amount of sales then there should be the necessary copy of the said agreement/contract. It is understood that the ORIGINAL agreement/contract has already been handed in to the administration department for vetting and approval purposes. A copy of the agreement/contract must be submitted with the WAR each week.

3. "Original business cards or company letterheads or compliment slips": We have already discussed this above so we will not deal with this now other than to say that this is simply included as a reminder in the check-list of items to be submitted with the handing in of the WAR each Friday.

4. "Photocopies of this week's calendar, diary or Day-Timer": Dealt with above but another reminder on the final check-sheet of items to be submitted.

5. "Current account report sheets": These must be COMPLETED IN FULL before submitted.

6. "Photocopy of assigned sales leads:" All necessary feedback must be completed BEFORE submission.

# CURRENT ACCOUNT/CALL REPORT

**CURRENT ACCOUNT/CALL REPORT**

COMPANY NAME: _____        DATE OF VISIT: _____

ACCOUNT CONTACT: _____        POSITION HELD: _____

CURRENT SERVICES IN PLACE: _____

NEW SERVICES PROPOSED: _____

ACCOUNT CATEGORY: _____        CONTACT TEL: _____

REMARKS: _____

_____

_____

_____

_____

I hereby acknowledge that I have performed the abovementioned CURRENT ACCOUNT visit. I have also performed a complete analysis of the client's needs with a view to identifying potential future business.

_____                _____

(PRINT NAME)                                            (SIGNATURE)

# WEEKLY ACTIVITY REPORT ("WAR")

WEEK # _____     WEEK ENDING: _____     SALESPERSON: _____

*SUMMARY SHEET*

**QUOTES (PROPOSAL) REPORT**
| | | | |
|---|---|---|---|
| 1. | QUOTES OUT | : _____ | (number of quotes i.e. 4, 5, 6 etc) |
| 2. | QUOTES VALUE | : $_____ | (total value of all quotes for the week) |
| 3. | QUOTES BUDGET | : $_____ | (weekly target as given by S.M.) |
| **4.** | **QUOTES SURPLUS / SHORTFALL** | **: $_____** | **(the difference between 2+3)** |
| | | | *Reflect negative figures between ( )* |

**SALES REPORT**
| | | | |
|---|---|---|---|
| 1. | NEW BUSINESS | : _____ | (number of new accounts i.e. 4, 5, 6 etc) |
| 2. | SALES VALUE | : $_____ | (total value of ALL sales for the week) |
| 3. | SALES BUDGET | : $_____ | (weekly target as given by S.M.) |
| **4.** | **SALES SURPLUS / SHORTFALL** | **: $_____** | **(the difference between 2+3)** |
| | | | *Reflect negative figures between ( )* |

**GENERAL REPORT**
| | | | |
|---|---|---|---|
| 1. | Number of cold calls this week | : _____ | (add bus-cards, comp slips or letterheads) |
| 2. | Number of appointments this week | : _____ | (must match photocopy of diary) |
| 3. | Number of appointments for next week | : _____ | (must match photocopy of diary) |
| 4. | Number of AAA accounts visited this week | : _____ | (must be supported by Current Account Report) |
| 5. | Number of AA accounts visited this week | : _____ | (must be supported by Current Account Report) |
| 6. | Number of A accounts visited this week | : _____ | (must be supported by Current Account Report) |
| 7. | Number of sales leads received this week | : _____ | (must be supported by COMPLETED document) |

REMARKS: _____
_____
_____
_____

**Please note:**

1.  This document must be completed in FULL each week (Hand in to S.M. **before** 3:00pm on Fri.)
2.  This document must be accompanied by:

    a.  Photocopies of all quotes as given to prospective clients
    b.  Photocopies of all authorized (signed) orders
    c.  Original business cards or company letterheads or compliment slips
    d.  Photocopies of this week's diary (completed)
    e.  Photocopy of next week's diary (completed)
    f.  Current account report sheets (completed)
    g.  Photocopy of assigned sales leads (completed)

*To the best of my knowledge, I hereby declare the above report to be an accurate reflection of my sales activities for the week. I understand that false reporting may lead to disciplinary action against me which may mean termination of my employment.*

_____          _____
(PRINT NAME)                                          (SIGNATURE)

# Conclusion

By now you must think that I dislike salespeople intensely. I hope that you don't feel this to be the case and maybe I should qualify this statement. I absolutely love working with salespeople that want to work and who have a drive to succeed. I do not waste my time on "salespeople" who are not serious about sales, and in the process, they cause the demise of young business. I have seen the likes of what I have come to term as "job-hoppers" who quickly "run" when the going gets tough. I have also seen the disappointment in well-meaning entrepreneurs who place their trust in a smooth talking salesperson only to find out that they have been deceived into believing that the salesperson can actually sell.

My advice, ALWAYS check at least three business references BEFORE you employ a new salesperson. Ensure that the references are current and legitimate, and while you are at it, do a credit check and ensure that the salesperson is able to manage their personal finances – you will be amazed as to how desperate people lie.

On the other hand, when one comes across a newly employed salesperson, and they achieve, now this is what I call a blessing. You need salespeople that will understand your heart to grow your business and you need these people to be totally committed to you and the growth of your business. Professional salespeople are always a pleasure to work with as they know what needs to be done and they are simply good at doing what they know – SUCCEED! These types of salespeople wake up in the morning knowing exactly what they are about and what needs to be accomplished for the day, the week and the month. They are not afraid of cold calling but do very little of it because they are kept busy with referrals due to their commitment to excellence in service.

Therefore, adhering to a WAR will not be considered out of the ordinary for the professional but for the "chancer", the liar and the deceiver the WAR will always be a "noose around the neck" and he/she will hate it from day one. Salespeople that say they don't need a WAR of some sorts are those who will take a good entrepreneur for a financial ride in no time at all. WAR's are thus not developed for the professional but for the unprofessional. WAR's are developed for the LAZY salespeople of the sales world and in a new business you will do well to head my advice in that you should NEVER hire a salesperson that you have not cleared at least three character/business references for, that you have not requested a credit report for and that is reluctant to work within the bounds and scope of a WAR. There are three very good reasons why we call it a WAR:

WEEKLY means that you monitor the progress of your salespeople on a weekly basis. Monitoring them at least once a week will allow you to stay in touch with both their progress and lack thereof. It is far easier to help someone to achieve quotas if you are in touch and in control of the salesperson's time. What is the point of waiting till the end of the month before you realize that the salesperson will not deliver the desperately needed sales in order to grow your business? Monitoring the salesperson on a weekly basis will also force you to give attention to one of the most vital parts of your business and that is sales for business growth and an improved cash-flow. Assessing the salesperson's progress, or lack thereof on a weekly basis will also help the salesperson to understand that you are not the kind of person who is easily fooled and they will be more diligent in their actions knowing that they will have to report to you on a regular basis, and this, without fail week after week.

ACTIVITY means that you and the salesperson must be able to account for literally EVERY minute of every day. AFTER ALL, is this not the time which you are paying for? Allowing the salesperson to "roam on the prairie" without a reporting structure is like sending a child to a candy bowl and telling him to have all he can eat. There is no doubt in your mind and mine that a child would get very sick indeed, and while most salespeople are not children (close in some cases though) they too will get "sick" and will abuse and squander the time on activity that will have no bearing on their job description and their ability to bring you what you want to grow your business – SALES. You set the activity and by doing so you set the direction for success. Salespeople ALWAYS need direction and simply cannot be trusted to function without the parameters which make up clear direction. Guiding activity will set the pace and the direction. Once you have achieved this then stand back and reap the sales rewards.

REPORT lends itself to much needed accountability within the sales environment. Not having accountability for your salespeople or taking away accountability in the name of "freedom" will spell disaster for you and your business. As the business owner you have accountability to your bank manager or bankers (unless you finance your own business of course), to your suppliers, your clients/customers, your wife and your family. This is why I can never understand entrepreneurs who are smart individuals who will not set the time aside to share accountability with a salesperson that could, if you allow him/her, break you financially or make you in the same way! Reporting to someone has in the action a keen sense of accountability and the fear of pending consequences for poor and non-performance; however, on the other hand it also holds the key to success for the business and positive reinforcement for the successful professional salesperson who understands all of what you and I have dealt with in the chapter.

# Action Stations!

May I take this opportunity to say yet again that KNOWLEDGE IS NOT KNOWLEDGE UNTIL YOU PUT IT INTO ACTION!

You may be good at reading and thereby absorbing the theory; however, in order to be a MASTER ENTREPRENEUR SALESPERSON/SALES MANAGER you must transform all the theory into practice. You see, it is only when you apply what you have read in this book will you see positive results. It is only when you seriously consider the admonitions contained herein that you will determine whether you qualify as a MASTER ENTREPRENEUR SALESPERSON/SALES MANAGER or not. It may seem to you that I am against salespeople and this is the furthest thing from the truth. Of course, like you, I believe that more and more people should own their own business and I promote this daily. However, what I am not in favor of is the continual failure of both businesses and homes, and this due to a lack of focus on professional sales.

It is now your turn to act! It is now your time to shine! Focus on producing sales and your business will grow. You must understand that not to focus on sales, and not to employ and manage the right salespeople, WILL mean the demise of your business, your dreams and your family goals.

To now call YOU to action I mean that you must ACT. You must ACT on the information now in your head for the sake of your own future and the future of your family. It will now take DEEDS in order to assess whether the contents of this book has helped you in any way at all. It will be easy to criticize what you have read and experienced between the covers but as they say "the proof of the pudding is in the eating". I admonish you to exploit your new found knowledge and measure your results to those entrepreneurs around you. Become enterprising and endeavor to apply the sales principles BEFORE you enter into a business of your own. Learning about sales management and sales techniques is a process and any process requires ACTION!

I do not want you to fail at sales as you WILL then fail at business and this is the very reason why I recommend that you seriously consider acting upon the contents of this book.

## "ACTION SPEAKS LOUDER THAN WORDS!"

## "NOTHING HAPPENS WITHOUT A SALE!"

# Spreading the Word

Nothing will drive home the realities of this book more than a personal appearance and motivational CHALLENGE by the author himself. Trevor K. Whittaker's passion for the entrepreneur, salespeople and business people around the world is evident in his lively and enthusiastic approach to public speaking.

The message is spread and is clear, concise and hard-hitting. What the listener will come away with are the "clear and present dangers" which they will face BEFORE they enter the much sought after title of Master Entrepreneur Salesperson/Sales Manager. Many will also understand that entrepreneurs are needed worldwide but that the need relates to Master Entrepreneurs that remain in business and grow the business. This, simply put, WILL NOT happen without implementing the knowledge of generating sales. The world community and governments are concerned about the mounting new business "casualty rates" and the statistics which reflect the high failure rates of entrepreneurs. Look no further than the entrepreneur's inability to focus on and generate sales.

It is time to face the reality that the blame for the high failure rates with start-up businesses may have to be laid at the door of the entrepreneur. "Nothing happens without a sale!" The world needs start-up businesses that actually stick around and nothing will ensure this more than a constant flow of new business through sales-this is the secondary message! The primary message is that losing one's life investment due to a failing new business may destroy more than just the business-THE FAMILY! The best way to save the business, the investment and the family is to ensure that a prospective entrepreneur considers what qualifies such a one for the position, and then, focus as much attention as is possible on producing income through sales. This reality is communicated and brought to bear during a session with Trevor K. Whittaker.

Trevor K. Whittaker is a highly motivated speaker with a passion for getting his message across for the purpose of assisting the struggling and potential entrepreneur. His sense of humor makes his presentation fun while maintaining an inspirational flavor. Life lessons, which are highlighted during his presentation, cement the reality of possible business failure but his passion and solution minded approach to challenges leave the audience with hope and determination and the will power to succeed.

Please contact Trevor K. Whittaker at:

trevor@trevorkwhittaker.com for availability and bookings regarding workshops, seminars and conferences worldwide.

# About the Author

**Trevor K. Whittaker** has had more than thirty-five years of personal experience in business and has gained his experience in the United States, Canada and South Africa. His passion, as a long-term entrepreneur, is passing on his many hard learned lessons to those who believe that they no longer want to work for a boss – a noble wish but a dangerous desire.

Having lived, studied and worked in North America for at least sixteen years of his life he has gained valuable insight into the international business environment and has used these skills to assist and mentor entrepreneurs throughout his business career. While much of his personal experience has come from the international service and supply industries he has also owned business within the retail and restaurant environments. Many mistakes were made and many lessons were learned some costly and others simply valuable lessons.

**Trevor K. Whittaker** is currently the Founder and President of his own workplace services company located in Johannesburg, South Africa and the business has a national footprint. Trevor has commented as follows on many occasions: "Starting a business in North America is one thing but being an entrepreneur on the most southern tip of Africa takes pure determination and genius!" South Africa has often been referred to as the "America of Africa" and is one of the richest countries on the continent. During the year in 2010 Trevor's business – Crystalmount Workplace Services (www.crystalmount.co.za) – was nominated out of more than 32 000 businesses and was invited to participate as the business of the year finalist. At a gala dinner during November of the same year the business was announced as the BUSINESS OF THE YEAR 2010. As the MASTER ENTREPRENEUR for Crystalmount Workplace Services,

Trevor received numerous rewards, awards and national praise for the success of his business. The country is filled with geniuses, talented and highly motivated people who remain hungry for business success. Trevor is proud to be associated with his long standing business partners in the USA and his university associates in Greenville, South Carolina.

While much of his time is taken up by his passion for business in which he remains actively involved, he also has a long standing passion for writing. Trevor has authored many pertinent sales training modules and has presented these to many audiences throughout the years. He has also authored Operations and Procedures Manuals (OPM's) for the franchise community most of which are still in use today. **ENTREPRENEURSHIP (*minus*) 101** (Publisher: Austin Macauley-ISBN 978 1 78455 148 3 Paperback; ISBN: 978 1 78455 150 6 Hardback www.austinmacauley.com) is Trevor's first work and was borne out of the disturbing statistics relating to the rampant demise of start-up enterprises by well-meaning but misinformed people. The financial devastation of families based upon business failure is Trevor's main concern and he has attributed this failure to a lack of sales knowledge hence the development and publication between these covers known as **ENTREPRENEURSHIP $ALES 101** – Trevor's second book.

**Trevor K. Whittaker** is a successful entrepreneur, author and motivational speaker in his own right and currently lives with his wife Sunly-Ann in Johannesburg, South Africa. He has two sons namely Donovan and Ricky and three beautiful daughters in Kristen, Natasha and Shamarie. A few years ago he was blessed with two gorgeous granddaughters Savannah and Taylor-Reece and has also become "Grampy" to a new addition to the family named Matthew.